second

GUEST SERVICE

~ *in the* ~

Hospitality Industry

Kendall Hunt
publishing company

PAUL BAGDAN

Kendall Hunt
publishing company

www.kendallhunt.com
Send all inquiries to:
4050 Westmark Drive
Dubuque, IA 52004-1840

Brief Contents

Contents

SECTION II

Relating Service to the Sectors of the Hospitality Industry: How Service Relates   91

CHAPTER 4

The Guest Service of Food   93

CHAPTER 5

The Guest Service of Beverages 121

CHAPTER 6

The Guest Service of Lodging 141

CHAPTER 7

The Guest Service of Events 157

CHAPTER 8

The Guest Service of Travel and Tourism   179

SECTION III

Assessments and Planning   215

CHAPTER 11

Quality Tools 243

CHAPTER 12

Systems, Ratings, and Awards 279

CHAPTER 13

Developing a Staff 299

CHAPTER 14

Marketing and Establishing an Image for Service 331

Preface

Introduction

Taking care of the customer is the heart of hospitality. Students of and professionals in the hospitality industry must understand this in order to be successful. Their futures depend on it. They must understand and anticipate what the customer needs and know how to best meet and exceed those needs. Not only does one need to know how to serve a customer, but also how to acquire customer-related problem-solving skills, such as conducting basic surveys, and using other tools and techniques to identify and then solve problems. They must be able to plan and deliver quality service because it does not just happen on its own. And then, they must be able to manage other people to effectively accomplish all of these things.

Guest Service in the Hospitality Industry—Second Edition continues with the premise that there is no one simple solution to managing people who provide customer service. It does not claim one absolute answer, but, instead, takes an approach that incorporates various thoughts from different parts of the industry, differing from property to property. By providing several frameworks for instituting approaches, this book opens readers' minds to the idea of taking care of the guest. It discusses issues and debunks myths about customer service with concepts that are solid and proven in the industry. The methods of teaching utilized for this book have been proven in the classroom with the contemporary college student and, as a result, these teachings have served them well.

About This Book

Guest Service in the Hospitality Industry includes all of the major areas of the hospitality industry as they relate to delivering quality customer service. It not only provides a history and overview of guest service but then goes much further to include other essential topics, including problem-solving, quality tools and assessments, staffing, marketing, and strategic planning.

The need for this text, *Guest Service in the Hospitality Industry*, came about as a result of my teaching as a Professor at Johnson & Wales University, Providence, RI, Campus. I was pioneering a newly designed course in customer-service management. It was a general course, taught to all of our hospitality students in their first or second year. The students encompassed majors specializing in food, lodging, travel, and events. Furthermore, they each had concentrations within and among the majors, making their particular interests quite varied. I could not find a textbook that met all of their needs.

The first-generation of guest service books were from the 1980s and 1990s. They featured the guest service/quality movement as seen in its heyday. They were very heavily focused on total quality management (TQM) and continuous quality management (CQI). They referenced manufacturing-focused techniques and adapted them to the service industry. Times have changed and hospitality is now secured in its own sector of the service industry. TQM and CQI principles have since left our common vocabulary, but the ideas of serving the guest and performing well have not left our missions.

Since the guest service books either made general reference to hospitality or were extremely focused on just one aspect, I wanted a book for hospitality students. My aim was to combine some of the classic material, the current material, and focus it all on the areas of hospitality:

- ► food
- ► beverage
- ► lodging
- ► sports and events
- ► travel and tourism
- ► casinos.

Guest Service in the Hospitality Industry applies guest service to the hospitality discipline as a whole, whereas other texts have either a very general business theme or concentrate on a highly specific component of the industry.

✦ TO THE STUDENT

Guest Service in the Hospitality Industry is written as a textbook for hospitality students within any of the individual disciplines. It is also relevant to anyone wanting a survey of the past and present findings of customer service as they relate to the hospitality industry.

Written in a straightforward manner intended to introduce the topic of guest service to students of hospitality, the text incorporates a variety of learning features that facilitate various learning styles. Such features include:

- ► **chapter points and concepts** with visual diagrams
- ► stories and **real-life examples**
- ► **"Service Insights"**—tips incorporated throughout the text that provide extra guest service-related information to build and support points
- ► **review questions** that reinforce chapter concepts
- ► **case studies** that reinforce the learning.

Guest Service in the Hospitality Industry dedicates a chapter to each of the primary areas of the hospitality industry. All of the examples are related to hospitality, and the case studies and Service Insights relate to the industry as it truly is. It goes further to provide a history and overview of guest service, and then goes much further by exploring problem-solving techniques, quality tools and assessments, staffing, marketing, and strategic planning in guest service.

❖ ORGANIZATION OF THE BOOK

Guest Service in the Hospitality Industry is organized into three sections. The first section introduces the concepts; the students become acclimated to the topic of guest service through these chapters. The book then shows guest service in each of the major areas of hospitality: food service, beverage, lodging, events, travel and tourism, and casinos. Students learn about guest service in their focus area and in accompanying areas. A by-product is that they learn more about their discipline as a whole. Learning about other parts of the hospitality industry is great for student internships and their future in the industry, as areas are often blended and many professionals move from one area to another. The last section relates the best of remaining, related topics within the industry: staffing, tools and surveys, strategic planning and marketing.

Section I: Introduction and Essentials of Managing Guest Service

This section lays groundwork for the course. An overview of the meaning, the origin, and the progression of guest service is covered. This section includes:

- ☐ Chapter 1: The Basics of Managing Guest Service
- ☐ Chapter 2: Defining Guest Service
- ☐ Chapter 3: Problem-Solving for Guest Service

Section II: Relating Service to the Sectors of the Hospitality Industry: How Service Relates

This section relates guest service to each major area of the hospitality industry. A specific chapter dedicated to each of these areas:

- ☐ Chapter 4: The Guest Service of Food
- ☐ Chapter 5: The Guest Service of Beverages
- ☐ Chapter 6: The Guest Service of Lodging
- ☐ Chapter 7: The Guest Service of Events
- ☐ Chapter 8: The Guest Service of Travel and Tourism
- ☐ Chapter 9: The Guest Service of Casinos

Section III: Assessments and Planning

This last section takes all of the other major aspects of instituting and managing guest service in the hospitality industry. A specific chapter is dedicated to each of the following topics:

- ☐ Chapter 10: Strategic Planning for Service
- ☐ Chapter 11: Quality Tools
- ☐ Chapter 12: Frameworks for Quality: Systems, Awards, and Certifications
- ☐ Chapter 13: Developing a Staff
- ☐ Chapter 14: Marketing and Establishing an Image for Service

Supplemental Offering

A comprehensive online *Instructor's Manual* with Test Bank accompanies this text.

I sincerely hope that you find it as rewarding as I intended.

Best Wishes,
Professor Paul Bagdan, PhD CHE

Acknowledgments

I would like to thank my immediate family for their support through this process:

Kathleen Harrigan
Florence Bagdan
Luke Bagdan
Samuel Bagdan
Cassandra Connelly
Michaela Reed

Finally, thanks to the readers in advance for their time.

Professor Paul Bagdan, PhD CHE

Introduction and Essentials of Managing Guest Service

Chapter 1

The Basics of Managing Guest Service

CHAPTER OBJECTIVES

After reading this chapter, you should be able to:

► Identify and describe the history, ages of change, and current status of guest service in the US.
► Identify the uses of various reasons why guests may not outwardly complain.
► Identify and explain the reasoning behind why guests share their poor experiences with others.
► Describe the expectations of guests as they relate to hospitality.
► Explain and apply the concept of using quality service as a competitive advantage.
► Describe the influences of leaders of guest service.

TERMINOLOGY

Age of Communication
Age of Service
Age of Technology
Deming Chain Reaction Model
Economies of Scale
Functions of Management
High-Tech vs. High-Touch
MBWA
Moment of Truth
Paradigm
PDCA
Quality Customer Service
Service Profit Chain

Introduction

Guest service is not just a term, but an overarching field of study involving customer focus, teamwork, continuous improvement, empowerment, planning and analysis just to name a few. It cannot be studied in a vacuum. The concepts of this book are a unique blend of the materials essential to deliver quality guest service in the hospitality industry. It involves history, terminology, tools and instruments, human resources, problem-solving, strategy, marketing, and technology. It must also be applied to each sector of the hospitality industry.

This book is aimed toward the hospitality management student in the first, second, or third year of their college studies. It may also be easily applied to practitioners, laymen, and other secondary education.

THIS EDITION

The textbook has been fully updated in this edition to include the newest research, theories, and technologies. While the first edition was good, this edition includes more case studies, technology inserts, and an additional chapter to support the added material.

A SCIENCE AND AN ART

This book aims to explain all that is involved in customer service management within the hospitality industry. We all know that you should be nice to people, so why do we have so many negative guest experiences in the hospitality industry? Because it is not that simple. *Good service doesn't just happen by itself.* It requires a special blend of procedure, technique, and skill combined with the human element. It is both left-brain and right-brain. It can be anticipated, but not precisely calculated because it is continuously evolving and is unique with each experience. It requires training and Standard Operating Procedures, but also requires the human element of reading an individual and individualizing the interaction. It is, essentially, *both a science and an art.*

INTEGRATION OF CUSTOMER SERVICE

There is so much more to providing good service than simply being nice to people. In order for customer service to be successful, it must be integrated into the overall business. Customer service must be part of the company's identity, or brand. It must be tailored to the individual operation and customized, planned, and executed with systems that support it. The employees must be knowledgeable of the brand, the products, and the operations. Also, the customer must be properly gauged or assessed to ensure proper alignment with the brand image. So, the brand image, operations, and employees of the business must all align with the target customer who they are aiming to attract, serve, and retain. In other words, providing quality customer service is more than being friendly. It is part of the

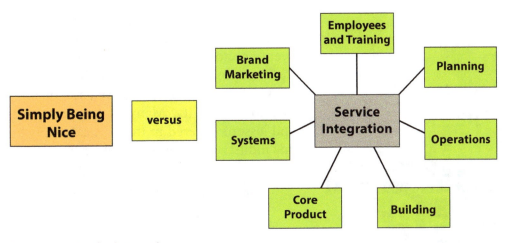

Components Service Integration
© Kendall Hunt Publishing Company

core of the business. It is integrated into nearly every decision. It is calculated and planned. It is evident in all of the operations, the people, and the plan.

DEFINING QUALITY CUSTOMER SERVICE

There are a variety of definitions for customer service. Essentially, anytime patrons, or even prospective patrons, interact with a facet of the organization, customer service is rendered. **Quality customer service** is meeting and exceeding the individual customer's expectations. If service meets or surpasses customers' expectations, in any situation, it is said to be quality customer service.

Meeting or exceeding the expectations of customers, or quality customer service, can occur anywhere and at any level of establishment. Good service can occur at a concession stand or a fine-dining establishment.

In fine dining or at a 5-Star hotel, a guest's expectations are very high. Many things establish this including star ratings, reviews, past experiences, brand, and price. The threshold for quality guest service is quite high. More will be covered on the topic of expectations later in the text, but it is important to note that it is a difficult balance for the establishment.

Quality Customer Service

Meeting and exceeding the individual expectations of the customer.

HOSPITALITY IS CUSTOMER SERVICE

The Hospitality Industry is a service industry. The guest is served through many different means. The industry has many segments. Food, lodging, and travel are the primary three. Controversy has recently entered the industry. Arguments supported that events, sports, gaming, health care, and assisted living are other major segments. Some argue that: "almost all of the industry is travel and tourism," or "marketing," or "business management." Despite this controversy, almost everyone would agree that *all of these disciplines fall with the service sector of the economy*. Being a service industry means that *customers determine the success of the operation and business*. The customer can make a business the most popular business in the town. The customer can also shut down a giant operation by choosing not to patronize the operation.

Hospitality Service Management
© mypokcik/Shutterstock.com

This text dedicates specific chapters to the food, beverage, hotel, casino, travel, and events sectors of the industry, recognizing the individual nature of each sector.

Customer service, however, is not limited to hospitality. Many of the principles and lessons covered in this text can apply to any industry that serves people.

WHY ACCEPT BAD SERVICE?

Why does bad service exist? There are many reasons for bad service. The reasons are endless and often appear to be out of direct control. Some even appear acceptable to the staff, the manager, or even the guests. Below is a list of common excuses. While many may appear legitimate, none are truly acceptable.

© Macrovector/Shutterstock.com

EXCUSES FOR BAD SERVICE

Staffing

▶ They are under-staffed.
▶ They aren't paid enough.
▶ They aren't properly trained.
▶ They are just having a bad day.
▶ No one or system is present to monitor.
▶ They are in training.
▶ They are overworked and tired.
▶ It isn't their responsibility.
▶ The boss isn't present or doesn't care.

SERVICE INSIGHT

I'm In Training

A nametag states, "I'M IN TRAINING." Employee turnover, cross-training, system changes, and employee development means that there will always be someone in training. How should this best be handled? Does it always have to be simulated behind the scenes? Or, can it be an assisted training in front of the guest? Surveys suggest that customers are generally more patient and have lowered expectations of service when they see that an employee is in training. Others, though, are immediately intolerant because they feel the business has provided them with less-than-adequate attention and errors are likely.

Systems

- ▶ The computer is slow.
- ▶ The kitchen is slow.
- ▶ The _____ is broken.
- ▶ We just got a new _____.

Capacity/Customers

- ▶ There are too many customers.
- ▶ They didn't expect this many customers.
- ▶ The customer is rude.
- ▶ The customers are too demanding.
- ▶ The customers don't know what they want.
- ▶ The customers don't pay attention.
- ▶ The customer doesn't seem to mind. No one has complained to corporate.
- ▶ The other reception is loud.

Setting

- ▶ Everything in this neighborhood stinks.
- ▶ This place is all about low-cost.
- ▶ We are renovating.

SERVICE INSIGHT

Renovations

Renovations are inevitable. Some upgrades can be made with little or no notice to the customers. Sometimes, however, this is not possible. How should a business communicate to the customer that it is performing renovations?

Some businesses announce: "please pardon our appearance." Others decide to say nothing and simply conduct business as usual. If it is mentioned prior, some customers will summarily avoid it. If it is noticed at the time of service, some will forgive and others will be very disappointed. Their expectations will not have been met.

There is no one-best-way to approach a renovation. Customers will be inconvenienced, and allowances must be made. Keeping the inconveniences and loss of expectations are a key. A good contractor and project manager also helps.

There are numerous reasons why poor service is delivered. Most of these reasons are common to all customer service settings. They are used regularly. It is important to have a mindset that none of them are truly acceptable.

REASONS WHY CUSTOMERS DO NOT COMPLAIN

An Irritated Customer Waiting in Line
© Matej Kastelic/Shutterstock.com

Most customers do not and will not complain. They will not give the business a chance to know what is wrong. Instead, they simply will not return. They may not tell you because they think you do not care or you don't deserve to know. They may think that you should figure it out for yourself or that it would be too difficult for them to complain and actually be heard. Or, they tried and the complaints fell on deaf ears. Perhaps no system was in place to receive or correct the issue.

Also, a lack of complaints doesn't always imply that service is great. Even the best-run companies struggle with issues. It has often been said that *if you think that you have no problems, then you aren't listening hard enough*. Below is a list of reasons describing what might be going through the minds of guests.

> ► I don't think it's worth it.
> ► I tried before and no one listened.
> ► I am in a hurry.
> ► I don't want to make a scene.
> ► I feel bad for the staff.
> ► It isn't the staff's fault.
> ► I don't want to get anyone in trouble.
> ► There seems to be no solution in sight.
> ► I'm afraid that they'll mess with the food.
> ► I don't think that it will make a difference.
> ► I don't think anyone cares.
> ► I just hate this place and I want to leave.

You may not always know the reason why a customer doesn't complain. While they won't tell you, they will be sure to tell many of their friends.

GOOD SERVICE CAN MAKE UP FOR BAD FOOD

Service may just be one reason why an experience is poor. What do you remember most about a poor hospitality experience? Was it the service? Was it the decor? Was it the event, the room, or the food? Or was it a combination of these things? It has often been said that:

> "Good service can make up for a bad food,
> but good food cannot make up for poor service."

Consider the following two scenarios.

Scenario A: Poor Service

You are at a nice restaurant with a date. Your evening plans are for dinner and an evening show. You mention to the server that you have show tickets. The server says, "OK." You are unsure what that means, but continue to order a medium-rare steak. Your date orders the pasta special. Within a reasonable amount of time, the dinners arrive at the table. You cut into your steak and discover that it is over-cooked to the point of almost being well-done. You look around and cannot find your server. After a few minutes, you catch a glimpse of your server walking back into the kitchen. You spend the next few minutes trying to get the server's attention and as he runs around tend-

Customer Left a Note on Table in Ketchup
© Matt Benoit/Shutterstock.com

ing to others guests. You are finally successful and able to explain the situation. The steak is returned to the kitchen and you are left with nothing in front of you while your date sits uncomfortably waiting for your new steak to arrive. Despite your requests for your date to begin eating, they feel awkward. After preparing a new steak, your order eventually arrives. By that point, nearly 20 additional minutes have passed and you have to eat quickly with no time to enjoy your food. You are nervous that you will be late for your show. You try to get the check as soon as you can, but spend the rest of the time anxious that you will be late for the show.

Scenario B: Excellent Service

You are at a nice restaurant with a date before an evening show. You mention to the server that you have tickets. The server inquires if it is at the nearby theatre and confirms the time. The server then smiles, nods, and says "Very well. We will do our very best to ensure that you have a great experience and make the show in plenty of time." You order a medium-rare steak. Your date orders the pasta special. Within a reasonable amount of time, the dinners arrive at your table. You cut into it and discover that it is overcooked to the point of being well-done. You look up and realize the server has remained at the table to address any issues. He immediately apologizes and rushes the steak back to the kitchen to correct the issue. He promptly returns with a complimentary beef appetizer so that you and your date can both begin eating together. Before you know it, your new steak is delivered to the table. Again, the server stays to ensure it is cooked to your liking. This time it is. You are delighted that it was solved so effortlessly. You are asked if there is anything they could get for you. Your response is no. At that point, your check is placed on the table and you are told that there is no rush but that it can be settled at any time that you would prefer. You finish your dinner and pleasantly arrive at your show in plenty of time.

Shortcomings will occasionally occur. When they do, good service can help to make them much more manageable. Remember that good service can make up for other problems, but those other items cannot make up for bad service. No matter how great things are, good service must be present.

COMPETITIVE ADVANTAGE OF SERVICE

Repeatedly, poor customer service is found to be the main reason people stop patronizing a business. On the other hand, a highly satisfied customer is far more profitable than an average customer. A recent Harvard Business School study determined that a typical customer patronizes a Starbucks store 4.3 times each month with an average check of $4.06 for an average of 4.4 years (Table 1.1). This changes dramatically if they are reported to be highly-satisfied. They patronize more, spend more, and remain customers for nearly twice the amount of time. A highly satisfied Starbucks patronizes at a rate of 7.2 times each month, with an average check of $4.42, and remains a customer for 8.3 years.

TABLE 1.1				
	Visits per Month	**Check Average**	**Average Life of Patronage**	**Total Revenue per Customer**
Average Customer	4.3	$4.06	4.4 years	$921.78
Highly-Satisfied Customer	7.2	$4.42	7.2 years	$2,749.59

While each business is slightly different, most hospitality businesses offer a generic product (Deming, 1982). Nearly:

- ► Every hotel offers a bed in a private room with a bath.
- ► Every restaurant delivers a meal with seating.
- ► Every theatre has seats and a stage.
- ► Every plane flies you from gate to gate.

Of course there are different styles, settings, shapes, and colors, but what really makes the difference is the specific service of the business or establishment. This idea can generally be applied to all businesses that offer guest service. The tangibles and logistics can be patented but quickly replicated. Employees and managers transfer among brands, and companies benchmark each other's ideas. What competitors have the most difficulty with is replicating the service experience.

All businesses realize they need to be nice to the guest and deliver quality guest service, but a few are rising above the rest and actually meeting or exceeding guests' expectations on a consistent basis. Some boast of this as part of their brand marketing and use it as a competitive advantage. One such example is the Ritz-Carlton Hotel chain. This company has based its strategy on providing exceptional customer service. As a result, it won a prestigious Malcolm Baldrige Award two times. Much planning, training, and preparation went into this resulting in standards that are copied throughout many industries. Most notable is their motto stating: "We are Ladies and Gentlemen serving Ladies and Gentlemen." This statement gives the employees status to take pride in their positions while treating the guests with the expected high standards.

They also have a credo telling the employees to ". . . fulfill even the unexpressed wishes of our guests." The customers are referred to as "guests." The services provided are "wishes" that are fulfilled, and the employees should anticipate the needs above those verbalized.

They also implement empowerment to a high degree. Their service values include statements such as: "I own and immediately solve guest problems." It does not matter who caused the issue or what department it is in, the employee owns the problem and will see to it that it is solved immediately.

The Ritz-Carlton goes on to train their employees to think about the big picture. Another service value tells employees to, "build strong relationships and create Ritz-Carlton guests for life." (www.ritzcarlton.com/en/about/gold-standards)

✦ BAD NEWS TRAVELS FAST

Advertisements show happy customers and boast about award-winning service, but how convincing is that compared to a testimony of a friend sharing their personal experience? These experiences are especially impacting when they are about bad service. When a customer goes away unhappy, they are far more likely to tell another about their experience.

A woman and her friend were finishing their meal at a small café when she asked the waitress if they had decaffeinated tea. The woman informed the waitress that she could not have caffeine due to health reasons. The waitress replied that she wasn't sure but would check to see. The waitress quickly returned to the table and informed the customer that they only had regularly-caffeinated tea. The customer, prepared for this situation because she enjoys tea and cannot have caffeine due to health reasons, requested a cup of hot water and took a decaffeinated teabag out of her purse. A few minutes later the bill came and she saw a miscellaneous charge of $2.00 on her bill. The woman inquired about the miscellaneous charge

News Travels Quickly
© GoodStudio/Shutterstock.com

to the waitress who replied that the manager assesses a $2.00 charge for hot water. This was verified after the manager came to the table. Despite the reasoning, the manager simply ignored her feelings regarding the matter. Granted, it was only a small charge, but it wasn't about the money. As it turns out, the customer was a group session counselor at the local Weight-Watchers Center. She told everyone in her classes about the situation. She vented and they became worked up for her cause. This small café was dependent on the population from the small community. They will likely see the result of this seemingly insignificant incident amounting to much more damage than $2.00.

"Bad news travels quickly" is a common expression. By some accounts, *customers will share a bad experience with 8–10 people.* Those people may tell other people, who tell more people, and so on. While the actual number varies, it is a commonly accepted notion that bad news travels quickly. If the guest experience was poor, they will likely tell several friends or acquaintances, who will likely tell others, and so on. Occasionally, someone receiving poor service has a large audience as in the story above. Online ratings are especially important because of the potential audience size, or "reach" of the postings.

There are reasons why bad news travels so quickly. Perhaps they weren't heard, they want revenge, and other reasons come to mind. Below is a list of reasons why bad news travels quickly to help explain the reasoning behind this phenomenon:

1. *The customer still needed to vent.* Customers need to be afforded the chance to express themselves. Venting is a normal part of the customer service process. A customer will need to share if they believe they weren't given the opportunity to be heard or understood. As a result, they recount their experiences to anyone and everyone that will listen.

2. *Customers may seek revenge.* If the customer believes they have been wronged, they want to get even. When people feel as though they haven't received what they had expected and paid for, they feel the need to "level the playing field." They tell friends and write poor reviews or anything else that justifies their pain and loss.

3. *Customers remember unusual events.* Because we have so many experiences throughout life, we filter the mediocrity from our brains. Customers continually take in information and filter all but the most usual, emotional, or important information. They tend to forget typical or mediocre experiences. If the guest experience was "OK" or even "good," people are not as likely to share the experience because it is deemed insignificant and quickly forgotten.

4. *People love to repeat extreme events.* Really great and really bad events are more interesting and, therefore, more share-worthy.

5. *People can relate to these incidences.* Everyone has been wronged in the past. Bad news is particularly share-worthy because it has a sense of wronging that others can easily connect to.

6. *Service companies and providers appear impersonal.* Companies appear big. Employees can easily be lumped into this same disconnected state since they have no human connection and can be easily blamed and criticized.

While humans may make mistakes, businesses are faceless. Talking about people may be seen as gossip. Criticizing others may be seen as unforgiving and impolite. Talking about businesses are fair game. Hotels, casinos, restaurants, and their employees are not seen as people with feelings.

As a result, each service encounter is important. Each time that a customer is wronged is an opportunity for bad news to travel quickly. Management and staff should keep this in mind in their daily operations.

THE PICKLE PRINCIPLE

In his popular book, restaurateur and author Bob Farrell tells a story of a letter that he received from a regular customer who always ordered his hamburger with an extra slice of pickle. The new waitress wanted to sell him a side order of pickles. After she spoke with the manager, she offered to sell him an extra pickle for 5 cents. The customer was upset and left. Bob's response, "Give 'em the pickle." His rationale was that it was a small extra thing and that it made all of the difference to the customer, while costing the business very little.

Pickle Slices
© Hong Vo/Shutterstock.com

This idea of not worrying about it and "going the extra mile" is an idea that we see throughout customer service. It is part of exceeding guests' expectations. It is an integral part of the empowerment principle and the Kano model which will be reviewed later in the text.

https://www.giveemthepickle.com/pickle_principle.htm

THE VALUE OF A RETURNING CUSTOMER

Most businesses want a satisfied customer who will tell others, spread the good word, and return on a regular basis. Businesses that can align well-trained employees with processes that fit the needs of the customers can be very successful. This is cost-effective and ideal. Customers become loyal and even recruit others to patronize your business.

Imagine running a small restaurant, with a loyal customer base of 800 that eat at your establishment once a week. Out of a small town and surrounding area totaling 100,000 people, you have successfully captured just under 1% of them. You don't need to market, because you already have all of the customers you need. You and your staff quickly learn all of their names because they are all repeat customers and you don't need to attract anyone new. You know their likes and dislikes, and can tailor to precisely meet their needs. You know how many to staff for and how much food to prepare. You run at maximum efficiency and reap the rewards.

While this would be an ideal situation, the truth is, it is never that easy. Loyal, return customers are highly sought-after prizes. While businesses spend infinite amounts of money attracting them, they are undervalued as they arrive and experience the product. They are often treated as if it is the first and last time they are ever to be seen. A return customer costs far less to keep than obtaining a new one.

✦ SERVICE PROFIT CHAIN

Service Profit Chain

A HBR model theory that links employee satisfaction to increased profits.

The **Service Profit Chain** is a theory that links employee satisfaction to better customer service and eventually increased profits. It was first mentioned in a Harvard Business Review (HBR) article in 1994 by Sasser and Schlesinger and later became a popular book. Sir Richard Branson was quoted as saying, "Clients do not come first, employees come first. If you take care of the employees, they will take care of the clients." This exemplifies the idea of the Service Profit Chain. It begins with high-level internal service aspects that are built into the operation. It has had numerous iterations, but remains essentially the same. Examples of these might be job design, job recognition, comfortable work space, proper training, tools, and development for employees. The high level of Internal Service Quality produces Employee Satisfaction, which produces improved employee retention and productivity. Employees who stay longer at an organization reduce training costs and reduce lower levels of service associated with new employees. After these steps are in place, the chain consequently increases external service value, or how customers perceive the products and services. This produces an elevated level of customer satisfaction or Quality Guest Service. Lastly, a satisfied guest will likely return, which creates profit.

Service-Profit Chain

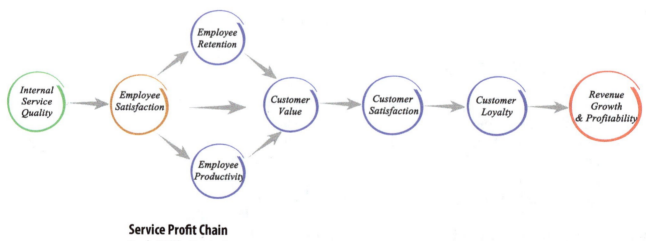

Service Profit Chain
© arka38/Shutterstock.com

✦ HISTORY OF SERVICE MANAGEMENT IN THE US

Service Economy

We live in a service economy. Service is the non-goods portion of a business transaction. A service could be simple or complex. According to the Bureau of Labor and Statistics, service industry sector jobs account for more than 80% of our total employment in the US.

The history of customer service is barely historical. At least from a scientific management point of view. References discuss innkeepers being hospitable and tavern owners "keeping people happy," but application of scientific methodology to the art of customer service has only expanded into what it is within the past 100 years.

Within that time, the US has seen ages of change advance relatively quickly. We have transitioned from an agrarian society to a service society in a period of just about 100 years. It is unlikely that neither agriculture nor industry will ever return as it once was, so the **age of service** should be present for quite some time.

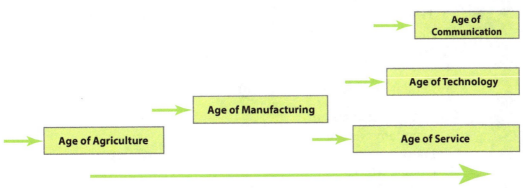

© Kendall Hunt Publishing Company

Age of Service

The present age of the US. As the US lost its manufacturing jobs, it was replaced with service-related jobs.

Age of Manufacturing

Originally the US was largely an agricultural nation. It evolved into a thriving manufacturing nation in the last century but then quickly lost its dominance to other nations. A large portion of the management techniques used in the service industries have been adopted from manufacturing, which dominated the literature before the late 1900s.

Age of Service

Presently, the US economy is largely comprised of service organizations. As the US lost many of its manufacturing jobs to other countries, it began replacing them with service-related jobs.

Age of Technology

Another recent age in the US. The increase and dominance of technology in U.S. culture and business operations.

Age of Technology

Coupled with service, the US also saw a boom in analog, then digital technology in the 1980s and '90s. This heavily influenced the way that businesses operate. Business functions were expedited by computerization. Customers enjoyed the many new conveniences associated with technology.

Age of Communication

The service economy combined with the proliferation technology created an increase in communication where services can be communicated instantly, information can be accessed cheaply, and ratings can be found easily.

Age of Communication

While service continues to dominate the economy and employment of the US, the advances and proliferation of technology spurred a new phenomenon of communication. Like never before could so much information be so readily available so cheaply and easily. This spread of communication has forever changed the way that customer service in the US and the world operates. Suppliers, businesses, and customers can now all communicate in real-time and have the ability to access records of each other. A bad service situation such as an airline attendant berating fliers, a food-borne outbreak at a restaurant, or bedbugs in a hotel can now be instantly seen around the world. Customers' opinions could be accessed by other potential customers, for better or worse.

List of most popular sharing websites

▶ **Communicative**
- ☐ Facebook
- ☐ Twitter
- ☐ Blogs
- ☐ YouTube
- ☐ Wikis
- ☐ Digital Pictures (Flickr, Picasa)

▶ **Customer Engagement**
- ☐ Company websites
- ☐ Fodor's
- ☐ Google Alerts
- ☐ Trip Advisor
- ☐ Urbanspoon
- ☐ Yelp
- ☐ Google places
- ☐ QR Codes

Sporting events could poll their fans on their cell phones. Conference attendees could tweet by use of a hashtag. New hotel guests could be recognized and their preferences known before they utter a single word. The Age of Communication certainly has an impact on customer service.

❖ BACKGROUND OF SERVICE

Until recently, a majority of people lived in relatively small neighborhoods where everyone knew each other. Traditionally, workers had a craft or trade. They took pride in their craft, so quality and service was natural. As a few businesses became larger, the smaller businesses could not compete with the lower prices of the bigger businesses. The small craftsmen went out of business. As more and more people began working for an hourly wage, craftsmen began to lose their sense of neighborhood and craft. More and more, a job was simply a job, and only a means to earn money. The idea of a proud neighborhood craftsman was lost.

This changed the idea and tradition of service forevermore. Management also changed to reflect the progression. Rewards, motivations, standard operating procedures, and punishments reduced craftsmen to a sub-human standard. Trust in employees dwindled and customer service suffered. Good economic times, coupled with an increase in disposable income, made the situation only worse. It wasn't until the 1950s and '60s that management began to change and treat humans as a resource, spawning the now common phrase, "human resource."

Since the end of WWII in the late 1940s, Americans developed a "need for speed." The world began to want and need all things fast. This cultural phenomenon also changed the way that the hospitality service industry operated. This shift gave way to an explosion of fast-food, fast travel, fast service, and fast communication. Suddenly, speed was added to the list of quality, comfort, personalization, and price.

The past two decades have also spawned the recent increase in self-service. Has the replacement of computers in customer service really made things better or worse? Presently, we have self-service at many places that we now take for granted, including:

- check-ins, check-outs
- banks
- ticketing
- streaming entertainment
- toll booths
- coin redemption

Over time, customers have adapted and the playing field has changed. Consider the following service examples of just 20 years ago:

- Most all banking was done through bank tellers.
- Only a few ATM's existed and many customers did not trust them.
- No Internet banking existed.
- Self-check-outs did not exist and bar code technology was not yet all standardized.
- Shopping was done in stores or by mail-order catalogs.
- Reviews were read in the newspapers, magazines, and travel booklets.
- No smart phones or "apps" existed.
- People went to the movie theater to see a new release.
- Air travel was only booked through the airlines or a travel agent.
- Hotel reservations were booked through reservations agents or travel agents.

Things have certainly changed. The idea of self-service is now ubiquitous. It has provided the industry with both advantages and disadvantages. Below is a list of each.

Advantages
- Decreased labor
- Increased speed of service
- Increased processing
- Smaller lines
- Increased access

Disadvantages
- Loss of human interaction
- Subject to input error

> ▶ May be difficult to fix errors
> ▶ Unfamiliar technology
> ▶ Unfamiliar with process
> ▶ Uncertainty of transaction

High-Tech vs. High-Touch Guest Service

A dilemma of balancing helpful technologies with the loss of the human touch or experience.

Despite the loss of the craftsman, the need for speed, and the increase in self-service, quality customer service remains the cornerstone of the hospitality industry. We seldom refer to TQM or CQI in recent times, but the techniques are still used to this day. Guest service has evolved but continues to be an underlying assumption of the hospitality industry. It is used as a differentiating factor and continues to set businesses apart from each other. Most businesses claim to have a passion for service, but only a few do it exceptionally well. When a business masters customer service, it truly becomes a strategic advantage.

Technology Update

High Tech—High Touch Dilemma

DIY, apps, e-tickets, queueless and electronic lines, self-service kiosks, mobile ordering, curbside pick-up, automated delivery services, robotic concierge, robotic room service, automated baggage storage, retina scanning, facial recognition, self-check-in, keyless entries, RFID, automated heat and lighting, self-checkout, self-pay, electronic surveys . . . There are many technologies available to assist with customer service process. Many of these are recent developments.

These technologies are wonderful. They reduce labor, which is becoming a large issue with the increase in wages. They make the process more efficient, permitting more guests to be served. They also enable staff to tend to crucial issues, because they are quickly alerted and more available. They have the possibility of adding mass-customization, allowing each transaction to be tailored to the individual according to their needs and profile. There are some restaurants and hotels that are nearly fully automated. While this might seem intriguing, there is a downside.

This proliferation of technology also has disadvantages. One of the largest complaints with these technologies is a loss of human interaction. The hospitality industry is an industry of people serving people. Humans are social creatures and desire the need for interaction. Patrons of businesses pay money and demand service. For many people, the idea of hospitality guest service typically means human interaction.

To balance the blend is a challenge referred to as high-tech vs. high-touch. A high-touch guest experience is one where the guest interaction is both crucial and extensive. A high-tech guest experience is typically, by nature, free of human interaction because technology takes its place. Since technology adds to the experience, is it possible to still involve the human touch and deliver a yet elevated level of quality?

Q: With a limited budget for capital improvements, which would you choose?
Q: How much human interaction is needed?
Q: Are there fail-safes in place?
Q: As a manager, what is the best use of your staff?

❖ MANAGEMENT INFLUENCES

There are quality references that date back to the Zhou Dynasty in the 12th century B.C., but in more recent years, Frederick Winslow Taylor is considered the Father of Modern Management.

Scientific Management: Frederick Winslow Taylor

Frederick Winslow Taylor wrote the Principles of Scientific Management in 1911. He embraced the idea of applying a scientific process to the management of people. He advocated for a thorough analysis of worker methods. Both industry and academics were ready for it. As an engineer by trade, he applied time and motion studies to determine the optimal efficiency of his workers. He would determine the optimal size shovel for loading coal so that workers could move the most amount of material. He proposed that management determine the optimal, most efficient, or "one best way" to perform any employee procedure. He did, however, recognize that there is a limit to how much you can expect to push a worker. He realized that if you overloaded a worker their work would eventually decrease. He was one of the first to announce that workers might not always favor cost-cutting, and resistance would likely form.

The Science of Management
© Anatoliy Sadovskiy/Shutterstock.com

Workplace Layout and Standardization: Henry Ford

Henry Ford is popular for his motor company that brought cars to the average American. As a result, roads were built and the hospitality industry was changed forever. What might not come to mind are the contributions to management and manufacturing that have found their ways into the way that we conduct operations to this day.

Henry Ford
© aradaphotography/Shutterstock.com

Henry Ford popularized the idea of an assembly line and standardization. He advocated for arrangement of the workplace. He wanted everything to be planned and laid out purposefully. He was very smart at creating interchangeable parts by reducing variances. In this, he reduced gross amounts of waste. He also demanded improvements to machines so there would be little downtime.

Another important point is that Ford advocated for **economies of scale**. This meant that he determined the optimum production level in which he could produce most efficiently. Too much production could lead to overtime, mistakes, and breakage. Too little production could lead to labor and machines not being used to their potential. He was one of the first to bring these newer ideas and technologies to his operation to promote: "work smarter, not harder." All of this made his automobile a household name for well over 100 years.

Economies of Scale

The optimum production level at which an organization can produce most efficiently.

Despite these praises, Henry Ford was not perfect. He believed in top-down control, which is now criticized by many experts. He was criticized for his social views. Also, he did not always adjust to changes in society and in the economy, which caused multiple issues.

Functions of Management: Henri Fayol

© Kheng Guan Toh/Shutterstock.com

In 1916, a mining executive named Henri Fayol devised the skills that a manager needs to be successful. These were referred to as the management functions in his book, *Administration Industrielle et Generale*. Originally, there were five distinct **functions of management**:

- ▶ Planning
- ▶ Organizing
- ▶ Commanding
- ▶ Coordinating
- ▶ Controlling

"Commanding" has been replaced by leading, to reflect a more progressive approach. Another skill, "staffing," shows up in literature but has since been primarily absorbed into the others forming the:

❖ FOUR MANAGEMENT FUNCTIONS

- ▶ Planning
- ▶ Organizing
- ▶ Leading
- ▶ Controlling

These functions were generalized to management of most industries. They have been adopted by schools into the curriculum of management since the 1950s.

Planning are the steps that you take to establish where you are and what you are going to do. You are planning your work. You observe the situation and establish your goals. Essentially, you decide what needs to be done. This requires knowledge of assessment and strategy.

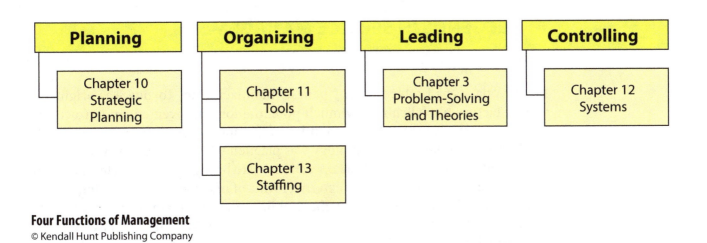

Four Functions of Management
© Kendall Hunt Publishing Company

Organizing typically comes next in the progression of operations. Once the planning is established, you can begin to organize your efforts to put them into action. In the first step you have planned your work. Now with organizing, you are beginning to work through your plan. You begin to allocate resources: human, financial, and physical. You begin to schedule to set yourself up for success. As you can see, this requires a knowledge of the entire operation.

Leading means working with staff to accomplish the goals. Whatever these goals are, a manager cannot accomplish them alone. You must begin to inspire your staff and properly motivate them to reach the goals. A leader's job is not to push workers, but to enable them to willfully strive toward the goals. This requires knowledge of motivation, personalities, and teams.

Controlling is last in the order. Controlling has a poor connotation, but is really quite the opposite. If properly managed up to this point, everyone wants to accomplish their goals. Controlling is the act of ensuring that operations stay on target to meet the goals. This means observation, measurement, oversight, and changes and improvements as they are needed. This requires knowledge of measurement tools.

The four functions of management fit well into the framework followed in this textbook that is adapted to guest service.

So, in a sense, you are still learning about the four management functions as business schools do. However, it is directly applied to guest services in the hospitality industry. Additionally, guest service is fully detailed and service characteristics are applied to each sector of the hospitality industry.

Functions of Management

Originally developed by Henri Fayol as 5, now are popularized as: planning, organizing, leading, and controlling.

❖ LEGENDS IN SERVICE MANAGEMENT

Kiichiro Toyoda

Mr. Toyoda saw a problem with Japanese manufacturing. Toyoda was originally a loom factory but Kiichiro saw much potential for improvement and growth in the automotive industry. As the founder of Toyota Motor Corporation in 1934, he observed that Japanese technology was plagued with poor quality. When there was a small problem, many of the operations were brought to a halt. He wanted to remedy this, so he studied many external forms of management, including that of Henry Ford. He combined management philosophy with manufacturing logistics which turned into what we know as Toyota Production System (TPS). Mr. Toyoda was a true leader of the ideas that have later been converted to Lean, Just In Time Inventory and other quality service methods.

Machine at the Original Toyoda/Toyota
Images © leodaphne/Shutterstock.com

W. Edward Deming

Dr. W. Edward Deming, a talented statistician and management consultant, is considered to be a leader in the customer service movement because of his work with the "total quality management (TQM) movement." While most of his earlier work was attributed to manufacturing, his efforts were transformed to non-manufacturing, including the hospitality industry. TQM management is an effort geared toward promoting quality products through many methods including suppliers, employees, and management working together.

Dr. Deming tried to lend his talents to the US manufacturing industries but his advice went unheeded. After WWII, Deming approached the Japanese with his ideas of applying statistics to automotive manufacturing. They accepted and embraced his ideas. He helped the Japanese automakers implement "continuous process improvement." As a result, the 1980s saw Japanese cars dominate the US, while domestic cars were left suffering. Deming was very direct at involving the employees in the process. He showed them that management cared and that they should also care about the product. He later involved the customers in the process. As a result, the Japanese automotive industry went from last to first. Later in the 1980s, Ford Motor Company came to embrace the philosophies of Deming, but it was already behind and it would take time to catch up to the Japanese manufacturers.

TQM movement advanced and was re-popularized throughout the 1990s, but then lost steam as the economy improved, and customer service had less of an impact because businesses did well regardless.

Dr. Deming was also popular for his Deming Cycle, most commonly referred to as the **Plan-Do-Check-Act (PDCA) Cycle**. This is a four-step process for implementing change or continuous improvement. It is useful for incremental or breakthrough improvement. It promotes the idea that a business can always improve.

W. Edward Deming and TQM Terminology
© Boris15/Shutterstock.com

PDCA

Plan-do-check-act cycle. A four-step process for instituting continuous improvement.

Instructions: Apply your change process to the following four-step process:

1. Plan
   Determine appropriate strategy
   Organize to conduct the change
   Team formation
   Problem definition
   Collect and review data

2. Do
   Test the change
   Pilot test
   Observe
   Change as needed
   Implement that change

3. Check
   Measure the effects of the change

4. Act
   Take action according to the results
   Document
   Standardize and formalize
   Promote the change throughout

Plan-Do-Check-Act Cycle (PDCA)
© Tanakax3/Shutterstock.com

This should continue onto step #1 making it a continuous process.

Another creation of Deming was the **Deming Chain Reaction Model**. It has similarities to Service Profit Chain. According to this principle, if an employee has pride in their product, they will produce quality customer service. This will allow the business to sell for less and create loyalty and growth revenue. If a business improves the quality of its products and services, it will bring pride to the employees and the business can enjoy a competitive advantage of quality and customer loyalty that was not possible before.

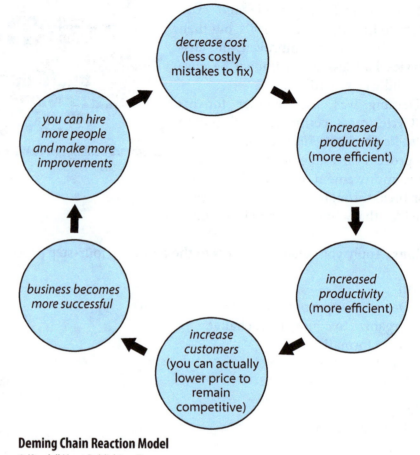

Deming Chain Reaction Model
© Kendall Hunt Publishing Company

An example is a hotel that received many complaints for being "run down" or "outdated." The employees did not feel pride in the hotel and when guests complained they had a "you get what you pay for" attitude. Then the hotel owners decided to do a complete renovation and the employees became proud of their place of business. Before the renovations, many guests would complain about their rooms "the beds are old and uncomfortable" which would lead to refunding stays and the hotel losing money. Now, instead of always returning money, they placed money into renovations and improving the quality of the resort. The level of refunds to guests greatly reduced. Employee morale is higher because they do not hear as many customer complaints. This should increase productivity. The quality of service will increase as well, making the guests wanting to return (i.e., creating customer loyalty). Loyalty becomes growth revenue and the business benefits from the improved product.

It is important to note that profit, the end-goal of most businesses, is the final link of the Deming Chain Reaction. Earning a profit allows the company to grow, prosper, reinvest, and continue to pursue quality in guest service, thus perpetuating the process.

Joseph Juran

Joseph Juran was credited as being the Father of Quality Service. A friend and colleague of W. Edwards Deming, Dr. Juran also helped to introduce quality to the Japanese. He first spoke to Japanese managers in a series of 1954 lectures promoting quality. He was a lecturer and business consultant in over 40 different countries. He published the Quality Control Handbook, among other texts. He established the Juran Institute to help develop and test new quality assessment tools. Steve Jobs, founder of Apple Computers, credits Dr. Juran's "deep, deep contribution" to the advance of quality.

Philip Crosby

Later in the Quality movement, Philip Crosby was originally a Quality Manager for ITT before leaving and setting up his own consulting firm in 1979. He published a well-known book, *Quality is Free*. He was able to show that quality programs would save much more money than they cost. He re-popularized, "do it right the first time" and "Zero Defects." He brought over many quality ideas that were originally developed for manufacturing. These ideas promoted processes and procedures that helped other businesses run smoothly and efficiently; thus, doing it right the first time. This reduced waste, repeats, the need for comps, and the need for service recovery efforts. This followed with the notion that, "if you don't have time to do it right the first time, how will you ever have time to do it over?"

Tom Peters

Author of numerous books, including *In Search of Excellence*, and a presenter and business consultant, Dr. Peters was one of the first and most influential gurus of contemporary management. He has advocated for service excellence through practical means. **MBWA** is a simple but highly effective premise that management should spontaneously walk around and talk to their staff and customers. Paperwork and other tasks prevented managers from walking around the department and property. MBWA promotes listening and qualitative assessment. The management can stay in touch with the staff and customers and identify problems and seek solutions more effectively than sitting in the office and looking at reports.

MBWA
Management by walking around. Idea that management should "get in touch" with the employees and customers to learn what is really occurring.

Peter Drucker

Drucker is commonly known as the Father of Modern Management. An author and management guru, he advocated for the human side as opposed to the numbers. He was popular for idea such as "management by objectives" and the "knowledge worker." He was very interested in the concept of permitting workers to think for themselves. He made many predictions; some of which came true. He, too, helped the Japanese and was also involved in helping General Motors.

Paradigms

Paradigm

A commonly held belief, accepted and presumed to be the proper method.

A **paradigm** is a belief that is commonly accepted as being the proper way or method that something is to be done. This was popularized by Thomas Kuhn in 1962. This promoted "thinking outside of the box" where a paradigm was considered to be "the box." The idea of a paradigm shift became very popular with the quality movement. The cliché of "thinking outside of the box" is still very popular today. Fast-food giant Taco Bell has a mainstream advertising campaign encouraging customers to, "think outside of the bun," imparting the idea that fast-fast doesn't have to be burgers.

Jan Carlson

Moment of Truth

A point of service at which customer service is either made or lost.

Most have heard the term "moment of truth." It is now something that is commonly used in society and applied to any challenging situation; however, the concept applied to customer service is extremely valuable. The term and concept was first popularized by Jan Carlson of SAS Airlines and has great meaning in the context of guest service. Carlson theorized that a service experience is comprised of many different "moments of truth" where customer service is either made or lost. Different situations have varying amounts of **moments of truth**. For example, a quick-service restaurant may have three to five, but a resort hotel may have several hundred. To do this, place yourself in the shoes and eyes of a guest. Record all of the points of interaction throughout the customer service experience. Flowchart the process if necessary. In breaking down the experience into moments of truth, management and employees can better analyze, realize, and monitor the crucial points in the process.

SERVICE INSIGHT

Paradigm Shift

In 1967 technology for the quartz watch was presented to the world at a watch trade show. The Swiss, who had led fine watchmaking for decades, dismissed the idea as being insignificant because that isn't how watches were supposed to be made. Despite being cheaper and having fewer mechanical parts, it went against the watchmaking paradigm. The Japanese saw the quartz technology as a new way to make watches. They saw the potential. They saw it as a paradigm shift and embraced it. Two years later, in 1969 Seiko introduced the first commercially available quartz watch. It caught on so well that the Swiss forever lost their hold on the traditional watch market.

For example, a typical hotel might begin with making a reservation, prepayment, arrival, valet, luggage, check-in, elevator, finding room, unlocking the door, entering the room and checking it, a call from the front desk asking if everything is OK, ordering room service, and so on.

> "The public—the most important people in our business. They are not dependent on us—we are dependent on them. They are not an interruption of our work. They are the purpose of it. We are not doing them a favor by serving them—they are doing us a favor by giving us an opportunity to serve them. They are not outsiders in our business—they are our business! They are not a cold statistic—they are flesh and blood, human beings with feelings and emotions, likes and dislikes. They are not there to argue with or match wits with, or try to outsmart. No one ever wins an argument with the public. The public—people who bring us their wants. It is our job to handle their requirements so pleasantly and so helpfully that they return again and again."

Gold, C. (1983). *Solid gold customer relations* (p. 22). New York: Prentice-Hall.

HOSPITALITY SERVICE PIONEERS

Conrad Hilton (1887–1979) Hilton Hotels and Resorts

Conrad Hilton built the largest hotel company of its time, building and acquiring some of the best hotels in the US. He is attributed to purchasing underperforming hotels. He would then improve operations and cut costs without cutting customer service. He helped to promote the concept: Quality guest service does not have to cost a lot.

Downtown Chicago, Conrad Hilton
© Jonathan Weiss/Shutterstock.com

J. W. (Bill) Marriott Jr. Marriott International

Bill Marriott is a man who still instills a strong sense of corporate culture. This is known as the "Marriott Way." He found people who had a "Spirit to serve" and prefers to be called Bill because he uses first names. He got to know his employees, their spouses' names, and even their children's names. This made employees feel a part of something special.

He promoted a hands-on management system. He still visits many of his properties and does his best to meet and shake the hand of each and every employee. He is a celebrity to this very day. Everyone remembers when they met him and shook his hand. This strong sense of culture builds up employees and makes them take pride in the brand.

Malaysia Marriott
© Augustine Bin Jumat/Shutterstock.com

Ray Kroc (1902–1984) McDonald's Corporation

Ray Kroc did not invent McDonald's. Instead, he applied the concepts of Henry Ford and automation to the fast-food industry. Kroc was also known for his strict operational guidelines. For example, no franchise owners can be silent partners. Instead, they must be actively involved in operations. These strict operational standards were applied to franchises across the nation and world, producing a uniformed product delivered with speed and accuracy.

McDonald's in Krakow, Poland
© Kkrakow.poland/Shutterstock.com

Norman Brinker (1931–2009) Brinker International

Brinker Food Concepts
© IgorGolovniov/Shutterstock.com

Norman Brinker is known as the Father of Casual Dining. Nowadays it is a natural service segment in the restaurant industry, but he helped to create a segment of reasonably-priced dining with full service. Prior to this, many restaurants were quick service or fine dining. This created a great sense of value in the eyes of the customer, surpassing many expectations of the guests. With Brinker's ideas of service, price, and value he was credited with creating or heavily influencing many popular brands such as TGIFridays, Chili's, Applebees, Bennigan's, On the Border, Romano's Macaroni Grill, Houston's, and Outback Steak House.

William Fisk Harrah (1911–1978)
Harrah's Hotel and Casinos, now part of Caesar's Entertainment

Harrah's Casino
© Page Light Studios/Shutterstock.com

Ironically, Harrah modeled many of his business practices after Henry Ford. He turned a small bingo parlor into what was once the largest gaming company in the world. He applied concepts of industrialization to hotels and casino. William Harrah wanted to bring quality, consistency, and efficiency to the hotel and casino market. He created a casino brand for the middle class that provided great quality service.

Mr. Harrah also had a strong sense of corporate culture. He brought a new way of treating both employees and customers to the casino industry. He learned names of many employees. He also empowered his managers and employees. He leaned on them for inspiration and introduced many of the great ideas of serving the customer that produced great success.

With guest service, he also brought ethics and honesty to the gaming industry. Standards were very important. Harrah encapsulated the mantra, "Do it right the first time" and was meticulous with his sense of detail. Everything needed to be planned and precise. These are many of the reasons why his name is still celebrated today.

Conclusion

All of these icons, pioneers, and legends have commonalities. They promote a strong corporate culture. They care about employees. They found a new way of promoting service. It is important to realize that many of the themes, lessons, theories, and philosophies of this book weave together into these few common themes.

❖ CHAPTER REVIEW QUESTIONS

1. What is the definition of quality guest service?
2. Why do some customers choose not to complain?
3. What "Age of Change" are we currently in?
4. List five examples of self-service that you have used in the past week.
5. How did Dr. Deming help the proliferation of quality management?
6. Why do we tend to forget certain events while remembering others?
7. When did the need for speed become popular in the US?
8. Why does bad service still exist?
9. List some of the major contributions to the development of quality guest service management as we know it today.
10. Who is the Father of Modern Management?

CASE STUDIES

A Loyal Following

A loyal following is very important. Giving customers what they want, when they want it, and how they want it can produce a great following. This has been extremely evident in the following of performances. DJ's, niche bands, and other events have struck a chord with the public to produce overwhelming results.

An example of this was the band The Grateful Dead. Led by the beloved Jerry Garcia, the Grateful Dead formed in 1965 and played over 2,300 concerts until his death in 1995. The legend of their music was much more than a performance. It gave society what it needed at a crucial time in California. They were part of the hippy movement of peace and performed more free concerts than any other band in history. It struck such a chord in society that few bands are even close to having the same impact on their fan base. Loyal followers, or Dead-Heads, as they were called, would follow the band anywhere they performed. They were easily spotted by a tie-dye shirt and famous dead art including dancing bears; Uncle Sam skeleton; and a red, white, and blue "Stealie Skull" with a lightning bolt going through it. People would camp out for days before a concert and follow them for lengthy periods. Networks were established in the days long before the Age of Communication. They traded and exchanged information regarding performances and band news like no other band at that time. They grew crowds of tens of thousands at nearly every performance. Tickets were difficult to obtain, no matter what price they charged. People weren't just entertained by The Grateful Dead, they knew and loved the band, its members, and its music. It was a lifestyle.

1. List the customer typical profile and traits of a Dead Head.
2. How did the band differentiate itself from the competition of other bands and entertainment?
3. What did the band do to produce such a loyal following before the Age of Communication?
4. Can you list bands that have a similar following today? What are the commonalities of the followers?
5. Which aspects of the Hospitality Service Pioneers did Jerry Garcia possess?

Club Me

Club Me is a new dance club in a downtown area, in close proximity to three colleges. It is located in an old factory building. It has a loft, balcony, and many cool private areas around the side of the dance floor. Its main target market are the students attending the three local colleges. Dance clubs are a very competitive market in this area. Being current is important and loyalty does not exist. The students can decide to go to one club or another within an instant and the whole scene changes.

Club Me was off to a great start. It was new and fresh and fun and had a mass of people waiting to get in, which only made more people want to get in for what is referred to as "fear of missing out" (FOMO). They had a great line-up of popular DJ's and regularly held contests with give-aways. It was packed every night of the week, and Club Me became more and more crowded. At first, it was a fun, packed atmosphere. As crowds continued to grow, it became apparent that Club Me couldn't adequately handle this volume of crowd. This became apparent when a fight broke out in one of the private areas. One female attacked another in one of the private areas. Security was stationed at the door, the dance floor, and the bar, but had little notice of the secluded areas which were largely ignored. When a security guard was told there was a fight between two females, he smirked and said, "Cool, a chick fight." He did not call for back-up, thinking it was just an argument and would soon be over. By the time he responded, a woman was badly beaten to the point of unconsciousness while others just watched. She had to be taken out in an ambulance and remained in critical condition. The security had clearly downplayed the incident to the point of neglect.

Club Me quickly hired more security, but the crowds stopped coming. The news of this had spread throughout the club scene. Females didn't feel safe. They felt unprotected against attacks and they stopped going to Club Me.

1. Why did large crowds go to Club Me?
2. How had Club Me met customer expectations?
3. How had Club Me failed to meet customer expectations?
4. Is it possible for Club Me to change the attitudes of the market? If so, what should be done?

Chivo's Banquet Hall

Chivo's Banquet Hall is a landmark. It is a family-owned hall and boasts the offerings of the Chivo family. Nearly everyone in the immediate and extended family can be found there during an event. The Chivos are very proud of their establishment. Mama Chivo, as she is called, can be found running the front of house operations. It is not uncommon to find her commanding orders to her staff, hugging and kissing repeat guests, and even offering advice to attendees. She is a true, old-style Mama.

Mr. Chivo runs the food. He is a proud Chef. He is very passionate about his work. Occasionally he and Mama will have an argument over the best way to serve an event. Mama usually wins and Chef Chivo retreats into the kitchen, cursing at times. As startling as it might seem, everyone is accustomed to it and most staff and customers consider it acceptable and continue on with the day.

Chef Chivo's way of ensuring customer satisfaction is by walking the room with his Chef's attire. After the food has been served, Chef Chivo works the room and stops by every table. With a proud smile, he asks everyone at each table how they liked the event and the food. Everyone usually says that everything is great. He looks at everyone's plates. If it is empty, he directly asks them if they would like more. If it has food on it, he asks them what was wrong with it. People almost always tell him there is no problem at all. He looks at them suspiciously and shakes his head letting them know that he is offended. Sometimes he will jokingly tell them that they need to eat more and that they look thin, even if they are not. Most everyone laughs, although it is not really funny.

1. Describe the tone of guest service at Chivos Banquet Hall.
2. Critique Chef Chivo's unique style of customer service.
3. What are some likely reasons why the Chivos seldom hear complaints?
4. If you could give the Chivos advice regarding customer service, what would it be?

Mount Will

Mount Will is a small, steep mountain. It features skiing and snowboarding in the winter, and offers other extreme opportunities throughout the rest of the year. It is known for having the most extreme offerings to make up for its small size. Its motto is little mountain, big adrenaline. Mount Will attracts many visitors who want a special challenge in a mountain experience. Luckily, it is located beside a major highway and receives much visibility from people traveling through the area. They try to change some options every year to keep it fresh. This year, they have arranged for a company to bring in a large crane to allow bungee jumping right next to the highway. Everyone passing by could watch the jumps and it would be great for publicity. They negotiated a great price with the subcontractor and are pleased to offer this attraction.

Unfortunately, they haven't been very successful. Very few people have dared to brave the bungee jump and their overall attendance is down for the season. Feeling the pressure in the loss of revenue, Scott, the Mountain Manager, decides to set up a small booth at a local grocery store to promote the event and hand out coupons. People are typically polite but he doesn't count it a success.

He decides to go out front to the crane by the road to discuss this matter with them. Scott usually takes the back road in and arrives at the property from a road. What he sees blows him away. From the front view, the cab of the contractor's crane looks dingy and dull. The cables appear rusty. The workers are unshaven and dressed poorly. Upon mentioning it, he is told that the cables are more than adequate and that it is only surface rust. The crane received inspections from the state and it is all of passing quality. Still, Scott is concerned with the image. He now realizes the issue.

1. How often should a manager perform full-view visual inspections of a property?
2. As a customer, list your expectations in a bungee-jumping crew and equipment.
3. What are the thoughts of potential customers passing by on the highway?
4. How could the expectations of the potential customers be best met?

REFERENCES

Branson. https://www.virgin.com/richard-branson/staff-come-first

Deming, E. "Quality, Productivity, and Competitive Position" MIT, Center for Advanced Engineering Study, 1982.

Heskett, J. L., T. O. Jones, G. W. Loveman, W. Earl Sasser, and L. A. Schlesinger. "Putting the Service-Profit Chain to Work." *Harvard Business Review* 72, no. 2 (March–April 1994): 164–174.

Chapter 2

Defining Guest Service

CHAPTER OBJECTIVES

After reading this chapter, you should be able to:

- ▶ Identify and explain the guest service principles.
- ▶ List and explain steps involved in providing guest service.
- ▶ Explain the unique characteristics of service.
- ▶ Identify different types and classifications of service.
- ▶ Illustrate the qualities of service such as perishability, tangible and non-tangible.
- ▶ Characterize guest expectations.

TERMINOLOGY

Brand Management
Explicit Expectations
Implicit Expectations
Kano Model
Primary Expectations
Quality Guest Service
Secondary Expectations
Service Promise

"In business you get what you want by giving other people what they want."

—Alice Foote MacDougall

"Being on par in terms of price and quality only gets you into the game. Service wins the game."

—Dr. Tony Alessandra

Defining Quality Guest Service

There are many definitions for **quality guest service** available. When summarized, most can be condensed to this one simple definition: exceeding guests' expectations.

This is often easier said than done. A challenge with this definition is that much work goes into consistently pleasing the guest. It is a collaborative approach that integrates all employees into a process of continuous improvement. There are many variables that must be accounted for. Below are many of the aspects that go into the coordination and execution of guest services.

Quality Guest Service

Exceeding guests' expectations.

ASPECTS OF GUEST SERVICE

© Nelosa/Shutterstock.com

There are many aspects that comprise guest service. Despite the initial definition, it demands much explanation. The following is a list of common ideologies that define customer service:

Welcoming the Guest

With a genuine smile and effort that makes the guest feel welcome. Make them feel recognized, respected, validated, appreciated.

Focusing on Serving the Guest

The guest is the primary focus. The guest can fire everyone by deciding not to patronize an establishment. Everything that you do should result in pleasing the guest.

Consistency in Service

Every guest experience is unique and important and cannot rest on its laurels. Dan Kaplan (Hertz Equipment Rental Corp.) makes a good analogy when he calls it "hitting 1,000 singles." Failing to provide quality service even 2% of the time can result in nearly 150 customers a week that may never return and tell others.

Efficiency in Service

People have a sense of efficiency on an unconscious level. They can detect ineffi-ciencies which often manifest themselves through irritability and impatience with a situation. Good service is often quick service with little wasted time or energy. Customers love to be a part of a well-run machine!

Guests Defining Quality and Value

Everything is subject to the guest's perception. The guest brings many ideas of what is acceptable and what is unacceptable. Every guest is different. It is impor-tant to be able to recognize the guests' expectations and accommodate as much as the system allows.

Knowledgeable Employees

Knowledge within your employees is often derived through proper hiring, on-go-ing training and motivation, and proficient shift management. This also brings a competence in your staff that feeds into the guest experience and helps to elimi-nate potential problems before they escalate.

Commitment From the Top of the Organization

Customer service must be supported by the top management of the organization. This will ensure that systems and resources are allocated and in place to effectively handle the demands of service.

Process That Allows It to Continually Improve

All good processes have a system of checks and balances built into them. You can learn a lot from your mistakes. Process improvement is done through a series of feedback evaluations where learning points can be derived and used to repair the system so that you are constantly getting better.

MEDIA REPORTS OF CUSTOMER SERVICE

The American Customer Satisfaction Index is a model developed by the University of Michigan's Ross School of Business. It is an industry standard and gets a lot of press coverage. It uses interviews to measure customer satisfaction on a scale of 0–100. Below are some of the top airline performers of 2018 with their ACSI Score.

2018 ACSI Top Airlines

1.	Southwest	80		6.	Delta	74
2.	Alaska	79		7.	All others	73
3.	JetBlue	79		8.	United	67
4.	Allegiant	74		9.	Frontier	62
5.	American	74		10.	Spirit	62

Some of the top airline industry for benchmarks included: ease of check-in, ease of making a reservation, courtesy and helpfulness of the crew, and timeliness of arrival.

Below are the results of hotel brands for 2018.

2018 ASCI Top Hotel Companies

1.	Hilton	82	6.	InterContinental	77
2.	Marriott	81	7.	LaQuinta	76
3.	Hyatt	79	8.	All others	75
4.	Starwood (Marriott)	79	9.	Choice	73
5.	Best Western	77	10.	Wyndam	70

Top Hotel Industry benchmarks included ease of check-in process, ease of making a reservation, courtesy and helpfulness of staff, and call center satisfaction.

ACSI 2018 Internet Travel Services—by Company

1.	Orbitz (Expedia)	81
2.	Travelocity (Expedia)	80
3.	All Others	78
4.	Expedia	78
5.	Priceline	78

Top Customer Experience Benchmarks included ease of booking and payment process, ease of navigation, site performance, and variety and selection of travel options.

https://www.theacsi.org/about-acsi/the-science-of-customer-satisfaction

It is not surprising that these same companies continue to rank highly on the lists. This type of publicity cannot be bought. These are companies that have taken service to new levels with training and innovation.

TYPES OF SERVICE

Another way to define service is by categorizing it by type. Service can be generally categorized into three different types: assistance, repair, and value-added. The first two types of service are expected. The third type involves exceeding the guests' expectations.

Assistance Service

This involves basic service. It is meeting the expectations of the customer. Providing assistance to others is crucial to any business.

> ► Example: I need help choosing a good seat for the show.
> ► Example: I need help choosing an appropriate wine.

Repair Service

Fixing a problem for a customer. It may have been a fault of the business. It is reactive, instead of proactive. It involves "putting out fires." Unfortunately, some people in the hospitality industry are better at putting out fires than avoiding them in the first place.

▶ Example: Repairing a leaky faucet in a guestroom.
▶ Example: Helping a traveler find an alternative flight in bad weather.

Value-Added Service

This involves exceeding the customers' expectations. This has a positive impact on the customer experience. It involves going a step past basic job requirements. It raises average service to the level of exceptional service.

▶ Example: Remembering a guest's favorite drink.
▶ Example: Offering a free upgrade.

Of course, being able to classify the levels of service is only the beginning. Next steps would include a training and guest service system that enables a sufficient amount of each type of service at the proper time.

❖ KANO MODEL

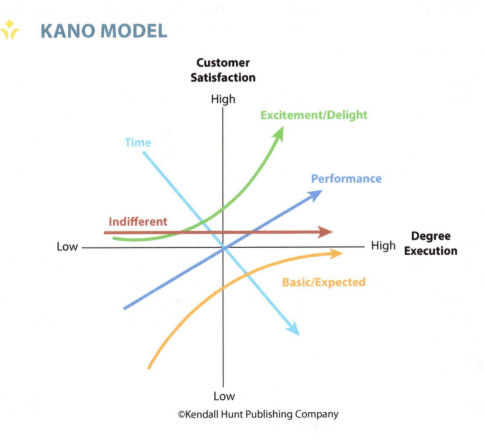

©Kendall Hunt Publishing Company

Kano Model

A model that uses an XY grid for classifying and analyzing types of service. Three main types are basic, performance, and excitement requirements.

The Kano Model is a similar description to types of service. It was developed by Dr. Noriaki Kano in 1984. The **Kano Model** helps businesses understand customer needs and how they influence customer satisfaction. It helps to determine which products, services, and features are important to the customer, and how they are important. In order to meet the needs of the guests, we must first understand their needs. Some would even claim that we need to know the needs of the guests better than they know themselves.

The **Kano Model** has two axes set up in a typical XY graph. The vertical axis is a measure of guest satisfaction. The horizontal axis is a measure of execution. It measures three types of service needs or requirements: Basic, Performance, and Excitement.

Basic Requirements

These requirements are obvious, assumed, expected, taken for granted, and must be present. Customers are upset when these requirements are not provided or missing. These were originally referred to as "Must-Be's" by Dr. Kano. Examples of these might be a proper air temperature in a plane, adequate security at a concert, or wholesome food at a restaurant. You would expect these items. Having them is obvious, and does not make you happy. Instead, they only upset you when they are missing.

Performance Requirements

These requirements are one-dimensional. Many of these are obtained or verified through market research. These are known, spoken, and obvious. They are used in evaluation of competitors. These are always good when supplied or fulfilled. The more of them that you can provide, the better. Examples of these might be extra leg room or a personal screen on a flight or extra amenities at a hotel.

Excitement Requirements

This requirement is considered to be awesome if present. It is something extra. This is the only type of requirement that is permissible if missing.

Dr. Kano originally referred to these as "attractive or delighters." It is also referred to by others as a "Wow factor" or a "unique selling position." It is a competitive service advantage. Examples of this will vary depending on the situation, but could be a complimentary umbrella on a rainy day, a free valet service, or a table visit from the Chef.

Shifting

It is important to note that categories will shift over time. There is a saying that "what is a wow-factor today, will be asked for tomorrow, and required the day after that." To illustrate this, consider the free Wi-Fi at a coffee shop. Some years ago it was a great extra feature that delighted customers, then it started to become common, and now it is quite noticeable and troubling if a business does not offer it to its customers.

Additional Requirements

Indifferent requirements: are those that customers do not care about. This is illustrated in the graph as a zone of indifference. Examples: restroom attendant, an elevator operator, or an extra copy of the menu with each Chinese take-out order.

Reverse requirements: are those that upset customers if present. This was not done on purpose. Instead, these extra amenities frustrate customers instead of helping them. This might be from a poor execution or design, or because it is inappropriate.

> ▶ Example: Guest not appreciating self-service in a 5-star hotel.

More details of how to implement the Kano Model will be reviewed in the tools section of this text.

CUSTOMER PARTICIPATION— INVOLVING THE GUEST

There are many levels and interpretations of self-service. The customer is usually present and involved in the service process, but the term self-service implies that it is to a far greater degree. This is sometimes referred to as "Co-creation of service" or "Co-production of service." Examples include airlines and hotels utilizing self-check-in, and restaurants employing customers to order meals on their own with tablet ordering.

In Chapter 1, advantages and disadvantages of customer participation were cited. An advantage was increased efficiency, but a disadvantage was potential errors in the process. In general, self-service can make wait times seem easier. Customers can proceed at their own pace. It involves the customer in new ways that can be entertaining and can speed up the process. It can save money and permit guests to even customize their level of service. In addition to being efficient, it can be empowering to the customer to have such control over the situation. In this section, we delve further into the management of the process.

Partial Self-Service or Self-Service
© Song_about_summer/Shutterstock.com

Customers Serving Other Customers

Another option is encouraging customers to work with each other. In this, the service provider's involvement is largely that of oversight.

The service point of contact could even involve guests helping other guests like in the case of chat forums, user-ratings, or even customer questions. In some cases, guests can even train other guests and support each other. This is very popular with technologies, but is beginning to transition over into the Hospitality Industry.

Customers can have a substantial influence on each other, be it in-person or electronic. They don't even have to know each other. This is why social media reviews are considered very important to organizations. In the case of user ratings, a customer's detail of an event is viewed as being even more credible than that of the company.

In certain cases, having customers involved in the process and even interact with other customers can be quite advantageous as mentioned earlier in this section. The most important aspect is to ensure it is managed properly.

To help better manage the participation of customers, consider these steps:

1. Assess what parts of the service experience best fit. Ask: do we need to do this for them? What are they able to do themselves? Would they appreciate being engaged in the process? Are there options?

2. Encourage customers to participate. Ask: What's in it for them? It might be reward points, membership, discount, efficiency, control, convenience, less invasive, and so on.

3. Make customer roles clear, but leave room for unexpected opportunities. Let the customers know what is expected of them. Provide clear instructions. Parallel the standard process. Provide a natural path of progression. Have a backup plan if something goes wrong, or they do not wish to participate. Test out these features ahead of time.

4. Show your presence. Don't let them ever think they are alone. Make yourself known and available throughout the process. Guests should always know that help is close by.

5. Monitor the participation. Learn and adapt to the curve of participation. Have easy options available for those who don't want to participate. Correct issues as needed. While most guests are fine, issues will occasionally arise and action must be taken. Customers should know that you can remedy issues very quickly or you will lose their business. Remember, the goal is to increase customer satisfaction.

Unique Characteristics of Service

TANGIBILITY OF SERVICE

Steak on a Plate With Red Wine and a Side
© Africa Studio/Shutterstock.com

Intangibility

Consider this, *What are we really selling?* Is it just a steak? Is it just a glass of wine? Is it just the rental of a room? Is it just a seat at an event? No, of course it is not. There is so much more in addition to the tangible items. In hospitality, we sell an entire experience. Thus, a great portion of your product is the experience. This experience turns into a memory of a pleasant event, exchange, or service offering.

To further understand what the customer experiences, it is important to take everything into parts or components. Two of the most common components are tangibles and intangibles. By breaking down each of the components, they can be monitored and evaluated and improved upon.

To do this, it is important to observe the entire customer service experience through the eyes of the customer. In doing so, you will find that most customers experience both tangible and intangible products. **Tangibles** are anything the customer can touch, consume, or take away from the experience such as a comfortable bed or a delicious meal. **Intangibles** are anything that cannot be touched or easily quantified such as an appropriate referral or a warm smile.

Tangibles and Intangibles of the Hospitality Industry

Tangibles	Intangibles
comfortable bed	suggestion to a nice restaurant
delicious meal	warm, welcoming smile
hot coffee	willingness to serve
chocolate truffles in the room	accurate reservation
luxurious bedspread	thank you and good night upon exit

After you have determined which tangible and intangible aspects apply to your business, you can help the situation by realizing that people often use tangibles to determine intangibles. So, monitor those tangibles. It might be a foul odor or a squeaky door, a coffee stain or an outdated entrance. Make your establishment a clean and welcoming environment. This will ease the customers' minds, drive new business, and increase sales. After you have them, then, of course, the intangibles also need to be in place and correct.

HETEROGENEITY OF SERVICE

Service will usually be unique. There will always be a certain amount of variability in the service.

Since there is typically a human element in the service process, each transaction tends to be unique. Even if a service is identically replicated, they are seldom perceived the same. Human beings are diverse, each with a different set of needs and expectations.

Humans provide variation in the delivery of service. In addition, the same service could be accepted in one location and totally unacceptable in another. Consider additional variations in time of day, season, and occasion.

It is subject to interpretation by the staff and the customer.

Intangible

services—Cannot be "touched"; airplane flight example. An issue with intangibility is that customers do not physically have a product until they purchase it. Therefore, they must base their expectations on the tangibles.

Tangible

products or goods— Ones the customer can see, feel, and/or taste ahead of time.

✦ THE CUSTOMER ULTIMATELY DECIDES—A DIFFERENT PERSPECTIVE

Restaurant Customer With Food Issue
© Branislav Nenin/Shutterstock.com

Consider these questions: Who pays the salaries of the management and the employees? Who pays the rent, the utilities, and the taxes? Who can fire the entire establishment? Who can bring the business to a screeching halt? The customer can. The customer's satisfaction is the reason that all of this is possible. The customer can fire everyone and bring the whole place down. They vote with their patronage. They return as little or as often as they wish. They may be easily swayed, but are difficult to convince. This is extremely important to know because they should be treated as the ultimate critic, because they ultimately are.

✦ INSEPARABILITY OF THE SERVICE (AKA SIMULTANEITY)

You cannot separate the:
—*provider* of the service

from the
—*act of providing* the service

from the
—*consumption* of the service.

Since it is often produced and consumed simultaneously, it is difficult to separate the two. Since the provider and the service are linked, and the act of providing the service and the consumption of it are simultaneous, all are judged as the same.

It is important to know this because a brand and reputation will be judged by the level of the service transaction. Dr. Deming spoke heavily of variability in processes. Your goal is to reduce this variability, or everything will suffer. To help remedy this, you must elevate guest service standards. This can be done by properly hiring and training with correct standards.

✦ PERISHABILITY OF SERVICE

Perishability
Cannot be used for later or future sale but must be made during the time of service.

You cannot inventory service. It is not a commodity. It needs to be ready as dictated by the customer. Most of what we do in the hospitality industry is perishable because service is produced and consumed simultaneously. This has a major effect on your staffing and cost of labor. You must be able to accurately predict what services are needed, when they will be needed, and to what extent they will be

SERVICE INSIGHT

Service Is Most Important Indicator of Revenues

A recent study by Cornell linked higher guest satisfaction with the higher revenues in hotels. A research report from PFK Hospitality demonstrated that guest satisfaction is heavily influenced by guest service. Key factors included:

—employee attitude,

—continuity of service,

—pacing of service, and

—order of services procedures provided.

This is one of many recent studies demonstrating what many have preached all along. Customer satisfaction is a key to a successful business. This means that satisfying the guest is one of the most important things that you could do. In fact, service was deemed far more important than location or even price! Also noted of importance was a well-kept property, hence reinforcing the idea of tangibles predicting intangibles.

(Cornell Hospitality Research Summit, report by PKF 2012).

needed. As an example, an a la carte restaurant has to be able to accurately predict the correct amount of properly trained staffing or it will face difficulties. Too few staff will save payroll, but not meet the demands of the customers. Too many staff will meet the demands of the customers, but will erode your profits, eventually forcing you out of business. Add to that situation, unions, call-outs, fluctuations in business, and emergencies and you will quickly realize how difficult this is.

Meeting Guests' Expectations

Receiving truly great service is receiving more than you expected. It is something that a guest would want to tell others about. They want to tell others about their favorite restaurant, or a fantastic hotel that they just visited, or a wonderful show that they attended, or a wonderful trip that they just took. You are selling, in a sense, bragging rights. Most people enjoy hearing these stories as they can see it in their eyes how much they enjoyed it. Is it the great product they received or did they receive exactly or even more than they expected? It was likely both. And the first step in "meeting expectations" is understanding them.

Expectations can be as complex as people themselves. Most customers do not ask for the unreasonable. Only a few want the world on a platter. Most customers simply want their expectations met. In fact, they even have tolerance if a few things are lacking but they are treated well. Meeting those expectations can be best accomplished through first understanding them. Expectations can also be categorized a few ways.

Customer Service Collage
© master_art/Shutterstock.com

The first is to evaluate the type of signals you are putting out as a business. These signals begin to establish or set the level of expectations. They can be explicit or implicit. They all make up the brand or image that you portray. This idea is commonly referred to as **brand management**. All decisions, both implicit and explicit, would be related to this central theme, from the wallpaper and décor to service-style.

Brand Management

The idea of organizing and controlling a theme that is consistent throughout the entirety of a company.

▶ **Explicit Expectations**: those expectations that are fully expressed. They are set by promises made by staff, contracts, menus, signage, advertisements, and **service promise**.
▶ **Implicit Expectations**: those expectations that are not fully expressed. They are set by prices, décor, location, and service style.

Explicit Expectations

Expectations of service that are clearly provided or given by the business.

LEVELS OF EXPECTATIONS

You can also define expectations by level. In the perfect world, you would want to achieve ideal expectations. Reasonable levels, however, are still quite meritable, particularly if accomplished on a consistent level.

Service Promise

Often stated internally and externally, a guarantee of goods or services that the customer will be satisfied. In the event that this is not achieved, the business promises to correct the error. Common in organizations.

▶ **Ideal Expectations**: The best possible outcomes, those that exceed the typical expectations. These experiences "WOW!" the guests. They create memorable experiences.
▶ **Reasonable Expectations**: These are typically met by following the standard protocol. They are the expected outcome and still very worthy and held in regard.
▶ **Minimal Expectations**: The least the guest will tolerate. Not ideal for most guests. This level opens the door for competitors. Some guests will complain, but many will endure, leaving the management and staff wondering what went wrong. Others will move on, particularly if lured by the competition.

Implicit Expectations

Expectations of service not fully expressed or stated, but certainly implied by a business.

ORDER OF EXPECTATIONS

Expectations are also defined by order: primary and secondary. The primary expectations are assumed, while the secondary expectations are initially less important.

Primary Expectations

Essential expectations. Crucial to the quality guest service experience.

▶ **Primary expectations** are generalizable to most hospitality settings. They are the main wants and needs of the service experience.

☐ Prepared and ready for the guest
☐ Attentive, professional service
☐ Efficiency
☐ Comprehension of the process
☐ Knowledge of the times
☐ Wants are heard and understood
☐ Follow-through of a product that is what it claims

► **Secondary expectations** are less important to basic, essential service and may be omitted with a certain level of tolerance by the customer. They are the things that take away from the guest service. Guests don't usually mind until they become a larger issue, although it would certainly be best to provide all of these expectations in a desirable situation.

- ☐ Knowledgeable, pleasant staff
- ☐ Options made known
- ☐ No transferring
- ☐ Competence
- ☐ Acknowledgment, know me. Or, respect my anonymity.

☀ INPUTS THAT SET EXPECTATIONS

Every customer is different. There are many inputs that determine the individual customer's expectations. Some come from the business while others come from the guests. As a result, the expectations may be low, high, or even undecided. To understand what the guest expects, let's look at examples of the different inputs that define their expectations.

Guest Expectation Inputs From Businesses and Guests

Inputs from Business	Examples	Guest Expectations
Marketing		
Advertisements	Nobody beats us . . .	↑high
Reviews	4 Stars	↑high
	Critics dislike	↔undecided
Operations		
Name	Is it vague?	↔undecided
	Does it instill high expectations?	↑high
	Cheesy? Cliché?	↓low
Menu prices	High prices	↑high
	Low prices	↓low
Menu offerings	High quality items, tableside . . .	↑high
Service Type	Full	↑high
	Limited	↓low
Décor	Food service: tablecloths, high-back chairs	↑high
	Hotel: valet, concierge, many amenities	
Inputs from Guests		
Self		
Personal knowledge	They took a course in wine appreciation	↑high
Standards	They mind seating themselves	↓low
Personal view of quality	They are accustomed to all meals being fine dining	↑high

Inputs from Business	Examples	Guest Expectations
Others		
Influence of others in party	Trying to make a good impression on others in the party	↑high
Competition	Competitors are weak	↓low
Word-of-mouth	Word-on-the-street says that you are awesome	↑high
Occasion		
To relax	Laid-back	↓low
To entertain	Business clients	↑high
To impress	First date	↑high
Professional	Business meeting	↑high

As you can see, there are many factors that go into assessing the expectations of the customers. Some can be managed, like menu offerings, prices, décor, and image, yet other factors can only be responded to. The individual customer's personal combination can range from low to high and can change depending on circumstances. It is important to identify and accommodate as best as possible.

Scenario A: Fast-Food Restaurant

Unsatisfied Guest
© Iakov Fillimonov/Shutterstock.com

Satisfied Guest
© Iakov Fillimonov/Shutterstock.com

You can have great customer service at a quick-service restaurant. Consider this scenario:

As you approach a fast-food restaurant, you have certain expectations. This is your first point of service. As you enter and move to the front counter, you have a certain set of expectations. This continues as you order, wait for the food, receive the food, and consume the food. You expect a moderately clean building, relatively short or fast-moving line, and a correct order. You would like to be able to place your order reasonably quickly without encountering a rude order-taker. You would like to receive the items ordered.

Point of Service	Expectations	Actual	Customer Reaction
Building	Safe, minimal litter, not too crowded	Average cleanliness, some straw papers on the floor, some trays stacked around trash can, semi-crowded	OK, because it's minimal litter and some crowd was expected
Line	Less than 3 minutes to order	Waited 3–4 minutes	OK, because it was close to the expected time
Cashier	Cashier mood: average, not disgruntled	Indifferent	OK, because cashier wasn't disgruntled
Order	Order accuracy: accurate as described, with minimal issues	Customer had to restate order, cashier was mostly familiar with menu (had to search for buttons)	OK, because the menu/order issue was minimal
Wait for Food	Less than 3 minutes	3 minutes	OK, because it took 3 minutes
Quality	Food quality: average	Average, fries were hot but not straight out of fryer, one onion ring mixed in	OK, because food was "average." One onion ring mixed in didn't bother them
Table	Available with minimal effort, all members in party can sit together	You find an adequate table, you clear off a few crumbs from previous customer	OK, because everyone can sit together. Small mess seemed reasonable
Was it a good experience?			Yes, because they received what they expected

Scenario B: Fine Dining Restaurant

Correspondingly, you can have poor customer service at a fine dining restaurant. Consider this alternative scenario:

As you approach a fine-dining restaurant, you have far higher expectations. These expectations are not met. There are a few recently discarded drinks outside the entrance. You wait 3–4 minutes before being noticed. They are indifferent to your arrival, mispronounce your last name, and are still setting your table. Once seated you had to restate your order. The timing of the food was otherwise good but the sauce was smeared and a few green beans were hanging off the plate.

Point of Service	Expectations	Actual	Result
Building	Safe, spotless, not too crowded	Average cleanliness, a few drinks discarded outside entrance, semi-crowed	Not pleased, but able to overlook these small issues at first
Entrance	Maître d' greeted within 20 seconds of arrival	Waited 3–4 minutes to be noticed	Mildly upset, 3–4 minutes seemed like a long time for such a nice place
Maître d'	Is pleased to see guests	Indifferent, somewhat hurried, no special recognition	The guests feel unimportant. They are paying a great deal of money and want to feel welcomed
Reservation	Reservation correct as requested and table ready	Correct with mispronunciation of last name	Perturbed. They have the reservation, but the mispronunciation conjures ill-recalled memories, causing the customer to roll their eyes
Table	Open and set	Open but busman setting it	Inconvenienced and dislikes having to stand in dining room, feels as if in the way of passing servers, patrons, stairs. Wonder why they were walked to table if it wasn't fully ready. Smell of cleaning solution emanates.
Server	Attentive, friendly, professional	Indifferent, rushed	Feels like a burden to the server. They wonder what is going on with management and operations.

Point of Service	Expectations	Actual	Result
Order	All accurate, memorized, server had a superior command of menu knowledge	Accurate, used a pad, customer had to restate order, average menu knowledge	OK, but frazzled from previous feelings
Wait for Food	Only reasonable timing is acceptable	Reasonable timing	OK, but frazzled from previous feelings, beginning to feel better
Food	Perfection	Perfect except for a smear of sauce and two green beans hanging off side of a plate	Preposterous! Wonders if the kitchen cares at all
Was it a good experience?			NO! Their expectations were not met. Food and service was not acceptable

Was it truly horrible? Probably not, but according to the guest it was preposterous! They believe that they were not provided with the level of service they expected. A customer might bring comments like, "What's the matter with this place?" and "The service was absolutely hideous!" Meeting expectations of service can make all of the difference.

Neither scenario was great, but although it wasn't an exceptional experience for either example, the customer at the fast-food restaurant left pleased and would likely return. The party at the fine dining restaurant will probably tell many of their acquaintances about the disappointing experience they had.

Also notice that some small issues are permitted in both cases. As the customer service encounter progresses and service points are not meeting expectations, the Customer B becomes quite upset. So, it is both meeting expectations and a culmination of several smaller points.

SERVICE INSIGHT

Meeting Expectations—Basics

To help meet or exceed the guests' expectations, consider the following:

Become familiar with your customers, survey them.

Demonstrate your dedication to your customers.

Tell your customers what they can expect, then keep your word.

Develop your expertise and maintain consistency.

Treat all of your customers and workers with the same high level of respect.

Apologize if you are wrong, and remember that credibility is much harder to regain than it is to attain in the first place.

ISSUES WITH EXCEEDING EXPECTATIONS

Can you always exceed customer expectations? Is this possible? Perhaps you should just meet them. Consider this:

If you are always "delighting" customers, logic might claim that you are consistently underselling and over-delivering. If this were the case, wouldn't the customers come to expect more than you say? And wouldn't they be disappointed when they did not receive more than promised?

Wouldn't your competition be able to make greater claims if you are underselling? What happens if you can only promise a 45-minute show (that is typically 55 minutes) and they are able to promise a 55-minute show? They look better than you do.

Aren't you going to lose money by giving everyone a free meal, a free room, a free show, and a free plane ticket? Of course you are. You cannot upgrade everyone to first-class, and someone has to eventually pay for all of the items that you comp. After all, businesses are in business to earn a profit.

Dr. Kano of the previously mentioned Kano Model also made reference to issue. His advice was to consistently re-evaluate the responses of the customer as they may likely change over time.

Consider this, the other part of the definition of quality guest service is "consistently meeting expectations." You can still exceed expectations, but it must be done with grace, tact, finesse, and logic that all properly trained hospitality professionals have. To give something extra doesn't mean giving away your business, it could mean personalizing a service, giving extra attention, recognizing a familiar face, extra help with bags or the elevator. Using the human touch is what makes hospitality what it is!

"Great service."

Great Service!
© Cartoon Resource/Shutterstock.com

Hospitality companies are quickly adopting an approach to getting to know the customer and adding a human touch by what they call, "developing lifetime relationships with the customers." They have developed a large database with all of their customers' information which is shared among properties. This database keeps record of the guests' profiles which stores items such as:

- ► Name and title preferences
- ► Likes and dislikes
- ► Pictures of pets
- ► Food and beverage preferences
- ► Past issues
- ► Lifetime usage and frequency

☀ DELIVERING A BETTER SERVICE

What is service? Consider the simple definition of providing a service. It is when something is performed for another. It could be help making a reservation, checking in a guest, delivering an entrée, or any number of tasks that we regularly provide in the hospitality industry. In short, we do things for other people, but is it really that simple? What makes the delivery of our services better? Why should customers patronize us? What makes our services more competitive?

Scenario 1

Imagine walking up to a concierge station and asking for a recommendation for a great Italian restaurant. Nearly any concierge will deliver the necessary information and provide a valid recommendation. That is providing a simple service to a guest. If it were a pass/fail test, the concierge would pass. The recommendation would probably be fine and the transaction between the concierge and the guest will soon be forgotten along with countless other forgettable encounters of the day.

Scenario 2

Now, suppose that the concierge immediately stops what they are doing and instantly meets you with a smile. They greet you and then begin to listen intently to your request. They then ask a few questions of clarification: occasion, price range, traditional or contemporary, distance, timeframe . . . to get a better sense of your precise needs. Then they recommend two or three choices based on your needs. They also have menus available on the computer monitor and suggest one of them as their personal favorite. They offer to make a reservation for you and help you with directions and transportation.

SERVICE INSIGHT

Picture of Pet on Nightstand

They review these in advance of the stay and include these in the meetings. They can do things like set the lights and temperature as the guests prefer, and print off pictures of their pet, place them in a frame, and set them next to the bed for a special touch. Now that's a special touch!

© ALife/Shuttetstock.com

This type of service takes planning, training, and the ability to go above and beyond the normal ability to provide a simple service. This is delivering a better level of service. Something as basic as a dinner recommendation can go from a simple service transaction to something that creates value in the eyes of the customer.

Conclusion—Quick Guest Service Advice

Be prepared by knowing the products and services. Know the procedures of your company and the industry. Use this information to make things better and easier for the customer.

Be professional. Present yourself well using verbal and non-verbal communication. Take pride in yourself, your company, and your job.

Listen to the customer. Empathize and assess the customer's feelings first. Let them know that you care for his needs and have a sincere interest in their satisfaction.

Exceed guests' expectations. Be responsible for the customer's satisfaction. Treat the customer as the most important part of your job. Notice the specific needs of each customer and provide those extras that are more than what the customer expects.

In short, deliver a *better* service.

CHAPTER REVIEW QUESTIONS

1. Apply the Kano Model to a local coffee shop.
2. What is the difference between implicit and explicit expectations?
3. Explain the difficulties with always exceeding expectations.
4. Define basic expectations of guest service and explain why they may be met but quality guest service may not be perceived in the eyes of the customer.
5. Provide three recent examples of a service setting when your expectations were exceeded.
6. List five tips for delivering quality service.
7. Explain why expectations differ between customers and establishments.
8. List and explain the characteristics of providing a service.
9. Explain the difference between tangibles and intangibles in a service setting.
10. What does the term "Perishability of service" mean in relation to the hospitality industry?

CASE STUDIES

Ghost Tours

Ghost Tours is a small tour company that specializes in walking tours through the town of Salem, Massachusetts. A small New England town, Salem is known for its famous witch trials. People come to Salem from all over the world to experience the history and lure of the town. Ghost Tours takes this opportunity to provide them with an opportunity to experience this firsthand.

Ghost Tours is a low-budget tour company. It was started a few months ago by Dana Robinson. She saw other companies doing this and thought that she could do an even better job with a little investment, some creativity, and a lot of hard work. She was right. Ghost Tours quickly gained a reputation of being the best in town. It won an award from a local magazine and was featured on the Best Small Businesses of the Year. It has also received great ratings on social media in the past.

She operates her business using a website and a cellular phone out of her home. Ghost Tours began in the spring with four tour guides and is now up to 10 employees since the late summer going into the busy Halloween season. The tours meet people at pre-determined locations to begin the tours. A popular starting point is her friend's coffee shop which enjoys the extra business before and after the tours. Dana's creativity has produced a great website which offers reduced payment if patrons pay online, in advance. Business is growing and, in general, it has worked quite well.

Many of the tours have gone quite well. Guests have returned to the coffee shop excited. However, Dana's friend at the coffee shop is noticing a trend. Guests are arriving unprepared for the early darkness and the cold, inclement weather. Dana originally presumed that people should realize what they are in for when they sign up for a walking tour. As she begins to send out e-mail surveys to her customers, and looks at the social media reviews, she is realizing that she is wrong. She is struggling with how to remedy this problem.

Dana looks at her reviews to see what could be done. It writes that "…you will be scared, on this walking tour. Be prepared and dress accordingly."

Despite what it said on their website, guests were not always dressed accordingly. The sun goes down and the temperatures drop quickly. The wind blows adding windchill, making it feel even colder. Dana decides to pass out inexpensive flashlights to help guests avoid tripping, but wonders what else she can do. Despite this, the complaints continue.

1. In what ways was Ghost Tours successful?
2. In what ways was Ghost Tours unsuccessful?
3. Do you believe that Dana has done everything possible to contend with unsatisfied customers?
4. If you could provide advice to Dana, what would it be?

Bar 229 Main

Bar 229 Main is a trendy, new bar. The owners had a vision to make it the coolest trendy place in town. As many places do, they used a common method of naming by the type of establishment and its address. This trendy name was accompanied by a trendy setting and décor. Being downtown, they were located in the nightlife and the pulse of the metropolitan neighborhood. They had a small window in front, and an open door. Eclectic music spilled out into the street. The inside was dim and intriguing, with small, changing LCD lights that illuminated the clear tables, chairs, and the bar. The place was exotic. People walked in and thought, "Wow, that's cool." It was the place that people wanted to be.

As trendy as the Bar 229 Main was, the owners also had a unique hiring technique. They hired the most attractive people that applied. The owners cared very little about background and qualifications and mostly concentrated on hiring good-looking people. The owners said, "Anyone can wait tables, and we could train a monkey to tend bar. If they don't know how, we can train them, or they can shadow another person who does. It's not rocket science."

Initially, this worked. A few of the applicants knew how to wait tables and worked with the others. This did not last, and soon service suffered greatly. The skilled workers became aggravated when they had to cover for the unskilled workers, and customer complaints began to greatly increase. To make things worse, the owners scheduled workers without taking skill into account. Long wait times and slow service continued. At first, the unskilled workers used charm to overcome their lack of ability, but it was not long before customers grew intolerable.

1. Describe the brand management of Bar 229 Main.
2. What experience was Bar 229 Main aiming to sell?
3. How could Bar 229 Main overcome the customer complaints?

Beachside Hotel

Beachside Hotel was a typical small hotel by the water. It had 32 rooms. All but two of the rooms had a view of the beach and the water. Beachside was once a branded hotel, but the owners didn't feel it was worth paying for the name, the standards, and the hassle of the inspections. In fact, it was questioned whether they gave up the name or lost it.

Eda and Surge were the owners of the Beachside Hotel. They were minimalist, placing all of their efforts into the hotel. They lived in a small apartment in the back of the hotel. They were frugal and strict with every aspect of their personal lives and business. They had acquired the hotel as a run-down property many years ago. Having spent all of their money to repair the property and pay the mortgage, they closely monitored all of the expenses.

Surge would often go off on a mantra telling the employees: "You just check them in and clean the rooms. They don't need anything extra. It just costs me extra money and they don't need it. They have the beach and water. What more could they want? You give them good, basic service. You smile. You take their money and give them a key to their room and that is it. What do you think that we are running the Taj Mahal here?" In fact, Beachside did provide the basics. The rooms were clean. They were basic, but did provide access to the beach and the water.

1. List the tangibles and intangibles of the Beachside Hotel.
2. Did the Beachside Hotel meet the expectations of the customers?
3. What suggestions would you make to Surge and Eda regarding customer service?

Bakery Pricing

Main Street Bakery is an upscale, trendy bakery that recently opened in a renovated filling station. It resides in a transitional, mixed neighborhood that is being rejuvenated by a local artisan crowd. The area still has a traditional class of blue-collar locals, but has recently seem an influx of a younger class of professionals and lovers of art, literature, and all things socially-conscious that has spilled out from the nearby city. Main Street Bakery features socially-responsible breads and pastries baked on-premise in an open kitchen. It also roasts its own coffee on-premise.

One day, two customers enter the bakery and begin to loudly complain about the size of the coffee for the money. One of the customers walks up to the counter and abruptly asks where they get off charging that much for coffee. The customer loudly states that the chain down the street is way cheaper.

The Owner-Manager of the Main Street Bakery hears this and walks over to introduce herself. She smiles and welcomes them to her bakery. She thanks them for entering her establishment to check it out. She explains that it is premium coffee, fair trade certified, and roasted in-house. She assures them it is a much better cup of coffee than the competitor down the street and offers to give them both a free sample. The two customers are hesitant but begin to cautiously let down their guard.

1. Describe the idea behind Main Street Café.
2. Describe the difference in clientele.
3. Rate the response of the Owner-Manager.

Chapter 3

Problem-Solving for Guest Service

CHAPTER OBJECTIVES

After reading this chapter, you should be able to:

► Contrast the expectations of guests and staff.
► Explain and apply the concept of Red Flags.
► Identify and assess the contradictions behind the premise "the guest is always right."
► Identify and apply the five steps to resolve guest issues utilizing the G.U.E.S.T. method.
► Identify the different types of problem guests and outline strategies for handling these problems.
► Explain the science of anger and apply specific strategies for dealing with angry guests.
► Provide an overview of psychological theories and relate them to customer communications.

TERMINOLOGY

Ambivert
DISC
Duty of Loyalty
Emotional Intelligence (EI)
Empathy
Extroversion
Four Temperaments
G.U.E.S.T.
Intent to Return
Introversion
Keep Important Stuff Simple (K.I.S.S.)
Keirsey Temperament Sorter
Lateral Service Principle

Lifetime Customer Value
Meyers-Briggs Type Indicator (MBTI)
Moment of Truth
Opportunity Cost
Rate of Dissatisfaction
Red Flags
Service Recovery
Transactional Analysis

"Customers don't expect you to be perfect.
They **do** expect you to fix things when they go wrong."

—Donald Porter, British Airways

Considering Different Points of Views

WHAT DO PEOPLE REALLY WANT?

At the root of it all, people need to be heard, understood, and appreciated. This is applicable to nearly every relationship and interaction.

People need:

- ▶ to be listened to.
- ▶ to be made to feel special.

People expect the host to:

- ▶ have their best interest at heart.
- ▶ be confident and competent.
- ▶ be believable in their statements and promises.
- ▶ give them what they ask for.
- ▶ surprise them, or at least they appreciate being surprised.

Waitress Serving Coffee
© wavebreakmedia/Shutterstock.com

K.I.S.S.

Keep
Important
Stuff
Simple

Keep Important Stuff Simple (K.I.S.S.), also known as keep it simple stupid. This is the idea that processes don't always need to be complicated. There is great merit to sticking to the basics. This term is widely used among many industries. Refers to keeping processes as simplistic as possible, thus reducing the tendency for error.

❧ LISTENING TO THE CUSTOMER

A woman ordered a cheeseburger at a quick-service restaurant. At her table, the woman immediately realized the cheeseburger was assembled with two bun tops on it. One bun top on the top and another bun top was on the bottom. She went up to the manager at the counter to just explain the situation. Before she could get a single word out of her mouth, the manager immediately handed her another cheeseburger. She didn't want another cheeseburger. Instead, she only wanted to explain what happened. As she tried to explain again, the manager quickly held his hand up stopping her and said, "It's OK, just take a new one." She only wanted to tell him what happened, and he only wanted to give her a replacement cheeseburger.

This is an example of a lose-lose situation. The restaurant lost a cheeseburger, and the customer felt unheard and disrespected. Problem-resolution is often more complex than people think. The solution isn't always what you would first believe and it isn't always about a quick replacement.

The term **Service Recovery** was originally popularized by Ron Zemke when he made a science out of fixing customer mistakes. He gave a system for acknowledging, apologizing, and fixing customer complaints. Other authors have devised their own variations of rectifying mistakes, each version being slightly different. Marriott International uses LEARN (listen, empathize, acknowledge, record, and notify).

> **Service Recovery**
>
> Popularized by Ron Zemke, a system for acknowledging, apologizing, and fixing customer complaints. Other authors have devised their own variations of rectifying mistakes, each version being slightly different.

SERVICE INSIGHT

Good Service Often Goes Unremembered

It is an exceptional experience that is remembered: exceptionally good and exceptionally bad. Our lives are filled with so much information and stimuli that we filter out unexceptional experiences. We forget mediocrity. We remember the "wows" in life. The same holds true to the customer experiences. Customers remember great experiences and horrible experiences, and forget the in-betweens. When they remember, they want to share with others. Review sites are filled with "love-its" and "hate-its" with little in-between. Most don't take time to write a review, a letter, or even share a mediocre experience. This leaves us with two options:

1. "Wow" the guest.

2. Seize the opportunity to fix it and make it right, and allow them to leave feeling special.

Certainly option #2 isn't preferred, but it is an option that reinforces service recovery. A problem is an opportunity to not only correct, but to have a guest leave with something great to remember and share. They can leave with a great WOWED memory, no memory, or great (fixed) memory.

Whatever the method, it is important that each business have one that fits their level of service and is adaptable to its customers. This provides a means to train and provide consistency throughout the organization. Below is an example of **G.U.E.S.T.** which can be easily adapted to resolving customer issues. It is straightforward and detailed enough to serve as a foundation for others to follow.

Other Popular Advice

Don't punish employees with negative feedback from the customers. Also, eliminate the complaint department because complaints should be part of everyone's job. Everyone should be able to, and responsible for, handling customer complaints. There should be a system in place to train employees on how to deal with customer issues.

G.U.E.S.T.

Greet
Understand
Empathize, Apologize
Solve
Track

> **G.U.E.S.T.**
>
> A system of resolving guest conflicts:
> **G**reet—
> **U**nderstand—
> **E**mpathize—
> **S**olve—
> **T**rack is an acronym used to remember how to handle customer complaints or issues.
> An easily-adaptable, problem-solving model.

G.U.E.S.T. is an acronym used to remember how to handle customer complaints or issues. It is an easy-to-remember, easily-adaptable, problem-solving model for service recovery.

Typically, it is not the fault of the employee, but the guest often does care. Most guests do not want to speak with the manager. They want it solved without much trouble. What truly matters is that it is resolved, quickly and effectively. Studies show that if that can happen, a guest satisfaction is significantly improved.

G—Greet

▶ Stop what you're doing when you see a customer.
▶ Turn toward them, make eye contact.
▶ Say your name and ask how you can help them. Customers are the reason you have a job. Let them know that you will respect their time.

> *"Hello, I'm Julie. I see that you aren't doing well. I am here to help. Can you help me to understand?"*

▶ If you are with another customer, acknowledge their presence and let them know that you will be right with them. Call for back-up if needed.

> *"I'm sorry. I'll be right with you in just a moment."*

U—Understand—Listen, Repeat

▶ A complaint offers you an opportunity to learn of a problem.
▶ Listen to the guest.
▶ Try to identify all of their needs and wants.

- Nod your head.
- Don't speak until they finish (even if you know what they are saying).
- Lean in slightly toward them.
- Don't interject your own beliefs (yet).
- Project a sincere face (practice in the mirror).
- Repeat by summarizing what they say to ensure that you heard it correctly and ensure that you have all of the facts. This will help you to determine the problem.
- Take notes if needed.
- Be sure not to complain about other departments and how it's their fault.
- Don't challenge them or trade wits.
- Don't argue with the customer because no employee has ever actually won an argument with the customer.

> *"So your luggage was lost on your flight over, and the air conditioning wasn't working in the shuttle? Your children are upset from the flight and now your room isn't available early?"*

E—Empathize—Apologize

- Respect them. Let them know you care. Customers like to be recognized most of the time. Human beings crave attention and recognition.
- Do everything you can to keep from embarrassing your customers.
- Thank the guest for bringing it to your attention (don't always wait until the end).
- **Empathize**—Acknowledge their feelings. Use phrases like "I understand." "I know how you feel." Consider illustrating your empathy by briefly relating to a similar incident that happened to you.
- **Empathy**—Understanding and compassion for someone else's emotion. When expressed, it often creates a connection between the staff and the customer. Crucial to customer service resolution. Different than sympathy which expresses regret. A much more personalized emotion, which means that you feel and can relate to their hurt. There is a belief that you can only feel a person's pain by "walking a mile in their shoes." This might not always be possible, but hopefully you can find some way to relate to it. Instead, envision what you might do if you were in the customer's position. Empathy feels their hurt and can relate to it, making them share the emotion.

Apologize for what happened to them and how they feel even if it wasn't your fault, or beyond your control, it does not matter. Briefly restate what they said and then say, "I apologize." If in person, be sure to look at them in the eyes with a sincere look. Look at them for 2–3 seconds after you finish speaking.

Don't get caught up in the small points. You aren't admitting blame. Instead, you are apologizing because it happened to them. Even when it's not your fault, don't make it look like it's a big hassle. Don't bring up problems from the past. Don't let your anger get a hold of you.

Also remember that each customer is a new experience. You may have heard it 10 times today, but it is probably the first time for the guest today. Be careful not to relate to other customer experiences, because it may not be viewed as professional.

"I apologize that happened to you. Thank you for letting me know. That makes for a difficult beginning to your trip."

Studies show that spoken words account for about half of the communication. Other variables are the tone of your voice, facial expressions, and other non-verbal body language. Remember that how you say something is just as important as what you say.

S—Suggest—Solve

► Suggest—If you can, offer some type of suggestion. Be careful to be tactful and to not overestimate your own agenda by strongly interjecting your own opinion.

► Solve—If you can, solve it right then and there. Improve the service you can. Try to solve a customer's problem immediately using all of the possible resources at your disposal. Look for solutions and select the right one. Anticipate their needs, but be careful not to provide much more than they want/will except. Look for a win-win. It doesn't have to be a win-lose. Consider the wins and losses of both sides. Envision what the customer may lose versus what the business may lose.

► Observe the impact of the resolution. Did it work? Was it effective? What are the implications?

► Assure them the situation will be resolved. Explain what is happening. Let the customers know that you are working on their problem instead of just getting back to them with the resolution sometime afterward. They may not know that you are working on it or that you're going to get on it right away.

► Ask for an opportunity to continue to resolve the situation and to continue to do future business. Let the customer know that you're going to make things right and that you want to satisfy and keep them as a customer and that you care.

"Let me see if the concierge floor is available so that you get some refreshments in the air conditioning. There are couches up there and a corner with a television for the children. I will call up there right now and let George, our Lead Concierge, know of the situation."

T—Track—Record/Document/Write-Up

► It is important to let someone know by documenting the issue. Most businesses have a manager's log or an incident report and/or a reason for void/comp. Note the likelihood of future business, or, the customer's **intent to return**. These can be troubling to fill out and are easily over-looked. Be sure to look for patterns.

▶ Tracking is important to identify weaknesses in the processes and be proactive in looking for future problems before they occur.

▶ Follow up with the person. Some people appreciate knowing that the cause of the problem has been remedied and is not likely to occur in the future.

▶ Try to have class about it afterward by being professional.

▶ Envision scenarios of alternative positive resolutions. Store those in your memory for future instances.

▶ Take care of yourself. Realize your feelings. Are you stressed?

▶ There is much reward and personal satisfaction from being able to please others.

Intent to Return

The belief of a customer that they will patronize the establishment or services in the future.

Types of Customers

It is important to realize that while all customers are unique, they can often be categorized. It is important to understand different types of customer categories. Each customer is a bit different, so you will need to adjust to them, but you should have tactics for dealing with each type of customer.

Some refer to it as "games" while others merely categorize them. Either view works, providing that it is effectively handled.

1. One of the first things to do is to identify which type of customer they are. This may be done by recognizing familiar catchphrases.
2. Understand where they are coming from because you will want to address what is behind this. Understand the premise or motivation behind their type.
3. Employ your strategy or solution.

You will quickly learn to recognize these popular customer tactics. Occasionally, you will encounter a new twist on them. Place all of these in memory for your mental tool-bag of skills.

This list of Level I customers requires some work, but is generally easy to deal with. The tactics are relatively harmless traits of humanity, but can detract from the customer service experience. Be ready because these softballs can turn into strikes if you aren't prepared.

Unhappy Diners
© Fancy Studio/Shutterstock.com

❖ LEVEL I—HANDLING DIFFERENT TYPES OF CUSTOMERS—REQUIRES LITTLE WORK

Type	Catchphrase	Premise	Solution Strategy
Advice-giver	You know what you should do?	I know more than you. I can improve any situation.	Welcome ideas. Let him know that he is valued, but you have to keep moving. Agree to pass them on but keep transaction moving. Show that you are noting the advice.
Anxious	Is this going to take long?	They have constraints that concern them greatly (travel, bed bugs, phobias).	Show confidence. Give specific praises. Instill confidence in them. Assist them in taking actions.
Arrested Youth	Lighten up.	They are an adolescent in an adult's body.	Be friendly, but guard your boundaries. Let them know that they are accepted, but must follow basic rules.
Bliss	Isn't this awesome!	This person is thrilled.	Keep it friendly. Ensure they focus on the transaction at stake. They may forget essential pieces. Ensure their needs are fulfilled.
Compliments	That's a pretty name.	They want you to like them. They may be afraid of bad service.	Acknowledge and accept the compliments when appropriate. Don't lose sight of transaction. Let them know what you are doing to serve them.
Friendly	Let me show you a picture of my grandson.	They love to share. They desire attention at any cost.	Be polite, but be sure not to allow too much time and attention. After the transaction, tell them it was a pleasure meeting them, and that you now have to tend to another task.
Gossiper	Is there something going on in the ballroom? Was that guest OK?	They like to talk and are hoping for gossip.	Some knowledge can be shared, while other information is highly confidential. Learn what is permitted to share. Respond empathetically by stating you don't know or cannot say in a curious way.
Hot-Mess	It's in here somewhere . . .	Disorganized. Cannot get things together.	Have patience. Sensing anxiety in you will likely make him worse. Make them feel welcomed, understood, and accepted. Suggest alternative methods and service as appropriate.
Jokester	I just flew in, boy are my arms tired.	Desperate for attention. Wants to humor others.	Show good humor and smile at his jokes when appropriate, but direct them toward the business transaction.
Pleaser	It's OK, really.	Concerned to please everyone. Often wants others to be at ease.	Politely let them know what he deserves. Ensure they get everything needed so they aren't secretly unsatisfied.
Ponderer	Umm, what was the first choice again?	Fear of making the wrong decision.	Suggest options when appropriate. Assure them of his decision. Let them know the options available if they change their minds.
Shy	None (and no eye contact).	Some people are shy, afraid of things: looking foolish, making mistakes . . .	Give them an easy out. Respect their shy nature. Reassure them. Attend to them as sincere and low-key as possible. Keep transaction discrete as to minimize their exposure.
Too much information	I just lost my job.	They will talk to anyone that will listen.	Handle with compassion, but expeditiously. Note and help if appropriate. Wish them well with their situation.
No questions please	Yes. No.	They don't want to interact for some unknown reason (shy, tired, cranky, ill).	Respect that. Use caution in trying to get them to open up. Small talk isn't always essential or welcomed.
Questioner	What time is the 3 o'clock parade?	Want to ensure they have the best possible information. Disbelief in information. He believes in the security in redundancy.	Calmly answer each question. Point out where information is available. Repetitively reassure. Be sure to complete necessary transactions.

Level II Customer
© Antonio Guillem/Shutterstock.com

LEVEL II—HANDLING DIFFERENT TYPES OF CUSTOMERS—REQUIRES MODERATE WORK

The list of Level II customers are more difficult to deal with. Their tactics tend to be more coercive with a goal of achieving more out of the situation. Boundaries are key to dealing with this group. Realize what you can give and what you cannot.

Type	Catchphrase	Premise	Solution Strategy
Controlled	The menu does not state that.	This person is very exact. They have precise expectations.	Knowledge of your operation is key. The more that you know about your product the better. Let him know how it could be interpreted that way. Apologize for the oversight and assure him that you will mention it to the person in charge of communications. Matter-of-factly let him know what you can and cannot do at this time.
Flirt	I'm much better now, thanks.	Can be from a male or female. Trying to charm their way into a perk.	By the book. Stick to the standard procedures. Don't use emotion. Don't gag or swoon. Be sincere. Stand your ground. Let him know that you are providing great service.
Free is good	Got any specials going on?	Either they have a genuine desire to save, or they like to play the game of manipulation for self-esteem.	Remind them of the values in your product and service. Let them know of discounts when appropriate.
Grumbler	We paid all this money and . . .	Mildly aggravated. The world is against him and owes him. Many complaints, but non-specific in his demands.	Try to get him to tell you how you can please him. Assure him that his comfort is our #1 priority.
Manager Request	Let me talk to the manager	Assuming you've performed your job, he wants special privileges.	Offer to solve, but then call manager if you are refused. Realize it is not likely about getting you in trouble. It will happen on occasion.

Type	Catchphrase	Premise	Solution Strategy
Space Invader	I just have to go backstage because . . .	This person likes to go where others are not permitted. He believes he is special and rules do not apply to him.	Be straightforward and direct. Maintain boundaries with him. Smile, but be firm in your limits. Suggest all permissible options.
Partier	Which way to the bar? Woo— Partay!	Cannot be bothered with formalities.	Let them have fun, but ensure he does not interfere with others. Politely, be sure transaction or business is still conducted.
Royalty	I'll have the usual.	Likes to be made to feel special. Feels entitlement to be acknowledged as more deserving than others. I'm not just anybody, I am me!	Let them be king. Show respect. Remind him of all of the services being given.
Whiner	I have had such a bad day . . .	Wants someone to listen. Cannot handle situation alone. Wants others to help.	Listen, then let him know what you can do. It may be nothing this instant. Offer hope as you can. Tell him what he can do. Be constructive in your advice.

Level III Customer
© CREATISTA/Shutterstock.com

LEVEL III—HANDLING DIFFERENT TYPES OF CUSTOMERS—REQUIRES SUBSTANTIAL WORK

This list of Level III customers typically requires substantial work to resolve their situations. Watch for changing of tactics and escalations of anger. Separate any of these customers if they begin to cause a scene. Many of these tactics are directed at you personally. Stay focused, respond to the tactic, maintain professionalism, and successfully complete the transaction in mind. In the end, you want it to end well.

Type	Catchphrase	Premise	Solution Strategy
Bully	I pay good money . . .	Wants special attention and will say just about anything to get it.	Give the attention, but realize that you aren't there to knock him down. Stay on your game. Know your limits and the limits of the business and stick to them.
Campaigners	I'm going to start an Internet boycott!	He sees himself as a leader who speaks up.	If possible, immediately separate from other customers and present options or ask what you can do to resolve situation. Realize that others are not as likely to follow as they would believe.
Embarrasser	Well if you knew how to . . .	Pent-up issues.	Similar to a bully. Don't allow yourself to digress. Direct him to stick to the business transaction. Be specific to obtain the needs. Keep professional and don't let it get personal. Finish as quickly as possible.
Excuse	The menu board was confusing.	Fear of something and looking to blame.	Apologize. Reassure. Don't be critical. Know the boundaries. Present solutions.
Inappropriate	%^$#@#$%	Another tactic to gain the upper hand in the situation. May be intoxicated.	Similar to embarrassers. Don't lose momentum by being offended. Know the limits and professionally, but directly, let him know when it has been crossed. Call security if intoxicated.
Injured	I have never been more insulted in all of my life!	Lives on extremes utilizing drama to their gain.	Separate from other customers if possible. Acknowledge the purported struggle. Realize that it may take time to recover from the drama before they are rational. Meanwhile, apologize, present options, and maintain boundaries.
Narcissist	Do you know who I am?	He is a self-centered person that cares only of himself.	It should be about him. Let it be about him, but you must also balance to make sure that he doesn't compromise service to others.
Nasty	Are you stupid?	Places others on the defense without concern.	Similar to embarrassers and inappropriate tactics. Let him know that you don't wish for him to feel that way. Put on your most professional face and don't take it personally. He has issues that you cannot solve. Realize this is a tactic to get the upper hand. Know the boundaries and stick to them. Complete the transaction as soon as possible.
Promised	I was promised . . .	Perhaps he was promised, or manipulating and controlling.	Be straightforward: "I am really sorry. This is what we can do: I can promise you that . . . Does this seem reasonable?" Or, "What would you suggest as alternative?"
Seeker	Oh, you must help me to . . .	Enlists the help of others to get things accomplished.	Only help if appropriate. Build their confidence. Let them know what you do within your limits.
Slur	Are you (fill in protected class here)?	They are looking for a weakness. They likely have a prejudice.	Answer only if appropriate. Tell them that you would prefer to continue the business conversation. Complete transaction as soon as possible. Note.
Unacceptable	This is unacceptable.	Accustomed to getting everything their way.	Reassure that you are working toward a solution. Act promptly. Show respect.
Unchangeable	That's how I am.	Resistant to change, childish.	Inform of the policies and how much can be accommodated. Expect him to push as far as you will allow. Also expect a shift to another role, such as bully, royalty, or a manager request.

Realize that you are not going to change many of these people. You can only work with them to make this guest service situation work well for them at this time.

SERVICE INSIGHT

Codes and Systems

Hospitals have codes, supermarkets have codes, police and rescue have codes, hospitality have very few. Should they? Having a system of codes is a great way to communicate to management and staff. Guests can be categorized according to sales, importance, and difficulty with terms or numbers. Requests for help can also be coded. It eliminates embarrassing situations, laborious descriptions, and facilitates immediate communication. It can be a very simple system.

► Tables and seats should all be numbered.

► A bell, a shout-out, and a pager are all old-school techniques.

► A tap on the manager's left shoulder means assistance requested when possible, and a tap on the manager's right shoulder means an emergency situation.

► Customer intoxication can be relayed as a green light, yellow light, red light system.

FOUR CHEMICALS THAT DETERMINE BEHAVIOR

Dopamine
Oxytocin
Serotonin
Endorphins

Chemical Behavior

As we continue to interpret and understand guests, we should also be aware of what drives their behavior. Oddly, much of human behavior is believed to be caused by the release of four chemicals: Dopamine, Oxytocin, Serotonin, and Endorphins. You can remember it by the acronym: DOES, EDSO, DOSE . . . however you would prefer to remember it. We prefer DOSE, because it is what you get from the chemical.

► **Dopamine**—this chemical motivates us to do things and achieve things. It makes us competitive.

► **Oxytocin**—this chemical produces a feeling of warmth associated often with belonging or safety.

► **Serotonin**—this chemical provides that proud feeling that you often feel in your chest when you realize that you have done well.

► **Endorphins**—this chemical makes you feel happy. It hypes you up and contributes to your staying awake longer. It can also dull a sense of physical pain to help you to push on through something.

Let's place these into a guest service setting:

► Your manager called everyone together for a pre-shift meeting. Everyone is in uniform and in a circle. You are going to work together and have a great shift. You feel a part of something. (oxytocin)

► You know that you are being audited and you really want to perform well on this next guest satisfaction survey. You have this urge. (dopamine)

► You help a guest and they are really pleased and compliment you. You feel proud and know that you really handled it well. (serotonin)

► You are nearing the end of your shift, but you still feel great! You kept moving and the time flew past. In fact, you might even notice that you have a difficult time relaxing after the shift ends. (endorphins)

Angry Customers
© magic pictures/Shutterstock.com

HANDLING ANGRY CUSTOMERS

Sometimes even the best systems fail. It would be great if all customers were reasonable and rational and if systems worked, but that is not always the case. When things go wrong, emotions run high, and employees must be ready for the unexpected. This is when anger heats up.

True anger manifests itself within our bodies. The blood is pumping, the stomach may be turning, and the face may be reddening. People often say things they may not mean and shouldn't say.

When a customer is to this point it may be very difficult to immediately diffuse and resolve the situation because they are no longer hearing, comprehending, or thinking with great ration.

Anger often has three phases:

1. Building
2. Exploding
3. Cooling

Realize that it may take some time once they explode. Don't take it personally. Mentally remove yourself from the situation. One way to mentally remove yourself is to understand what is behind their anger. It can help you to form a defense, or at very least, categorize it. This can also help in the aftermath as you process what happened.

What is their primary goal behind their anger?

▶ Fun: they have power and actually enjoy anger as a hobby.
▶ Wear you down: they achieve success through repetition.
▶ Bullies: they desire power and often get their way by getting angry.
▶ Unexplained: something else happened in their life.
▶ They don't care who's to blame: they are venting and want to blame someone and you are in front of them. Remember, they may not always be logical.

It is natural to want to respond in the same manner as the customer. If someone picks a fight, your natural reaction might be to get defensive or fight back. While no one should ever be subjected to physical abuse, occasionally you will encounter an angry customer. While no one should have to take verbal abuse, it will occasionally occur.

Call security or the police. Call for the assistance of other staff and managers. Be direct. Get them away from others. Record facts as soon as you can and note witnesses.

When dealing with angry people, consider these tips

▶ Try to keep your voice low and quiet.
▶ Deal with the emotions first. Otherwise, logic won't be appreciated.
▶ Get them out of view if possible.
▶ Realize they need to vent. When people are angry, it often takes a few minutes or more for their body and emotions to adjust and logic to prevail. During this time, don't be overly pleasant, because it won't be appreciated. Instead, slow your speed and be factual. Speaking quickly will only elevate their mood.
▶ Use phrases like: What can I do to help you?
▶ How can you neutralize the situation?
▶ Increase continuous eye contact.
▶ Focus on the options, not the limitations.
▶ Involve them if appropriate: How can we solve this?
▶ Don't take negative customer comments personally.
▶ Mentally remove yourself from the situation.

- Let them know when you are thinking or looking or calling. Don't just leave to "surprise them." Instead, let them know that you are working on it.
- Pause to think and pause for emphasis.
- Don't argue. If you have to disagree, it doesn't have to be personal. Perhaps you can agree to disagree? They don't always have to agree with your side and you don't always have to agree with theirs. In which case, you should re-emphasize what can be done. Try to stick to facts.
- Do your best to remain calm. No one ever wins a shouting match with the customer. Try to get them to use logic as the anger subsides.
- Keep your eye on the prize/goal—your aim is to get past the anger and solve the problem. Remember that it is not a contest.
- Keep in mind that your inside/private thoughts may show. If this happens, you will appear as forced and insincere. Most people are discerning enough to know.

> **Emotional Labor**
> Psychological demands of customer service.

SERVICE INSIGHT

Handling Stress

In addition to the physical demands are the psychological demands of customer service. Dealing with customers causes stress on a personal level. This stress can be referred to as *emotional labor*.

Stress can be good. It can be a motivator. It can show that you care. It helps to reinforce your determination, and it is part of life. More typically though, people are plagued by the inability to effectively moderate their stress.

Below are three categories: Pre-Stress, Occurrence, and Post-Stress. By breaking stress apart into these categories, it can be evaluated and monitored more effectively.

Harmony versus Chaos
© Adrian Niederhaeuser/Shutterstock.com

Pre-Stress

- Are you going into the shift of already stressed?
- Realize stress will likely occur.
- Visualize how you will act differently when it occurs.
- What motivates you?
- Do you need a challenge?
- Do you have both professional and personal goals to work toward and look forward to?

Occurrence

- Mentally remove yourself out of the situation.
- How is your body reacting to the stress?
- Label the stressor, or reason causing the stress.
- Is it yours to own stress or are you assuming the stress of others?
- What steps can you do to fix it?
- Can you allow time to pass? Realize it will take time for your body to adjust.
- Do you have to have this argument?

Post-Stress

It is important to think about what happened. Change what you can, then leave it alone.

- ▶ What did you do correctly?
- ▶ How could you have improved?
- ▶ Can it be avoided in the future?
- ▶ Can you talk to someone about it?
- ▶ Can you change your environment?

Other tips:

- ▶ Exercise.
- ▶ Give yourself permission to make mistakes.
- ▶ Realize what you are presently doing to cope with the effects of stress. Realize if a vice is taking hold of you.

SERVICE INSIGHT

Dealing With Other Cultures

The world is becoming a smaller place. A majority of the new customers come internationally. Foreign travelers spend about three times as much as the domestic traveler, so businesses find them lucrative as customers. It can be difficult to exceed their expectations when you don't know them. Language, customs, and cultures are different.

It is important to remember that we are not alone. Our town, city, or country is our world. The circle of friends and co-workers that we currently have are usually not representative of the customers that we will encounter and they are certainly not representative of the world's population. And with the increase of travel and communications, it is vital to understand, and be able to relate to others that are unlike you.

When you do business with foreign guests, it is important to understand them if you want to succeed. First, it is important to make them feel comfortable. Begin with a smile. A smile is welcoming around the world. For most foreign travelers, their top priorities are:

1. Safety
2. A new experience
3. Comprehension of all that is occurring

Then, consider these tips for delivering proper guest service to foreign travelers:

- ▶ **Communicate:** This might be difficult, but communication is a key to customer service. Find a translator, learn basic terms, or find other ways to communicate. Signage is also very important. Most international venues have brochures available in many languages. Technology is also a new key in translation.

- ▶ **Understand their cultures:** Understand their customs and traditions. Good service is not universal. Expectations vary much between countries and cultures. Make it a point to understand the meanings and importance behind their requests and actions.

- ▶ **Survey your clients:** Determine what they are thinking and feeling in an effort to better serve them. It is important to know the areas you need to improve.

- ▶ **Get educated:** Make it a part of your ongoing training to get to know them. Learn how to say hello, good-bye, and thank-you in 20 different languages. Counting is the next step. Even just a few phrases or gestures could be very impressive to them. They will understand that you are trying to serve them and they sincerely appreciate it.

- ▶ **Smile:** A smile is the most widely recognized form of guest service across the world.

STAFF EXPECTATIONS

There are many expectations of a front-line service worker. They don't just represent the company, they <u>are</u> the company! There are several qualities management would expect to be present in anyone that works directly with customers. Most of us would think that these are common sense, but to quote Mark Twain, "common sense isn't all that common." Therefore, as a manager, it is important to tell them in orientation, at reviews, and whenever else needed.

Personal Care: Make it clear that it is the employee's responsibility to stay in proper shape and rest before a shift so that they are comfortable. They should be well-groomed.

Attitude: We expect employees to care about the guests, the business, and their co-workers. Let employees know and be able to understand that they have a **duty of loyalty** to the betterment of the business. This means that they should:

- ▶ want to help.
- ▶ be empathetic.
- ▶ give their full and personalized attention.
- ▶ have a sense of pride.

Duty of Loyalty

Regarding the employees, it implies they have a responsibility to act in the best interest of the business in all of their actions. This means they should want to help, be empathetic, give their full and personalized attention, and have a sense of pride regarding their work.

ANOTHER VIEW: PROBLEM HOSTS

For a different viewpoint, consider how organizations appear to the customer. The host represents the business. What type of host will you be? There are many ways to host guests, but below are some of the types to recognize and avoid making the same mistake.

Hostess With Look That Raises Questions in the Guests' Minds
© Balchugova Maria/Shutterstock.com

TYPES OF HOSTS

Insincere Pleaser—they offer a fake front, they have to say certain things and appear sincere to some but not all. Everything is an act.

Relaxed—they are seemingly relaxed about customer service and life in general. They believe that things will work themselves out. Not all of their customers share their relaxed attitude.

Bragger—they love to brag. They view their job as an opportunity for others to behold and listen to how great they are. In truth, they have probably done some great things, but customer service is about serving the guest.

Zesty—they LOVE the business. They tell that to everyone, all of the time. They almost can't work enough. They are usually a bit rough in appearance because of always wanting to Go-Big.

Formal—they are extremely formal, proper, and operate by the book. They thrive on procedure and protocol. While this isn't inherently bad, they are usually not open to deviating to better accommodate a guest.

Judging—they appear to be judging the customer to determine their view of suitability. They almost seem to be determining if customers fit into their culture. Sometimes accompanied with a painfully disapproving expression or a condescending niceness.

Undertaker—they are quiet and sincere. They are so very sincere that they are almost sorry for your loss.

Busy—they are almost too busy for the guests. They always seem busy, except it isn't with serving the guests!

Apathetic—they have low energy and display little interest in serving the customer or performing their job.

Favorites—they obviously have their favorite customers. This creates an us and them with the other guests. Making one guest publicly feel important is at the risk of making the others feel less important. All guests are important, but VIP's should be handled with tact.

Problems—they almost have too many problem to deal with serving the guest. Similar to "Busy" host. They have to fix things. Customers get in the way of business!

Absent—not typically around. Customers wonder why, then go away, usually forever.

Realize that corporate culture will typically dictate which role that the host decides to take. In smaller, private establishments, it is up to the owner, which also might be the host. Realizing how a host appears to the customer is a crucial step in improving your guest service system.

✦ IS THE GUEST ALWAYS RIGHT?

The guest is always right! Everyone has heard the claim, "the guest is always right." This phrase frustrates both the business and the customer because it simply cannot apply to every situation. It sets up unreasonable expectations on both sides.

Is the guest always right? The answer is that there are contradictions to this claim.

Employees disagree arguing: How can a guest always be right? How can anyone always be right? That is theoretically impossible. What if they are overly demanding? Or what if it is impossible to fulfill their requests? What if it compromises other customers? Employees feel bullied. Why should the guest always be right? What if they don't realize or won't listen to the entire situation?

Guest Is Not Always Right
© Rommel Canlas/Shutterstock.com

Owners want the employees to please the paying customers, so the statement is made. They also think they have to give away profits. Often, they do. Sometimes, it is merely "the cost of doing business." Other times, the customers may be trying to get something for nothing. Owners wonder if the customer is lying. Occasionally, people lie, especially when it is to their benefit and associated with a business's profits instead of an individual.

In the end, it is a very difficult statement to make. You should serve the customer, but a situation may occur when the customer is unreasonable. The customer can be very rude, and believe they have more rights than they actually do.

Others say, "While the customer may not always be right, the *perception of the customer should be right.*" This does change the notion, but it is still difficult to consistently apply it to real-world scenarios. It continues to set up a difficult situation for all parties involved. In an effort to better explore the notion of "the guest is always right" you are essentially implying that your answer should always be yes and that a guest should never be refused.

CAN YOU SAY NO?

If the idea is to always please the guest, and the guest is always right!

- ▶ Should your answer always be yes?
- ▶ Can you say no to a customer?
- ▶ Can the guest be wrong?
- ▶ Are there limits?

Yes. Yes. Yes. And Yes.

It may seem odd for the answer to be YES to all four of these questions, but consider this. Always saying yes does not have to mean total compromise. The customer does not have carte blanche, the employee doesn't have to be frustrated, and the owner doesn't always have to give away the profits. Your answer should be yes, but in a way that you can accommodate their needs. In a sense, you are saying NO to a customer, but in a way that still accommodates their wishes and needs.

Are there limits to what you can do? Of course there are limits. There are budget and legal restrictions. You have other customers to serve and a business to run. *The point is to not get caught up in the details and look at the larger picture. Look for alternative "win-wins" where you can say YES while remaining within your limits.*

Keep your eye on the prize. Remember that your goal is problem resolution in everyone's best interest.

- ► Occasionally the business will take a loss.
- ► Occasionally you will make a mistake.

Use these as learning opportunities so that you can change your system to minimize the likelihood for future reoccurrences.

Other thoughts that would help your decision to say "Yes" or "No" would be:

Lifetime Customer Value

- ► The total amount that a customer might spend at a business when combining all purchases. This would be all potential future sales from the customer. Also consider word-of-mouth.
- ► The entire amount of worth generated from a patron. A combination of all potential sales revenue and unquantifiable word-of-mouth.

Opportunity Cost

- ► All of the cost associated with obtaining a potential customer.
- ► How much would it take to replace or obtain another customer? This is a complex estimate of your marketing expenses and time. Estimates claim that it takes between 4–20 times the amount of money to obtain a new customer than to retain an existing customer. It really depends how much you spend on marketing and what they are asking for.

Rate of Dissatisfaction

- ► The amount or percentage of errors in a system. If calculated through a survey, the amount of low-scoring results.
- ► How often does it happen? If it occurs often, then there is likely a process error that is of most importance.

❖ IT'S ALL THE LITTLE THINGS

The customer service experience starts even before they enter the establishment. It is with their first contact with the business. It could be when they make a reservation or buy a ticket. It is all the little things. It may not be one, single issue that influences or bothers a customer. Or, it may be a series or combination of seemingly small, insignificant issues. Essentially, those red flags—a squeaky door, an extra minute to wait, dust in the corner, or a few crumbs from a previous customer—may not independently seem like much, but can quickly add up to a less-than-stellar encounter.

Jan Carlzon popularized the phrase and best-selling book, *Moments of Truth*. In it, he wrote about how the service encounter is made up of many individual "moments of truth." Within one encounter, there are many points at which quality guest service can be made or lost. It is a nice way to think about all of the little things that go into quality guest service.

Lifetime Customer Value

The total amount that a customer might spend at a business when combining all purchases.

Opportunity Cost

All of the cost associated with obtaining a potential customer.

Rate of Dissatisfaction

The amount or percentage of errors in a system.

Moment of Truth

Popularized by Jan Carlzon of SAS Airlines, a phrase and best-selling book, *Moments of Truth*, explains how a guest experience is made up of many individual "moments of truth." There are many points at which quality guest service can be made or lost. These might also be referred to as touch-points.

WATCHING FOR RED FLAGS

Red flags are now another commonly used expression.

You cannot be all things to all people. Even the best businesses have problems. To further complicate things, customers bring in preconceived notions and expectations. Employees need to be able to read the subtle signs of the customer who probably won't tell them exactly what he or she wants. When customers do not receive what they need and expect, issues arise. As this occurs, red flags go in a customer's mind. Like a warning flag on the beach, a red flag is an indicator of something potentially wrong.

Red Flag
© Yakov Oskanov/Shutterstock.com

Some of the obvious signs may be a reddening face, a change of posture, a glance at their watch, or a sigh. Other signals may be difficult to detect. The customer may not even be aware of this. Others may be unable to verbalize all of the issues. The red flags are indicators of a gap or disparity between what the customer needs and expects and what they actually receive.

When just a few red flags pop up, most customers are tolerant because they are resistant to change their behavior. They don't typically want to find another place to do business or stop the transaction midstream. They aren't "wowed," but they file these red flags away in a mental folder. The red flags are totaled. Too many red flags at once, one that is huge, or too many small ones build up and they complain, blow up, or never come back. A great question to ask when evaluating service and serving the customer is, "Are they getting what they need and expect?" Look for the signs. Use empathy. Place yourself in their shoes, or try to see it from their perspective.

Red flags

Indicators that go off in a customer's mind when they do not receive what they need and expect. Not easily detected. The red flags have a cumulative effect and result in a poor service experience.

SERVICE INSIGHT

"Miss" versus "Ma'am"

Women are usually concerned about their appearance and age. Most women, particularly those above 30, prefer to be seen as young. Women feel old when referred to as "Ma'am." It isn't typically anything they will outright remark on, but they will notice; and we want people to feel comfortable. Miss implies a younger connotation. Make it a point to refer to women as Miss, despite their age. This also has regional variations between the North and the South of the US, making the rules ambiguous. Nonetheless, be aware of your personal jargon that may unintentionally upset others.

REMEMBERING NAMES

Everyone likes to be recognized and remembered. It is especially important in customer service. It makes customers feel special to be remembered. Calling them by name helps to create a special guest experience. It is never a good feeling to be without a name, so consider using the following tips to remember names:

Remembering Names
© sspopov/Shutterstock.com

- ▶ **Listen** intently to the pronunciation.
- ▶ **Repeat** it immediately and then at least a few more times in the conversation.
- ▶ **Memorize** their appearance—anything unique?
- ▶ **Relate** it to something or someone that you know. This is sometimes referred to as an anchor, or anchoring their name. For example, Bob is my uncle's name and he reminds me of my Uncle Bob. Mrs. Supperski is a Polish name and it reminds me of supper—Polish Supper—Supperski. Mr. Ross reminds me of Ross of the television show *Friends*. So, Ross from *Friends*—Mr. Ross. Whatever it takes. Sometimes obvious or odd associations commit better to memory better than practical, boring ones. You could also relate or anchor it to their appearance. Also consider rhyming as an anchor, but be careful it doesn't come out embarrassingly incorrect.

Lateral Example: a guest has an issue. Someone else is sitting in her seat at a concert. She mentions it to the ticket counter. The staff at the ticket counter know that it isn't their specific job and they could simply send her to security, but they stop and help her regardless. They verify the ticket, then ask her to wait just a minute while security is called to the ticket office. Once security arrives, they explain the situation and escort the woman back to her seat to resolve the rest of the issue. Security is also informed of another available, upgraded seat that is available in case it cannot be resolved.

Lateral Service Principle

The idea that employees are to stop what they are doing and help to solve customer problems even if it is not in their department.

Actions: We expect that employees should do things, but don't always state the obvious. Ensure that employees are told they should:

- ▶ always stop what they are doing and acknowledge the guest, smile, and make eye contact.
- ▶ be adaptable and flexible to meet customer needs by utilizing the lateral service principle to solve customer problems that they are aware of, even if it not in their department.

Related Psychological Theories

There are numerous models, theories, and assessments that interpret and explain human behavior. These can be used to understand what motivates people and what might cause them stress. Hence, it describes how people might act in conflict or problems. With these results, you can use these to begin to classify situations and people to better gauge and to determine an optimal outcome by influencing people's emotional behavior.

Many people take these tests or use these models to first better understand themselves and then how they would relate to others. These tests create a common language that can be used to identify characteristics and describe others. Most of these instruments are quick to deliver and there are no right or wrong answers. Also, many would claim that they are influenced by education, experiences, and maturity.

Dr. Carl Jung popularized the terms introversion and extroversion. These are terms that describe personal preferences.

- ▶ **Introversion:** interests and gratification come from within self; quiet, shy, closed.
- ▶ **Extroversion:** interests and gratification come from outside of one's self, like crowds, open.
- ▶ **Ambivert:** balance of both introversion and extroversion.

Introversion and Extroversion
© GrAl/Shutterstock.com

Many people learn to do both as they mature, but where is your preference? What energizes you?

These instruments are not new to describe personalities. Many remind people of the four fundamental personality types believed to originate from ancient Greek times. Those four are still seen today in some classifications.

The **Four Temperaments** are sanguine, choleric, melancholic, and phlegmatic.

- ▶ **Sanguine:** extroverted, social, talkative, enthusiastic, difficult to sit and do nothing.
- ▶ **Choleric:** extroverted, goal oriented, and ambitious.
- ▶ **Melancholic:** introverted, perfectionists, analytical and detail, deep thinkers.
- ▶ **Phlegmatic:** introverted, relaxed and peaceful, caring.

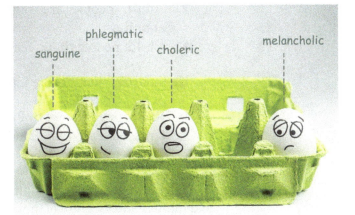

Four Temperaments
© TanyaJoy/Shutterstock.com

❦ TRANSACTIONAL ANALYSIS

Dr. Eric Berne was a psychiatrist who first captured the idea of transactional analysis and brought it into the mainstream. He released a book in 1964, *Games People Play*. It was originally written for practitioners but quickly went mainstream and hit the NY Best-Seller's list. It spawned a field of analyzing all human encounters as transactions that either benefited or manipulated those involved. He devised levels of the closeness that encounters can experience: withdrawn, ritual, pastimes, games, activities, and intimacy. Its application to the service industry revolutionized how we deal with customers. Many programs and ideas began to see it as more of a methodology. As a result, the field of customer service adapted many derivations of this science.

Every time two people come together, they are constantly evaluating and making assessments. Some people claim that they do not judge. But consider this situation: you are alone working night audit at a hotel. You look up and see a man is walking quickly toward you, approaching the front desk. It is late at night. He is wearing sunglasses, a hat, an overcoat, and his hands are in his pockets. You must quickly decide whether this person is nervous and walks quickly, has recently had cataract surgery, is a rock star, or is going to rob you. Dr. Berne provided a system for understanding and controlling the behavior of others.

This struck a chord with the general public. He referred to anger as a racket, writing that it may be self-righteous, adversarial, or even fun. Regardless of the reason, he viewed it as a choice within one's control. This influenced how we deal with angry customers. Just because they are mad, doesn't mean that we have to be mad. We choose how we will react to any situation. We also help by realizing that they are after a goal and are leveraging their behavior. When identifying the goal and the behavioral tactic, we can react to this in constructive ways to achieve our desired outcome—quality service and customer satisfaction.

Parent—Adult—Child

There are three types of ego-states:

1. **Parent:** people mimic their parents. Some shout, while others nurture.
2. **Adult:** people are rational, informed, and free from overwhelming emotion.
3. **Child:** people think, feel, and behave as they did when they were a child.

He theorized that people interact three different ways:

1. **Reciprocal:** Parent to Parent; Adult to Adult, Child to Child
2. **Crossed:** Parent to Child; Child to Adult
3. **Covert:** when messages have both parent and child responses combined.

To look at it in another light, we can process this as a game, trying to analyze and manipulate, or control their attitude, hopefully before it reaches the blown-up stage. We can let them vent, and we can help them to calmly reach a solution. The options are ours. If it goes wrong, it is likely that we didn't perceive and adjust correctly.

MEYERS-BRIGGS TYPE INDICATOR

The **Meyers-Briggs Type Indicator (MBTI)** was developed by Isabel Briggs Meyers and based on the theory of psychological types outlined by Jung. MBTI is another tool used to explain personalities and temperaments. It is useful to explain why we do something or may react in a certain way. It is also helpful in understanding and relating to others. You may not agree with them, but at least you can modify your strategy and understand their premise. Modified versions are also helpful to assist in job selection. It includes four dimensions, producing 16 different personality types.

MBTI Results

- ▶ How do they view the outer-world: **E**xtroversion–**I**ntroversion
- ▶ How do they take in information: **S**ensing–**IN**tuition
- ▶ How do they make decisions: **T**hinking–**F**eeling
- ▶ How do they structure things: **J**udging–**P**erceiving

MBTI Types
© Amir Ridhwan/Shutterstock.com

KEIRSEY TEMPERAMENT SORTER

Another labeling tool is the **Keirsey Temperament Sorter Instrument (TSI)**. Produced by David Keirsey, the Keirsey TSI correlates with the MBTI. In it, four different temperament types are produced. These categorical names can serve as quick labels for understanding, communicating, and relating to personalities.

Artisans, Guardians, Idealists, Rationals

- ▶ **Artisans:** who are observant trouble-shooters that want to make an impact.
- ▶ **Guardians:** who are responsible and dutiful organizers.
- ▶ **Idealists:** who seek inner-meaning, mediate and use diplomacy, and,
- ▶ **Rationals:** who use self-control and strategy.

EMOTIONAL INTELLIGENCE (EI)

As mentioned earlier, it is helpful to know yourself and how you react to situations. Much of this logic is also present in Goleman's more recently popularized, **Emotional Intelligence (EI)**. EI is one of the most popular instruments on personalities in the last 20 years. EI claims that IQ does not tell the whole picture in relating

The Meyers-Briggs Type Indicator (MBTI)

Tool used to outline personality and temperament types.

Keirsey Temperament Sorter Instrument (TSI)

Tool used to outline personality types into four primary categories.

Emotional Intelligence (EI)

A view of personalities, personal encounters, and success. Four dimensions: Self-awareness—knowing your emotions; Self-management—controlling your emotions; Social awareness—knowing others' emotions; Relationship Management—the ability to manage interactions with others.

Emotional Intelligence Matrix
© arka38/Shutterstock.com

to others and being successful. Instead, it uses four dimensions to assess an emotional quotient (EQ).

▶ **Self-Awareness:** *understanding emotions* or knowing your emotions.
▶ **Self-Management:** *managing emotions* or controlling your emotions.
▶ **Social Awareness:** *perceiving emotions* or knowing the emotions of others.
▶ **Relationship Management:** *using emotions* or managing interactions with others.

Emotional Intelligence Mind Map
© dizain/Shutterstock.com

Goleman claims that none of these skills are independently best. Instead, one should be proficient in all to be successful in working with others. The theory of EI claims that a blend of ability to read emotions, know your own, and alter accordingly to produce your intended outcome.

A developed EI can be associated with:

- improved decision-making and performance in teams,
- reduced job-related stress,
- and an increased feeling of well-being.

It is suggested that a person can develop their own EI. Some of the suggested ways are to begin to train yourself to:

- Embrace your emotions by acknowledging them and taking responsibility for them.
- Reduce compulsive behavior by thinking before acting.
- Avoid situations that might cause you extreme stress, if possible.
- Practice humility and empathy toward others.
- Also, be aware of your non-verbal behavior as others will use it to interpret you.

DISC ASSESSMENT

This is an older model that has received much recent attention as a behavioral profile and is quite popular in service organizations of all types. Dr. William Marston originally developed the model in 1928, but others have built upon this work to more recently create DISC assessments and other tools.

The **DISC** assessment attempts to explain characteristics that influence people's emotional behavior. The questionnaire uses phrases instead of words to provide a better idea of the questions in the instrument. The tests results can be applied to better understand how individuals approach work and relationships. It can also predict how they might act in conflict or problems.

The results of the assessment predict the level of individuals within four primary areas: Dominance, Influence, Steadiness, and Conscientiousness.

- **Dominance:** is specific, direct, and decisive. They are strong at solving problems, and a self-starter who takes risks.
- **Influence:** is optimistic and trustworthy. May be talkative, impulsive, and persuasive with others.
- **Steady:** is also trusting, but a good listener who is understanding. Very predictable and works well on a team.
- **Compliance:** is very conscientious, works systematically, uncovering facts and producing precise accuracy.

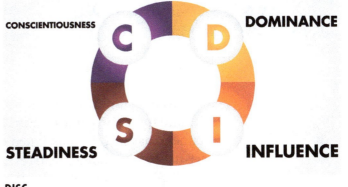

DISC
© dizain/Shutterstock.com

SERVICE INSIGHT

Ethics Checklist

When analyzing a specific action in question, consider the following:

- ▶ Is it legal?
- ▶ Is it fair?
- ▶ How do I feel about it in my conscience?
- ▶ Would the court of public opinion find my behavior incorrect?
- ▶ Am I fearful of what those and I trust and respect would say about my actions?

CHAPTER REVIEW QUESTIONS

1. In every service situation, a customer has certain expectations. List and briefly describe these expectations.
2. Is the guest always right? Explain the argument and provide support to your answer.
3. Recall a service encounter in which you became angry. Apply it to the phases of anger and provide five tips of advice for the service provider in dealing with the situation.
4. Recall and describe a recent experience where you encountered a problematic host.
5. How does G.U.E.S.T. help a business to train for customer service?
6. Customers have reasons for acting out the way they do. Recall four of the "types" listed in the chapter that apply to you and your personality.
7. List three reasons why you would have to politely tell a guest, "No."
8. What should you do after a stress guest contact situation? List ways to effectively handle the situation.
9. Explain why mediocre service often goes unremembered.
10. Would you consider yourself an introvert, extrovert, or ambivert? Explain.

CASE STUDIES

What's Going On?

5-A's Event Planning is a medium-sized event planning group. They have five full-time and three part-time event planners. Allison, one of the newest full-time event planners, has just been assigned this event. It was originally assigned to another part-time event planner who resigned after difficulties with the event and pressure from 5-A's. Allison welcomes the challenge. She is competent and energetic and full of new ideas.

The event is a corporate promotional dinner to thank their customers. The corporation typically handles small events in-house, but is enlisting the help of a professional meeting planning company to ensure this event goes as planned.

As soon as Allison receives word of the event she immediately calls Sam, the direct contact person at the account to set up a meeting. Allison quickly finds herself deep in the project. She realizes the company has many different ideas and very high expectations for the event. They were promised many great things that Allison keeps finding out about. She wonders how this is even possible with their budget. She listens to everything they say and diligently takes notes. Then, she reports back to her supervisor, the Director of Operations. She explains the dilemma. Allison is told to make it work or they will get someone else who can make it work. She feels unsupported. She goes to the purveyors to review the prearranged details. They explain that they cannot deliver what she is asking. She continues to negotiate and tries to determine what exactly the purveyors can offer and all of the real possibilities for the event. Armed with this information, Allison calls Sam to discuss the issues. Sam tells Allison that the customer is always right. Sensing that this will be an involved issue, Allison sets up a meeting with Sam and the Director of Operations for the following day. When Allison arrives at the meeting, she finds that Sam is only one of four people at the company making the decisions, and all of these people have different ideas.

1. List the issues regarding the promotional dinner event.
2. What would you guess happened with the planner that Allison replaced?
3. How could the Director of Operations be more helpful?
4. What are Allison's options at this point?
5. How should Allison handle this meeting?

Two Different Groups

Buena View Resort is a 3-1/2 star property located in Tampa, FL. It is a beautiful property that boasts splendid views of the ocean from the endless pool in a tranquil environment. The artwork and the landscaping are palatial. It typically accommodates business travelers during the week and leisure travel and catered events during the weekends. Mr. and Mrs. Baker traveled to Tampa for an extended weekend getaway to celebrate their 40th wedding anniversary. The rates were relatively high for what they were accustomed to, but they decided to splurge because of the occasion and the wonderful property that they would surely enjoy.

The Bakers checked in on Thursday evening and enjoyed a quiet arrival. They noticed a few other couples and business travelers quietly scattered around the pool area enjoying the view. They decided to have dinner to enjoy the tranquility. It was a delight! After dinner, they had a few cocktails and then retired to their room for the evening. They were off to a great start in celebrating their anniversary. They rose early the next morning and had breakfast by the pool. It was so beautiful.

Just after breakfast, a number of vans filled with young girls began arriving. The girls would immediately run out to the pool area with their luggage and lounge in groups. They were laughing and joking and performing small, theatrical dance routines throughout the pool area. Other groups arrived and began congregating in the other public areas of the resort.

The Bakers questioned a few of the girls near them and soon realized that they were the early arrivals of what would be a cheerleading competition at the resort. From that point forward, the resort was filled with groups of texting tween and teen cheerleaders and their chaperones.

The Bakers realized the cheerleaders had a right to be there, but their tranquil experience was being infringed upon. They couldn't go anywhere around the resort without being inundated by spontaneous chanting and cheer practice of groups.

By Saturday morning they were very aggravated. They approached the front desk and described their situation. They explained they had paid a lot of money and that they expected a tranquil experience. The front desk attendant quickly apologized. He admitted that it can be distracting with all of the commotion and that he would speak to the organizers of the event. He gave them both a free pass to the spa for a massage. He told them that he hoped the massage would help them to regain the tranquility. The Bakers thanked the attendant and took the passes and left to get a massage. However, the cheering and groups continued. They overwhelmed the couple and they left feeling very aggravated.

1. Describe the issue between the two sets of guests.
2. Rate the service recovery effort. How could it have been helped?
3. List ideas for accommodating both groups.
4. What are the potential consequences of this situation if it is not handled correctly?

Let Me Tell You What You Want

Mr. Garrison is a seasoned business traveler. He travels in excess of 200 nights a year. He typically stays at another popular 3-star hotel because of the brand and the reward points, but tonight decides to try a new, sleek hotel named Y.

After a long flight, Mr. Garrison's cab pulls up to the curb of the Y. He gets out and looks around. It is a great-looking property, but something is odd. It is very quiet and he sees no one. He grabs his bags and enters through the front doors. He looks around and small stations with computer modules are arranged around a small lobby. It is oddly small, very quiet, and he sees no one. He walks up to one of the computer stations and begins to look at it. Within a few seconds, Josh, an attendant in a fashionable uniform, comes out of the back office and greets him. The attendant asks if he is checking in, to which Mr. Garrison looks at his bags and replies "of course." Josh then asks him to step over to another computer station at the end of the lobby where he is logged in. Josh is very polite and smiles the entire time. Mr. Garrison is a bit troubled because Josh did not notice that Mr. Garrison is new to the property and the protocol. Josh quickly finds the reservation with notes that there are no preferences. He asks if Mr. Garrison has any allergies. Mr. Garrison, acting troubled, replies, "I am allergic to cats, does that count?" Josh assigns a room and then asks him if he would like help with his bags. Mr. Garrison refuses stating that since he has already brought them in it doesn't matter at this point. Mr. Garrison is directed to the elevators. Upon looking at the room number, he realizes that it is on a higher floor than he expected. He prefers lower floors so that he won't have to deal with traffic and ease when entering and leaving his room and also in the event of an emergency. He says nothing and proceeds on. Upon entering the room, he sees that it doesn't have the king-sized bed as he is accustomed to. It is also very cold in the room because the thermostat was set to 55 degrees. He tries to change it but is unable to do so. He calls the desk to ask about it and is told that it can easily be changed by using the hotel app on his smartphone. He then turns and opens the curtains to find that it also doesn't have much of a view. He tries to connect his computer and realizes that he isn't sure how to connect to the WiFi. Shortly after, Josh calls his room to see how everything is going and if he needs anything else. Mr. Garrison begins to take Josh up on his offer. He replies, "Yes. There are many things. No one helped me with my bags. I prefer a low floor, and I received a high floor. I need Internet before I can go to sleep. I prefer a king-sized bed. What kind of view is this? Who lives in temperatures this cold and needs an app to change it? I need a normal hotel room now! In fact, I think that I need a new hotel!"

Josh is surprised to hear this. He thought things were going well.

1. Describe the expectations of Mr. Garrison.
2. Describe the gap between Mr. Garrison's expectations and the service provided.
3. How should Josh handle Mr. Garrison at this point?
4. What should the hotel have done differently to avoid this disparity?

Sunset Cruises

Sunset Cruises is a small family-owned and operated sailing operation located in the quaint port of Grand Island. It provides sightseeing cruises throughout the tourist season. It features music and provides appetizers, wine, and cocktails. It accommodates mostly couples and groups. It provides breathtaking views in a relaxed setting.

Ken and Stan were a middle-aged couple that had been vacationing in the area and decided to attend the evening cruise during an evening walk. They saw the price on the sign that read:

- ► sailing nightly
- ► $45 per person
- ► reservations encouraged
- ► sorry, no refunds

The pier was busy. They did not have a reservation, so they approached the counter. Ken asks if there were openings on this evening's cruise to which the attendant responded, "Sure. We sail in just a couple of minutes. Two?" They were pleased, because the boat appeared to be filling. He replied, "Yes. Two please." Ken then asked, "Do you have any discounts?" The attendant replied, "No, I'm sorry there are no discounts available at this time." It was Sunset Cruise's policy to not offer discounts or negotiate at the counter. Only previously-negotiated discounts would be honored. Ken was reluctant at having to pay the full price of $90.00 for two, but agreed, paid, and he and Stan moved over to the side to wait for the cruise to begin.

Next in line was a young couple. The attendant asks if they have a reservation, to which they smilingly reply, "Yes, Mr. and Mrs. Drew!" They had reservations that were made through their inn, a preferred vendor who had discount coupons for 50% off a cruise for two. The couple had received it as part of a mid-week promotional package. Ken and Stan, just off to the side, heard the attendant ask the couple for $45. Concerned, Ken waits until their transaction is complete and then immediately approaches the counter, pushing in front of the next person in line. He begins to raise his voice and state to all that could hear the previous couple only paid $45 for two. He then accuses the attendant of lying to them because she "does not like their type" because she didn't tell them about the deals. Ken demands that they receive an apology and a half-price discount or a refund immediately.

1. Describe the issues. Was the attendant at fault?
2. Should the same discounts be made available to every guest?
3. What should the attendant do to remedy the situation?
4. What are the potential consequences of not handling this situation appropriately?

❧ EXERCISES

Exercise 1: Answering a Customer Complaint Letter

Directions: Below is a complaint letter. Consider the type of customer, their service experience, and the impact of the situation.

1. In this letter, draw a circle around each red flag.
2. As the owner, compose a letter of apology. Take any actions you deem most appropriate.

October 1, 20XX

Dr. E. Harrigan
10 Main St.
Boston, MA

Mary and James Swanson
The Jan House on John's Pond
Covington, New Hampshire

Dear Mr. & Mrs. Swanson:

This is the first time that I have ever written a letter like this. We are so upset that we felt compelled to let you know of our recent experience. We had dinner reservations at the Jan House for a party of six under my wife's name, Dr. Harrigan, for Saturday evening, October 1. We were hosting my wife's sister and her husband visiting from New York.

We were promptly seated according to our reservations at 6:00 p.m. in the dining room. The dining room was nearly empty with at least three fourths of the tables unseated. We were given menus, a wine list, water, rolls, and butter. We then sat for nearly 20 minutes until the cocktail waitress asked us for our drink orders. I think that she was out back smoking, because she smelled of cigarettes. My sister-in-law said, after being asked what else she would like, "I'll have a Grey Goose martini straight up with an olive"; a relatively standard drink. The cocktail waitress immediately responded, "I'm not a stenographer." My sister-in-law politely repeated her drink order. There was no apology for the lateness.

The dining room was quite so we could hear the kitchen and bar area. We sat there for the next 10 minutes listening to our cocktail waitress tell the bartender about her broken-down car and her boyfriend troubles. By the end, we felt as if we knew her life story. It was troubling to listen to, and she should have been tending to our drinks! Finally our waiter arrived, informing us of the specials of the evening. I do not remember his name, but he had blonde hair, wore glasses, and had his sleeves rolled up displaying tattooed arms. Our drinks had still not arrived, so I asked about them and he said that he would check right on it. He immediately left to check on the drinks. It was so quiet that we heard him ask about the drink order and a small argument erupted between the cocktail waitress and our waiter. We could hear the whole thing! He returned promptly with our drinks. He acted concerned but was unaware that we heard the entire dispute.

We then requested appetizers so that we could get started with the meal. He politely informed us that he could not order appetizers without ordering our entrees and dessert at the same time since it was a pre-fixed meal. We felt placed on the spot, so we decided to order everything. When the waiter asked my wife for her order, he addressed her as "Dear." When he served her the meal, he also called her sister "Dear." They did not appreciate this term.

As of 7:00 p.m., we requested that our salads be brought to us as soon as possible. I then asked an assistant to bring us more rolls as each of us had been served one when we were seated. His response was "Who wants a roll?", upon which, caught off guard, we went around the table saying yes or no so that he would know exactly how many "extra" rolls to bring to our table. It seems as if rolls should automatically be refilled at an establishment such as yours.

Our salads were finally served at 7:15 p.m. At 7:45 p.m., we asked about our entrees. They were served at 8:00 p.m. This was 2 hours after we were seated in a restaurant which was three quarters empty. I must also add that we had to make constant requests for water refills and a butter replacement.

The food was excellent and the property is delightful. Despite all of this, our dinner was a complete disaster. We were extremely upset and insulted with our experience at the Jan House. Your staff is not well-trained and very unprofessional. We will not likely return to the Jan House. Also know that we will share our experiences with friends and business associates.

Sincerely,

Dr. E. Harrigan

Exercise 2: Handling Difficult Guests

Directions: Below is a chart with customer catchphrases. Fill in the chart the most appropriate customer type, premise, and solution strategy.

Customer Type (fill in)	Customer Phrase	Premise (fill in)	Solution Strategy (fill in)
	You people are so up-tight in your suits. Why don't you wear flip-flops?		
	This whole process is so confusing that you need an MBA to figure it out.		
	I think my 15-year-old son is having a party at home and my husband is about to leave me.		
	I would like to know all of your specials and the lowest price available.		
	I've had better days.		
	I am doing so much better now that you are waiting on me.		
	Don't they train you people?		
	I'm going to call my friend, the CEO of the company!		
	I have never been treated this way in all of my years!		
	Why did the chicken cross the ice skating rink?		

Exercise 3: Defining Service Expectations

Directions: Service encounters occur many times, every day. For this exercise, recall five of your recent customer service encounters. They can be anything from a meal to a telephone call with your cellular provider. Briefly describe the situation, your expectations, and provide an explanation of whether your expectations were met by completing the chart below.

Date and Time	Description of Service Encounter	Your Expectation	Was Your Expectation Met?	Explanation
1)			Yes / No	
2)			Yes / No	
3)			Yes / No	
4)			Yes / No	
5)			Yes / No	

REFERENCES

Berne, E. Dr. (1964). *Games people play: The basic handbook of transactional analysis.* New York, NY: Ballantine Books.

Carlzon, J. (1987). *Moments of truth.* Cambridge, MA: Ballinger Pub. Co.

SECTION II

Relating Service to the Sectors of the Hospitality Industry: How Service Relates

Chapter 4

The Guest Service of Food

CHAPTER OBJECTIVES

After reading this chapter, you should be able to:

► Identify and describe all the major service styles.
► Identify and define FOH and BOH positions as they relate to service.
► Identify and explain the uses of various service wares.
► Contrast typical place settings.
► Explain and apply the service procedures of a full-service restaurant.

TERMINOLOGY

A la carte
BOH
Chit
Classical Brigade
Cover
Crumbing
FOH
Frontline Worker
Gueridon
Mise en place
Recheud
Service Styles
Turnover

Introduction: About the Service of Food

There is much more to the service of food service than meets the eye. To the customer, the service of food represents many things sacred. It may not initially come to mind, but is certainly noticed when absent. It represents:

- ▶ **Offering:** a gift, although you pay, it is offered.
- ▶ **History:** the idea, rules, and rituals associated with the serving of food dates back to the beginning of civilization.
- ▶ **Artisanship:** the pride and skill of mastering a craft.
- ▶ **Community:** of time with family, friends, or even others at the counter or in the dining room.
- ▶ **Function:** a meeting or a business transaction.
- ▶ **Occasion:** an appreciation, a date, or a celebration.
- ▶ **Retreat:** to a memory, an adventure, or an escape.
- ▶ **Indulgence:** a deserved reward or a welcomed treat.
- ▶ **Promise:** a trust that food is wholesome and safe.
- ▶ **Statement:** of status or religion, belief or consciousness.
- ▶ **Rest:** a signal to stop work briefly and relax.
- ▶ **Nourishment:** it may be basic calories, as provided in a quick lunch, or very formal, but everyone needs nourishment for life. It is at the base of Maslow's Hierarchy of Needs.

Dinner Toast
© Rawpixel.com/Shutterstock.com

Food Trucks in Denver, Colorado
© Arina P Habich/Shutterstock.com

Food Service is much more than the serving of food! Consider this, when something goes wrong it may represent far more than a simple breach of a rule. It may represent:

- an insult to someone's religion.
- an important celebration or business transaction.
- the only rest of their day.
- something they were looking forward to for a long time.

Treat these things as sacred and you will be on the way to successful service of food with quality guest service.

Positions

Most food service operation positions are divided into two separate areas:

- Front of the House (FOH)
- Back of the House (BOH)

The FOH is in plain view of the customers. The staff in FOH positions are under close watch of the public eye. The **frontline workers** are those employees that work directly with the customer. Their presentation and professionalism is of utmost importance. The BOH is all of the area where the customers typically cannot go. Most of the actions of the BOH are behind the scenes, and out of view

Frontline Workers

The employees that directly serve the customers.

of the general public. Despite being out of the general view of the customer, their role in supporting the customer should not go unmentioned. They are essential to supporting customer service and the industry. The terms FOH, BOH, and front-line worker are used throughout the hospitality industry. Walt Disney World uses the terms "onstage" and "offstage" to impart the idea of a performance whenever an employee is within view of the public.

FRONT OF HOUSE

Front of House (FOH)

The service area in view of the customers.

In a small restaurant, there may just be a handful of employees in the FOH. In a large operation there may be as many as 50 or even 100. The positions that make up the FOH may be combined, but are as follows when separate:

▶ **Greeter or Host/Hostess:** This is often the first person guests see. They are the first point of contact and set the tone of the establishment. This may be on the telephone, at the door, or at the hostess station. Their primary duties involve welcome, receiving, guest concerns, safeguards for concerns (bottlenecks, warns kitchen, servers . . .). They seat the guests, provide menus, assign tables, give wait times, and provide general information. This position is not needed in quick-service or operations where the customers seat themselves.

▶ **Bartender:** This position may prepare drinks or "tend" the main bar or a service bar, which is designed for the dining room orders. This position is mentioned more in the next chapter.

▶ **Barback:** This position is the assistant to the bartender who performs lesser tasks.

▶ **Servers:** This is often the primary point of contact for the guests. They oversee the service of the table. Depending on the amount of support staff and level of service, they may make suggestions, take beverage and food orders, deliver food and beverages, present the bill, and provide general care for the table.

▶ **Busman:** This position is an assistant to the server. They clear and set tables, deliver bread and water, and provide general assistance to the servers.

FOH Pre-Shift Meeting
© Monkey Business Images/Shutterstock.com

BACK OF HOUSE

BOH is very different from the FOH. One can feel the entire climate change as they pass through the kitchen doors and proceed "offstage." The carpeted floor stops, air conditioning stops, and the fine décor is replaced with functional, militaristic décor. It is all about getting the job done in the BOH to support everything that occurs seamlessly in the FOH.

Part of the origins of the BOH as we know it comes from Augustus Escoffier. He was known as the Father of Modern Cuisine. He was the first credited with creating a system of organization for large hotels and kitchens, commonly referred to as the "Classical Brigade." He was also credited with creating one of the first versions of the modern-day menu. Escoffier ran his kitchen like a military. Everyone had a specific position, or station, with specific tasks. There was little or no duplication of these tasks. It was simple, effective, and efficient. Scaled-down versions of the

Back of House (BOH)

All areas that are not seen by the typical customer.

Classical Kitchen Brigade

A system of stations in the kitchen where everyone has a specific purpose.

Classical Kitchen
© Everett Collection/Shutterstock.com

stations and the militarist demeanor are carried over into today's Americanized versions of the classical brigade. French terminology is also still common, especially in upscale food service operations. Below are some of the stations of the *classical brigade*:

- ▶ **Chef du Cuisine:** the head chef, in charge of the kitchen
- ▶ **Sous Chef:** the second in charge of the kitchen
- ▶ **Saucier:** sautéed items and soups, sauces
- ▶ **Poissonier:** seafood dishes
- ▶ **Grillardin:** grilled dishes
- ▶ **Friturier:** fried
- ▶ **Rotisseur:** roasted, mostly meats
- ▶ **Entremetier:** warm vegetables
- ▶ **Garde-Manger:** cold food, salads
- ▶ **Patissier:** pastries

As kitchens progressed and less food was prepared from scratch, the positions were combined. Below is a table comparing the relationship between positions of Classical European Dining, American Fine Dining, and American Casual Dining. Note, many of the positions have been combined.

BOH STAFF COMPARISON

Classical European Dining	American Fine Dining	American Casual Dining
Chef du Cuisine	Executive Chef	Kitchen Manager
Sous Chef	Sous Chef	Combined
Saucier	Saute Station	Saute Cook
Poissonier	Poissonier	Combined
Grillardin	Grill Station	Grill Cook
Friturier	Combined	Fry Cook
Rotisseur	Combined	Combined
Entremetier	Combined	Combined
Garde-Manger	Pantry Chef	Cold station
Patissier	Pastry Chef	Combined

The Front of the House has also scaled down staff from the classical hierarchies. A few classical French terms such as Maitre D' and Sommelier remain in several settings. Recently French terms have begun to emerge as part of an organizational culture, bringing an elevated level of sophistication to the establishment. Despite the names, the job still gets done. The higher level of service, the more positions are required. Below are some of the typical positions present in fine-dining FOH:

- ▶ **Sommelier (chef de vin):** The lesser wine steward (certifications and levels). Professional dedicated to wine and beverage service and all aspects from menus, to sales, to inventory. This position is becoming more common in today's culture and renewed interest in wines.

- **Dining Room Manager (maitre d'hotel or maitre d'):** Supervises all dining room operations. More commonly greets and seats the guests.
- **Head Waiter (chef de sale):** In charge of all waitstaff and oversees the table.
- **Captain (chef d'etage):** Has the most guest contact once they are seated. Explains the menu, answers questions, takes orders, and performs the tableside cooking.
- **Front Waiter (chef de rang):** Sets the table for each course, delivers food, assistance to the captain.
- **Back Waiter (demi-chef de rang or commis de rang or busser):** The least experienced, fills water, clears the table, assists with lower end tasks.

Modern Kitchen Line
© Rawpixel.com/Shutterstock.com

The positions reduced and combined with levels of service and the American influence. The table below shows how the FOH Service Staff changed from Classical European style to American Fine Dining to Casual Dining.

FOH SERVICE STAFF

Classical European Dining	American Fine Dining	American Casual Dining
Receptionniste	Host/Hostess	Host/Hostess/Greeter
Maitre d'hotel	Dining Room Supervisor	Combined
Chef de sale	Head Server	Server
Sommelier	Wine Steward/Sommelier	Combined
Chef d'etage	Server	Food runner
Chef de rang	Combined	Combined
Demi Chef de rang	Bus Person	Busboy

SERVICE INSIGHT

Others Included in Guest Service

There are many other employees that are included in the service experience. This includes many people: the sales staff, reservations, staff fielding telephone or e-mail questions, and the groundskeeper or maintenance person that guests encounter while at the establishment. Every one of them makes a difference. People might ask what kind of flower a landscaper is planting. Their response is all part of the equation of service.

Wares and Their Uses

Below are several images illustrating various utensils used in the professional food service environment. Some are used by the customers, some by servers, and others during kitchen preparation. It is useful to be able to quickly identify these wares for proper service.

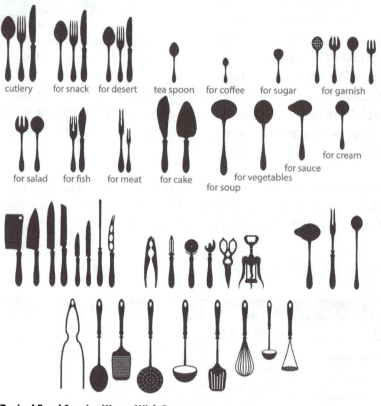

cutlery   for snack   for desert   tea spoon   for coffee   for sugar   for garnish

for salad   for fish   for meat   for cake   for vegetables   for sauce   for cream

for soup

Typical Food Service Wares With Purposes
© Strejman/Shutterstock.com

✦ PLACE SETTINGS

Every establishment has its own variation, each one claiming to be the correct interpretation and the absolute standard. Variations come from a blend of etiquette books, regions, time periods, necessity, and practicality. With all of the different rules the staff and guests are even left wondering. On the following page is a nontraditional place setting at a café that is quite acceptable!

Table Pre-Setting for Grand Event, With Show Plates
© Tsezarina/Shutterstock.com

A Variation of a Place Setting
© Africa Studio/Shutterstock.com

Despite the differences of opinion, there are general rules common to the industry. Below are three levels of service with general rules and variations accompanying each of them.

| Pause | Ready for second plate | Excellent | Finished | Don't like |

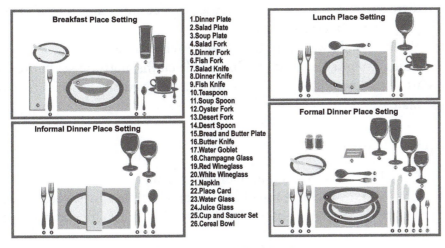

1. Dinner Plate
2. Salad Plate
3. Soup Plate
4. Salad Fork
5. Dinner Fork
6. Fish Fork
7. Salad Knife
8. Dinner Knife
9. Fish Knife
10. Teaspoon
11. Soup Spoon
12. Oyster Fork
13. Desert Fork
14. Desrt Spoon
15. Bread and Butter Plate
16. Butter Knife
17. Water Goblet
18. Champagne Glass
19. Red Wineglass
20. White Wineglass
21. Napkin
22. Place Card
23. Water Glass
24. Juice Glass
25. Cup and Saucer Set
26. Cereal Bowl

Table Etiquette and Place Settings
© Volodka28/Shutterstock.com

The above graphic displays typical table settings for levels of service. There is also a table etiquette on the top of the diagram. It is beneficial to memorize these signals; however, they are not used as much in recent years. Therefore, it is a good idea to always verify with the customer to confirm their communication.

Informal/Casual Place Setting

- ► Use: casual dining to upscale casual dining
- ► Courses included: bread and water, salad, main dish, coffee
- ► Left of plate: dinner fork
- ► Right of plate: dinner spoon, dinner knife
- ► Top left: Bread and Butter Plate (B&B)
- ► Top right: water glass
- ► Optional: salad fork, butter knife on B&B, table covering which may be glass over cloth, paper, linen, or matted. Single wine glass.
- ► Variations: all flatware may be wrapped in napkin or ring. Fork(s) can be on top of napkin and/or higher-quality disposable napkins may be used. More casual service omits all but a napkin, fork, knife, spoon, placemat, and water.
- ► Rules: salad fork is placed on the outside, knife facing inward toward plate

Formal Place Dining

- ► Use: upscale dining establishments, 3 stars/diamonds
- ► Courses included: bread and water, soup, salad, appetizer, entree, dessert
- ► Left of plate: appetizer fork, salad fork, dinner fork, dessert fork
- ► Right of plate: dinner knife, salad knife, dinner spoon, soup spoon, tea spoon
- ► Top left of plate: B&B
- ► Top right of plate: water glass, red wine, white wine
- ► Optional: plate may not be present. Contemporary interpretations may disregard many rules. Symmetry and space allowance may also take precedence in arrangement.
- ► Variations: flatware may be set with each course
- ► Rules: linen tablecloths, no disposable cloths, flatware set in order of use from the outside working inward, knives turned inward toward plate

Ultra-Formal Dining

- ► Use: classical, 4–5 star and diamond dining
- ► Courses may include: bread and water, multiple wines, soup, salad, appetizers, intermezzos, seafood, vegetable, meat, aperitif, fruit and cheese, dessert
- ► Left of plate: salad fork, fish fork, dinner fork
- ► Right of plate: salad knife, meat knife, fish knife, dinner spoon, soup spoon, tea spoon, oyster fork, coffee cup
- ► Top left of plate: bread and butter plate (B&B)
- ► Top center of plate: dessert spoon, dessert fork, dessert knife

- Top right of plate: water goblet, champagne flute, red wine, white wine, and sherry glasses
- Optional: top plate as a base or show plate removed upon seating
- Variations: there may be as many aspects of the settings as there are courses. When a place card is used it should be placed at the top right of the plate in front of the glassware. The napkin may be placed to the left of the forks, wrapped around the flatware, or folded anywhere else on table. Flatware and accompaniments may be reset with each course. The oyster fork may be slanted inward. Coffee may be served butler style (as requested). Symmetry of arrangement may not prevail.
- Rules: fine linen napkins and multiple-layer tablecloths are essential. Napkins are placed on guests' laps by staff upon seating. All flatware should be placed in the order of use, beginning on the outside and working inward. The flatware should be 1 inch from the edge of the table or placed on an invisible median line parallel with the table. Glasses should be an inch above the knives and in order of use; typically champagne, white, red, dessert, and water.

MISE EN PLACE

Mise en place is a very common term in the hospitality industry. It loosely translates to, "everything in its place." It is the assembling of everything that you will need to perform the job at task prior to beginning it. It requires thinking ahead of precisely how you will execute the task. It requires you to think about the steps and the materials needed. It eliminates unnecessary running around during the task, builds confidence, and demonstrates competence. Everything will be set up, making it much easier and efficient.

Mise en place

Loosely translates to "everything in its place." Having all materials assembled prior to starting a task. For example, a waiter obtains his mise en place prior to beginning his shift. He would ensure that he has his uniform in order, then checks his reservations and specials, notepad, corkscrew, crumber, pens, and so on.

Chef With Mise en Place
© Rido/Shutterstock.com

DEFINITIONS

A la carte: individual ordering of menu items

China: plates, dishes, cups, saucers.

Flatware: knives, forks, spoons.

Glassware: all cups made from glass, also carafes, pitchers, decanters.

Gueridon: a cart for tableside service.

Hollowware: larger ware items such as platters, coffee pots, trays.

Recheud: a heating source.

Service Ware: term for all wares used by the guests.

Side Items: Bread baskets, crumbing plate, doilies, flatware, napkins, sweeteners, wine bucket, ketchup, mustard, vinegar, birthday setup.

Service Styles

AMERICAN DINNER SERVICE

The term used to describe service of food is dinner service. It is appropriate for meals throughout the day, with the evening meal being the most formal. Full-service restaurants are also known as American Service or Sit-Down Service in the US. They are everywhere and everyone has been to them. Consequently they have developed opinions and preferences regarding their expectations. The typical pattern of sit-down dinner service is:

- ▶ Greet the guest
- ▶ Seat the guest
- ▶ Take drink order
- ▶ Serve drink
- ▶ Take dinner order
- ▶ Serve dinner order
- ▶ Clear dinner
- ▶ Present bill

Of course there are variations. Some guests will seat themselves, and other courses are added for appetizers and desserts, but the idea is generally the same: drink, food, and check. It would be great if it were only that simple to please the guests. Why do so many places get it wrong? Let's break it down and provide some tips:

1. **Greet the Guest:** Immediately acknowledge their presence
   - ☐ Smile. When you smile, it typically is returned with a smile.
   - ☐ Open and hold the door if possible.

Special Occasions

Many people celebrate special occasions at restaurants. Sometimes they are told it is a birthday, and other times the host needs to inquire. Every place has a unique way of handling birthdays. Many casual restaurants have a parade of servers, each dragged away from their table, often singing a version of happy-happy-birthday-birthday for the 28th time that evening, before quickly running into the kitchen to tend to their other duties. A complimentary dessert is common. Other restaurants have special drinks, sparklers, hats, and even rose petals. However the establishment decides to celebrate special occasions, a few considerations should be kept in mind:

► Make it fitting to the level of service you provide.

► Make it easy to tolerate for the others in the restaurant.

► Make it appropriate for the level of attention that the patron desires.

☐ Give them a warm welcome. Use their name if possible.
☐ Greet them appropriately.
☐ Don't label. Don't assume anything. A mother might actually be a wife. A daughter might actually be a date.
☐ Ask if they have a reservation.
☐ Ask the number in party and intentions (for dinner?)
☐ Ask if they have a seating preference.

2. **Seat the Guest:** Assess their needs, accommodate. Seat with a server as appropriately as possible. Walk them to the table or inform them of the wait time or options.

☐ Pull out chair for women if possible.
☐ Hand out menus.
☐ Inform them of the next step (Andre will be with you shortly).
☐ Inform server.

Also, let everyone know that it is their responsibility to greet guests, not just that of the host/hostess.

Tables are numbered in a system or pattern. Server stations are two to five tables with three being very common. This will also depend upon the level of service dictated. Food is typically taken in order of where they sit at the table.

Menu Knowledge

While a menu may be the silent salesman, the server is the talking salesman. The server should know more than the customer about the menu. They should be well-versed in nutritional information, allergies, tastes, favorites, portion sizes, substitutes, what is 86'd (out), and what is best for customers in a hurry.

SERVICE INSIGHT

Approaching the Table

Table approaches are as unique as restaurants. A few commonly used greetings are:

▶ Hello my name is _____?

▶ I'll be your waiter/waitress this evening.

▶ I'll be your server tonight.

▶ I'll be taking care of you tonight.

▶ I'll be taking care of you guys tonight.

▶ How are you tonight?

▶ Welcome to the _____! Is this your first time with us?

▶ Or, simply, "Drink order?"

What is the best way to approach a table? Most chains have standardized greetings of which *most* servers follow. Private restaurants tend to have less standard approaches and are subject to the server's discretion, which can bring in a caveat of issues. Most all greetings are pleasant, but most are insincere and forgettable. What is the most appropriate way to greet a table? It depends on the setting, the guests, and the expectations. A formal setting will dictate formality in a greeting, while casual operations are open to subjectivity. Some guests prefer a casual approach while others prefer formality and won't tolerate anything less. Gauging this incorrectly can really hurt the experience. It is always better to begin more formal. Lately, the trend has been to begin with formality and then adapt to allow the level of service to be tailored to the individual guest. However, always remain professional.

3. **Take Drink Order:** This step begins the tangible aspects of hospitality. Although they are paying, they still perceive it as a hospitable gesture.

4. **Serve Drink:** Quickly and accurately assess their needs. Do they want to order? Explain the menu, present specials, and answer questions.

5. **Take Dinner Order:** Beginning with the woman and continuing counterclockwise if possible, memorization is great, but it is more reliable if you write it down. In a full-service restaurant, orders are taken at the table and entered into a computer system. This system routes the orders to the proper kitchen station. The order tickets, or chits, are printed and then prepared. A chit is a slang term for an order ticket. Some kitchens have eliminated paper tickets and gone to a screen in the kitchen.

6. **Serve Dinner Order:** May use a food runner, ask if anyone needs anything else, stay or check back within 2–3 minutes.

> **Chit**
>
> Slang for order ticket. Often printed for line cooks to prepare. Sometimes referred to as a dupe (short for duplicate from the old carbon-copy checks).

There are strong differences of opinion. Different rules and cultures have blurred the map, each claiming to be an absolute authority. Some of the more contemporary operations are instructing their waitstaff to follow the general guidelines, while paying close attention to the guest, being reasonable and remaining flexible in an effort to keep the guest feeling comfortable. Generally, the more formal of a setting, the stricter the rules. The most appropriate for American Style Service is:

▶ Use a right hand to serve from the left side, and a left hand to serve from the right side.

▶ Appetizers and salads: served from the right with your right hand. Flatware preset.

- ▶ Soups: doily, bowl on plate, spoon on right. Preset. Served from right with right hand.
- ▶ Entrée: from the right with right hand. Logo or main item facing the guest. Flatware preset or reset. Side dishes to the left.
- ▶ Dessert: preset or reset. Flatware to the left. From the right with right hand.
- ▶ Beverages from the right, served or poured from the right.
- ▶ Clearing: from the right with your right hand.
- ▶ Envision a line between the face of the guest and the plate. Never cross over past this line.
- ▶ Always serve in a counterclockwise fashion.
- ▶ Always begin serving with a woman, usually to the left of the host.

7. **Clearing:** After each course, unless directed to leave. Always confirm before removing items. Look for signs: napkin on plate, plate pushed out of way, fork upside down across top of plate, both knife and fork together across plate, no food left, or too much time has passed. Crumb scrapers are an essential tool in fine dining. **Crumbing** is the process of scraping breadcrumbs, and the like, off the table between courses. Crumbs are usually scraped onto a napkin held by the waiter on the edge of the table.

Crumbing
Use of a tool to scrape bread crumbs from the table between courses in fine-dining restaurants.

8. **Leftovers:** How are leftovers handled? Everyone has a different idea. Some people consider it rude to take home leftover food. Others place it in a "doggie bag," although most pet owners wouldn't feed it to their pets for fear of making them sick. Others want to enjoy the rest of the meal at another time. For those guests, leftovers can be made special. Some are boxed at the table, while many are boxed out of sight. Leftovers made classy can be a great chance for the guests to have fond memories of the meal, associating the restaurant with class. It can also be a form of advertising. Consider this the next time a meal is thrown into Styrofoam and congealed on the side of the container.

9. **Present the Bill:** Discreetly present to the head of the table, or whoever requests. Thank the host and the rest of the table. Place in the middle of the table when unsure. This is one of the times where people may be ready to leave so settle payment as promptly as needed according to their terms.

SERVICE INSIGHT

Lingering Customers

Customers are wonderful for business. You want them to patronize your business. You want them to enjoy themselves. You also want them to leave in a reasonable timely manner so that you can "turn" the table. Many tactics exist to expedite the process without seemingly rushing the guests. The courses are kept moving along. The plates are cleared. A check is offered. Lights levels are changed. Despite this, some guests set up camp and linger for hours. What can you do? At a finer restaurant, there is little that you can do. It is considered rude and disrespectful to rush or push customers. In diners, there is an expectation of leaving once finished if other customers are waiting, so it might be acceptable to rush them if the table is desperately needed. If the level of service is between a diner and a fine dining restaurant, you could offer them a drink or dessert at the bar. If that doesn't work and you ask them to leave, you will likely lose the customer. Before you rush anyone, think about how badly you really need the table.

Service Style Overview

American Service is common but it is not the only style available. Below is a survey of the most common service styles with descriptions of each style.

AMERICAN SERVICE STYLE

- ► **Alias:** full-service, sit down service, plated service
- ► **Formality:** medium to high
- ► **Dynamics:** food is plated in the kitchen and brought out to the customers
- ► **Skill:** medium
- ► **Labor:** low
- ► **Personalization:** low to medium
- ► **Portion control:** high
- ► **Space required:** low
- ► **Speed of service:** medium

BUFFET SERVICE STYLE

Buffet Service Style
© LElik83/Shutterstock.com

- ► **Alias:** smorgasbord
- ► **Formality:** low to medium
- ► **Dynamics:** food is displayed on long tables. Guests pick up their own plate and choose their food. Can be assisted or unassisted.
- ► **Skill:** low
- ► **Labor:** low
- ► **Personalization:** low
- ► **Portion control:** low
- ► **Space required:** low to medium
- ► **Speed of service:** high

BUTLER SERVICE STYLE

Butler Style Service
© sergiovegafotografo/Shutterstock.com

- ▶ **Alias:** passed
- ▶ **Formality:** high
- ▶ **Dynamics:** similar to Russian Service but guests help themselves from the platter. They use the platter utensils. The guests may be standing as in a reception, or seated at a table.
- ▶ **Skill:** medium
- ▶ **Labor:** high
- ▶ **Personalization:** low
- ▶ **Portion control:** medium
- ▶ **Space required:** low
- ▶ **Speed of service:** low
- ▶ **Advantages:** guests choose
- ▶ **Disadvantages:** more space, clumsy guests, cold food, spilling . . .

COUNTER SERVICE STYLE

Counter Service Style
© Rawpixel.com/Shutterstock.com

► **Alias:** limited service
► **Formality:** high
► **Dynamics:** typical in fast-food settings, ordered, prepared in the kitchen, served at the counter. Other variations involve you deciding choices as they make it in an assembly line such as in Subway or Chipotle or coffee shops where they prepare it in front of you. Also, some will finish in the kitchen and bring it to your table.
► **Skill:** low/medium
► **Labor:** low
► **Personalization:** low/medium
► **Portion control:** high
► **Space required:** low
► **Speed of service:** high

CAFETERIA SERVICE STYLE

Cafeteria Service Style
© New Africa/Shutterstock.com

► **Formality:** low
► **Dynamics:** guests choose particular items from a display or buffet, and then are charged accordingly at the register. May also be one set price as in college dormitories.
► **Skill:** low
► **Labor:** low
► **Personalization:** low
► **Portion control:** low
► **Space required:** high
► **Speed of service:** high

DIM SUM SERVICE STYLE

Dim Sum Service Style
©Colin Woods/Shutterstock.com

- ▶ **Formality:** medium
- ▶ **Dynamics:** many different carts are wheeled to your table periodically, or platters are brought to your table, you choose what you would like. There is typically a system of stamping a card or the like for billing purposes.
- ▶ **Skill:** low to medium
- ▶ **Labor:** medium
- ▶ **Personalization:** low to medium
- ▶ **Portion control:** high
- ▶ **Space required:** low
- ▶ **Speed of service:** medium

ENGLISH SERVICE STYLE

English Service Style
©Norenko Andrey/Shutterstock.com

- ▶ **Other names:** family style (similar)
- ▶ **Formality:** high

- ▶ **Dynamics:** resembles gathering of families. All fully cooked in the kitchen. Mimics home-style cooking. Platters from the kitchen are brought to the head of the table or the host for inspection then set on table or passed. Typically in a private room instead of a main dining room. Variations—leaving salad in middle of table. Guests pass it around the table, or the captain serves around the table.
- ▶ **Skill:** low to medium
- ▶ **Labor:** low
- ▶ **Personalization:** medium
- ▶ **Portion control:** low
- ▶ **Space required:** low
- ▶ **Speed of service:** medium

FRENCH SERVICE STYLE

French Service Style—Tableside Preparation of Duck
© Chakarin Wattanamongkol/Shutterstock.com

- ▶ **Other names:** tableside service
- ▶ **Formality:** high
- ▶ **Dynamics:** tableside preparation of food in front of customer. Crepes, or bananas Foster is common in Americanized versions.
- ▶ **Skill:** high
- ▶ **Labor:** high
- ▶ **Personalization:** high
- ▶ **Portion control:** high
- ▶ **Space required:** high
- ▶ **Speed of service:** low
- ▶ **Advantages:** showcases food, entertains, warrants a higher price
- ▶ **Disadvantages:** must be highly skilled, timely, costly, lowers seating capacity, lengthens seating time therefore reducing table turnover. May bring unwanted attention to customer.
- ▶ **Tip:** consider a blend such as ladling a soup tableside

The Classical French multi-course menu may involve upward of 20 courses. Meals were times to savor the experience. America has reduced this to fewer courses. Some of the French terms are still present in today's restaurants.

Wine may be treated as a separate course. Sorbets or water and crackers may also be used to cleanse the pallet. See figure below for a comparison of courses among French and American menus.

Comparison of Courses Among Menus

Classical French Multi-Course Menu	(Translation)	American Tasting Menu	American Multi-Course Menu (Typical)
Hors d'oeuvre	Appetizer	Cold Appetizer	Appetizer
Potage	Soup	Soup	Salad
Oeuf	Egg	Fish	Main Course
Farineux	Starch	Meat	Dessert—Coffee
Poisson	Fish	Salad	
Entrée		Dessert—Coffee	
Sorbet			
Legume	Vegetable		
Salats	Salad		
Entrements	Dessert		
Fromage	Cheese		
Fruit			
Digestif	Alcohol		

RUSSIAN SERVICE STYLE

Russian Service Style
© Foodpictures/Shutterstock.com

- ▶ **Other names:** platter service
- ▶ **Formality:** high
- ▶ **Dynamics:** food is prepared in the kitchen and served on platters instead of plates. Plates are set and desired portions are served from

the platters with fork over spoon manipulation. Platter held in left and spoon/fork with right.

- ► **Skill:** medium, fork over spoon technique, easy to spill
- ► **Labor:** medium
- ► **Personalization:** medium to high
- ► **Portion control:** low
- ► **Space required:** medium
- ► **Speed of service:** medium

These service styles can be found in many types of restaurants and event settings. The figure below details the types of restaurants most common to these styles.

Relating Service Styles to Types of Restaurants

Types of Restaurants	Fine Dining	Upscale Casual	Casual or Family	Fast Casual	Quick-Service	Banquet or Private Events
Style of Service						
American	X	X	X			X
Buffet		X	X	X		X
Butler	X					X
Cafeteria			X		X	
Counter				X	X	
Dim Sum	X	X				
English	X					X
French	X	X				
Russian						X

Above are some of the most classic and popular styles. Other styles and hybrid service styles have recently come back into fashion. Below are photographs of Korean Barbecue and Fondue. Both of these styles involve customers heating or cooking their food at the table.

Customers Dipping Food Into a Cheese Fondue at Their Table
© Oksana Shufrych/Shutterstock.com

Customers Cooking in the Middle of a Table at a Korean Barbeque
© Wpixz/Shutterstock.com © Oksana Shufrych/Shutterstock.com

Related Points

❖ VOLUME

The amount of business that a restaurant achieves can be described different ways. Sales, **covers**, and **turnovers**. Sales are measured by the dollar per period, time segment, or shift. Covers are synonymous with meals served, and turnover is the number of times a seat is used and re-seated with another guest.

Cover

A dinner or meal for one person. Taken from the classical style of covering each dish when leaving the kitchen.

❖ TECHNOLOGY

Computers are now in nearly every food-service setting. Potential customers can check out the menu and view it on a map or in Google Street view. They can look at other customers' ratings. Customer profiles are created and reservations can be made online. Once they arrive, orders may be taken on a wireless system, or input into a computer at a server station. Orders are routed to the appropriate stations in the kitchen. Secure payments are accepted using the newest technologies. Redundancy and reliability are built into the system. Uninterrupted power supplies, back-ups, printouts, back-up systems, and the like are all configured and promise to ensure smooth sailing.

Turnover

Also known as seat turnover, customer turnover, dining room turnover, and churn in a full-service restaurant. Typically expressed for a shift, meal period, or day. The number of times that a seat or table has been seated with a new customer.

However, even the most robust system will occasionally fail. What happens when the system is not available? You can call for help from a technician, but meanwhile the show must go on! Tips are to have everyone trained on a back-up system. Have that system ready to go in the event of an emergency. This is typically a low-tech pencil and paper system with much verbal interaction. Everything but essentials are delayed, and business is reduced to a minimum until systems are restored.

SERVICE INSIGHT

Special Requests

Special requests can be a difficult task for servers. They want to please the customer, but the kitchen staff may not always be as accommodating. Some establishments refuse special requests, while others do anything in their power to make it happen. Most fall somewhere in the middle. A server should never promise until they are sure they can deliver. The kitchen staff must realize that it isn't the server's fault. Also, as competition increases, the customers realize that other businesses will accommodate their requests, and they will simply go there.

SERVICE INSIGHT

Serving Children

Children can be difficult in a restaurant. Some children are well-behaved with conscientious parents, others can bother the customers and create havoc. Consider the following tips when dealing with children:

► Let the parents serve the children. Give plates and water to the parents first, and allow them to pass it on to the child.

► Give them an out, offering food to-go, or an area where they can walk with the child until they calm.

► Remember that you are a stranger. The child does not know you. Don't expect them to answer your questions or easily welcome your presence.

► Follow the lead of the parents. They are the caretakers. They will often direct you.

► Don't place the children in highchairs. Set it out for the parents and allow them to do it.

► Place lids on cups when possible, and no ice.

► Remove knives, flames, and anything else from their close reach.

► Check the floor when you present the check. Children are notorious for dropping items, and the parents will appreciate it.

CHAPTER REVIEW QUESTIONS

1. List and briefly describe three reasons why BOH and FOH employees might argue.
2. Outline the primary differences between American, French, and Russian Service.
3. How many more courses might a Classical European Fine Dining meal have than an Americanized version?
4. List at least four things that a meal could represent to a guest.
5. What is the French equivalent term of the Dining Manager?
6. In your opinion, what is the most common service style in the US?
7. Should food be served from the left or right?
8. Who was Escoffier and what was his impact on food service?
9. Why do you think that buffets are considered to be less formal?
10. What is the purpose of table numbers?

CASE STUDIES

Midwestern French

Chateau le Petite was a small, French restaurant located in the Midwest. It was originally a casual family restaurant that closed after many years. The new owner did much research and determined that the town needed a fine-dining restaurant. He looked at the competitors and found his niche within the fine dining market. All of the other competitors served steaks, barbecue, or Tex-Mex cuisine. He would be an alternative with a sophisticated, authentic, high-end French restaurant. He decided the locals would appreciate the unique cuisine and they would use it for a special-occasion dining experience. He went on the Internet and gathered French menus. He combined and refined the items. He included many options of courses and kept the original French names on items whenever possible. He stocked a wall-displayed wine case with reasonably-priced wines from France and all over the world. He spent many hours stripping the walls back to bare concrete. He exposed the old wooden beams wherever he could. He wanted it to look old and feel as authentic as possible.

He also offered many tableside items. He hired the best candidates possible for the positions. Most of them were fluent in French and were instructed to speak to guests in French whenever possible.

Despite his best efforts and the research showing that the area could easily accommodate another restaurant, he was only busy for a few weeks in the beginning. After that, customers were not returning to his restaurant. The owner built an awesome restaurant and cannot figure why it won't work.

1. Describe the service style of Chateau le Petite.
2. Rate the level of service of Chateau le Petite
3. Why do you think that guests did not return to Chateau le Petite?

A Lost Art?

Tableside cuisine is thought of as a lost art. It brings guests to a place where the server is also a skilled showman who prepares your food right before you. He explains the process and shares his craft. The chef is also another prominent figure. His art is in the cuisine of the restaurant. Many consider themselves fortunate to have the chef come over to visit the table. Lately however, the trade of the elusive and exclusive chef and the art of French tableside service has been replaced with assembly lines of aspiring actors begrudgingly posing as order-takers and food-runners. When kitchens are closed, guests aren't certain how their food is prepared and they aren't sure that they want to know.

Taco Bell radically changed their system years ago to eliminate the conventional "kitchen" replacing it with an "assembly area." Food is cut, seasoned, and cooked by the distributor and shipped in a tube or a bag all ready to be chilled or heated and assembled. This has reduced training cost significantly. It has increased consistency and the safety of the food. Customers don't seem to mind, as Taco Bell is one of the leading quick-service names in America. Other kitchens are instituting the same type of changes behind closed doors.

On the other hand, there is a smaller movement for some to open their kitchen doors. Walls are lowered or removed. Guests can and do observe their food being made.

1. Outline the advantages of eliminating the conventional kitchen.
2. Is restaurant service becoming a lost art?
3. What is being done to preserve the artistry?
4. Make an educated prediction of the future of restaurant artistry in the next 25 years.

The Foundry

The Foundry is anything but a foundry. Originally a steel plant, the foundry retained its name as the neighborhood was transitioned. Recently, a new restaurant called The Foundry has moved into a small storefront of one of the renovated buildings. The Foundry features Upscale-American cuisine. It serves dinners only, and is open from 4–11 p.m. daily. It has an awesome steel bar with steel bar stools, steel tables, and steel chairs which can be seen from the street through the main window. Many people pass by the storefront and gaze in with curiosity. To help this, a telephone number and menu are posted in a steel display case at the front door.

Since it is a small place, a full-time receptionist cannot be afforded during the day. Instead, many calls are fielded when the cleaning and the prep staff are working. They regularly answer questions ranging from simple to difficult. Typical examples of questions might include:

► "Are you open?"
► "Do you take American Express?"
► "Can I bring in a cake?"
► "Can I bring my own wine?"
► "What is the dress code?"
► "Can I reserve for a private party?"

The prep staff is typically busy and ignores the telephone. The cleaning staff usually takes the calls. Most of them speak broken English, but try very hard to always accommodate all requests. They answer what they can, and do the best job possible. They leave notes, but occasionally leave out or miss details.

Recently, the owners have decided to remedy this by subscribing to an online reservation platform. This offers the ability for guests to view restaurant details, answer common questions, make reservations, and place special requests. While this is a great start, it might also cause issues.

1. Describe the telephone service at The Foundry.
2. Was this the best solution to this problem?
3. What potential problems do you foresee with this new technology?
4. What steps can be taken to ensure a smooth transition of this technology at The Foundry?

Reservation Issues

Fridays and Saturdays, college graduations, Mother's Day, and Valentine's Day can be some of the busiest days for reservations. Some restaurants do not accept advance reservations. For these restaurants, problems occur. The bar area may be too full, the waiting area full, and they end up crowding the entrance. When people have to wait for a long time in these conditions, it takes away from their experience.

For the majority of restaurants who do accept advance reservations, problems also occur. It is not uncommon for guests to make multiple reservations for the same date and time at different restaurants. They later decide which one to honor and disregard the rest. This causes great turmoil in restaurants who hold tables for parties that do not show. Industry average for no-shows is reported at nearly 15%! Most restaurants are relatively small and have very limited seating. The hostess has to stop walk-in seating in advance to ensure there are tables available for reservations. Customers become upset when they are waiting and tables appear open but are being held for late or no-show reservations.

To combat this, most restaurants take a telephone number and a name. Online systems penalize profiles that miss a certain number of reservations. These systems claim to have better success, but can be costly and awkward to use. Some restaurants have begun asking for credit card deposits to hold tables. Customers don't like this. Some give a bad card number or will dispute the charge. Other restaurants have overbooked, assuming that a certain percentage will be late or not keep their reservation. This works until the predicted percentage of no-shows is inaccurate, resulting in an overcommitment of acceptances. Despite the best efforts of restaurants, nothing has worked well.

1. Describe the issues with accepting advanced reservations in restaurants.
2. In your experiences, what have some restaurants done to remedy this?
3. In your opinion, is the practice of requiring a credit card for a reservation considered unacceptable?
4. What do you believe are the best solutions for tackling restaurant reservations?

❖ EXERCISE

Place Setting Exercise

Label the following wares:

© Amenhotepov/Shutterstock.com

1. _____

2. _____

3. _____

4. _____

5. _____

6. _____

7. _____

8. _____

9. _____

10. _____

11. _____

12. _____

13. _____

14. _____

15. _____

16. _____

17. _____

18. _____

19. _____

20. _____

21. _____

Chapter 5

The Guest Service of Beverages

CHAPTER OBJECTIVES

After reading this chapter, you should be able to:

► Understand and identify different liquors and their use in cocktail service.
► Identify common glassware and their association to specific drinks.
► Identify and describe different wines and their service.
► Understand the idea and flavor profiles of basic liqueurs.
► Identify and describe different types of coffees and waters.
► Explain how to serve a bottle of wine or champagne.
► Describe the staff positions involved in beverage service.

TERMINOLOGY

Alcoholic beverage
Aperitif
Call
Cocktail
Cordial
Corkage Fee
Decanting
Digestif
Neat

On the rocks
Premium
Proof
Speed Rack
Straight Up
Tall
Twist
Varietal
Well

Introduction

Beverage service is a unique niche of the hospitality industry. It is present in many other facets of the industry. It can also be a discipline in and of itself. Beverage service continues to change. The lost art of a bartender still remains a rarity, but is complimented by other additions such as mega-bars and bar-flare. To add, beverage appreciation has become an interesting hobby with many new demographics entering the mix. As a result, you need to understand and appreciate many uniquely different beverages in addition to preparing, mixing, and serving them. On top of all of this, you are also much more to the guest: you are part listener, part adviser, and part entertainer. The guests don't come to a bar purely for the drinks. They come to the bar for an experience and you make that experience.

Beverage Positions

Beverage service may be a portion of the job description or the entirety of a position. A bartender is typically responsible for the service at a bar. The duties typically involve serving the drinks and collecting the money. In addition, other responsibilities may involve bar preparation, greeting, ordering, receiving, setup and breakdown, inventory, and cleaning. A service bar may also be included in the position. This services the waitstaff who order drinks for the lounge or dining room.

Waiters With Red Wine, Rose Wine, and Sparkling Wine
© David Tadevosian/Shutterstock.com

BARBACK

A Barback is an assistant to the bartender. This is a position for aspiring bartenders who must learn the position and climb the ranks. They primarily replenish alcohol, ice, and glassware so the bartender can remain behind the bar and continue pouring. Busy operations could not operate without the backup support of this position.

Bartender Preparing a Craft Cocktail
© bogdanhoda/Shutterstock.com

COCKTAIL WAITRESS

Cocktail Waitresses are waitstaff that service the bar area. They may also supply lighter food or even full meals. They permit the bar to serve more people than the immediate dining room can accommodate. This position is historically a female-oriented position, but it can just as well be fulfilled by a male waitstaff.

SOMMELIER

Sommeliers are professional wine experts. The increase in wine consumption combined with discriminating and educated palates have given a rebirth to the term sommelier. A sommelier, also known as a wine steward, works the floor of a fine dining restaurant, assisting guests with their wine and beverage selections. He tailors his suggestions specifically to the guest. He establishes knowledge of their taste preferences, food order choice, occasion, and budget. While anyone can claim to be a sommelier or wine steward, few are certified. Many institutions offer courses and various levels of certification. The Court of Master Sommeliers is considered to be the most well-known and most prestigious.

SPECIALTY MANAGER

With all of the unique beverage operations, they may devise and employ a specialty manager in a niche area. This person differs from a sommelier in that they have less guest contact. This person may specialize in wines, liquors, or beer. They are likely in charge of inventory, promotions, and staff training. In the case of a micro-brew operation, this individual may also oversee production as well as service and inventory of beer.

BEVERAGE MANAGER

This position is the manager of all things beverage. It may be more BOH-oriented when combined with food as in the case of a Food and Beverage Manager. It may also be a service-oriented position in the case of a Bar Manager. In the latter case, this person establishes and oversees service protocol, pricing, promotions, inventory, customer service, regulations, and security. This position must be well aware of the actions of the customers and the staff. They make the difficult decisions regarding a balance between customer, staff, and organizational goals. They have likely been promoted through the ranks and are very "streetwise" in their dealings.

Wares

Glassware is essential to beverage service. There are many types of glasses available. Each has its specific purpose and holds specific drinks for a specific reason.

▶ **Stems:** are to keep the hands from warming the drink and permit ease of handling and storage. Stems also keep the bowl clean for observation. The staff should never touch above the stem.

▶ **Bowls:** are often over-sized to allow swirling of the beverage. This helps to aerate the beverage since leaving the bottle. They are usually clear to permit the guest to observe the "legs," "tears," or "curtains" of clear liquid running down the side which indicate alcohol content.

Wares
© Berezka_Klo/Shutterstock.com

- **Openings:** vary greatly. A smaller opening holds carbonation and fragrance.
- **Rims:** can be thick or thin, open or closed. A tulip-shaped rim closes to maintain the delicate fragrances. These qualities also force the mouth to open differently to allow the liquid to hit different parts of the tongue.
- **Over-Sizing:** is a very popular theme that appears to be here to stay. Average drinks have increased somewhat, but the size of the glasses and garnishes have nearly doubled in recent times. It makes for a spectacular presentation and warrants a higher check average.

History, style, use, theme, practicality, preference, and expectations all dictate the operation's individual selection and choices of glassware. Hence, there is a great variety in the field. Despite this, there are commonly-accepted glass shapes for most drinks. It is important to know the common glass types used and to be able to recognize them as an aid in preparing or identifying drinks during service.

Typical Glassware and Their Purposes
© A7880S/Shutterstock.com

Beverages and Their Service

KNOWING WINES

Wine Collage
© dizain/Shutterstock.com

Wine is typically made from fermented grapes. Winemakers occasionally use other fruit to make wine, or blend in other ingredients, but essentially, the fundamentals of winemaking has changed over the past several hundred years.

Wines may be classified by color: red, white, rosé (blush). Most of their color comes from the amount of time wine is kept in contact with the skins of the grapes. Therefore, red wine gets its color from being left in contact with its red skins after crushing. White wines are separated from the skins soon after crushing, and rose or blush wines are left in contact with the skins but for a shorter period of time than for red.

Wine may be also classified by the type of grape. This is referred to as a **varietal** wine.

> **Varietal**
>
> A wine referred to by the type or variety of grape used to make it.

Common white wine grape varieties are

- ► chardonnay
- ► chenin blanc
- ► pinot blanc
- ► riesling
- ► sauvignon blanc

Common grape varieties that make red wines are

- ► cabernet sauvignon
- ► gama (makes Beaujolais)
- ► merlot
- ► pinot noir
- ► Syrah/Shiraz
- ► zinfandel

Aging

Most red wines are aged for a period of at least a year or two. There are exceptions such as Beaujolais Nouveau, which is intended to be drunk soon after its release on the third Thursday of each November. Most of the better wines are aged in oak barrels before being bottled.

Sweetness

White wines can range from dry to sweet. Red wines are typically drier. Fortified wines are almost all very sweet.

Temperature

Everyone is familiar with the common generalization that white wines are served chilled and red wines are served at room temperature. In reality, wine temperature is a more complex subject than that. Over-chilling white wine can take away from its flavors. The idea of room temperature should be substituted with cellar temperature, which is about 55 degrees where the red wine is stored. Red wine served much over 65 degrees will bring out the harshness of the alcohol.

- ▶ White Wines: 45–50° F
- ▶ Red Wines: 50–65° F
- ▶ Sparkling Wines: 42–52° F
- ▶ Fortified Wines: 55–68° F

Regions

North versus South—Northern regions are colder and produce grapes that are lighter and more acidic. Southern regions are warmer and produce full-bodied and less acidic grapes.

Old World Wines versus New World Wines—Old World Wines are European wines which tend to be drier and less fruity. New World Wines are from the US, South America, Africa, and Australia and tend to be complete in flavor and do not need paired food.

Vintages

Most wines are dated by year the grapes were picked. Years are not prominently listed on most wine lists as debates arise from the attributes of aging. If a guest orders a vintage that you do not have, bring the closest year, and ask for further suggestions from the wine steward or manager.

Other Wines

- ▶ Champagne: all champagnes are sparkling wines but not all sparkling wines are champagnes. Sparkling refers to the carbonation in the wine. True champagne is sparkling wine produced in the Champagne region of France. Sparkling wine produced outside of this region is referred to as simply sparkling wine. Other regions also have their own names. Sparkling wine produced in Italy is called Prosecco or Spumonti.

Champagne Flutes
© Dasha Petrenko/Shutterstock.com

- ▶ Fortified wine: wines with additional brandies or other alcohols added. If this fortified wine is served before a meal, it is often referred to as an **aperitif**.

Aperitif
alcohol served before a meal.

Presenting, Opening, Tasting, Serving

▶ Glassware is either preset or brought just before service. It is also ordered/served by the glass.

▶ Lint-free. Hold by stem of glass. Avoid touching bowl of glass.

▶ Red and white wine service is very similar.

▶ White is chilled and red is served at room temperature.

▶ Present the bottle to ensure it was the bottle they ordered.

▶ Uncork it.

▶ Place cork on table beside them for inspection. A cork found to be in acceptable condition is an indication that the bottle was stored correctly.

▶ Pour the host a small portion—about two to three ounces.

▶ Hold up to light or against white tablecloth.

▶ Swirl to release aroma and aerate.

▶ Smell with nose over top of glass.

▶ Taste.

Decanting

Decanting

Separating sediments from the wine.

All wines have sediments which are yeasts, skins, and other organic materials. As red wines age, the sediments settle out of the wine. **Decanting** is the process of removing these sediments from the wine by slowly pouring it into a glass vessel referred to as a decanter. This allows the wine to "breathe" or allow air to come into contact with it. Most of the sediments stay in the bottle, and the rest settle to the bottom of the decanter. A candle is held up to the side of the glass decanter as it is poured to ensure it is not poured past the point that the sediments also pour out.

Decanting of a Bottle of Red Wine
© RossHelen/Shutterstock.com

Champagne and Sparkling Wine Service

▶ Present bottle.

▶ Remove cage (be careful not to point after removal).

▶ Cover with napkin.

▶ Thumb on top, slowly twist the bottle, not the cork.

▶ Pop cork, on the edge slowly permitting the pressure to release (otherwise it will fly across the room).

▶ Wipe.

▶ Pour, wrap napkin around it, and place in the bucket.

Mojito Cocktails
© Sunny Forest/Shutterstock.com

❖ KNOWING COCKTAILS

Liquors are the basis of mixed drinks. A **cocktail** is a combination of liquor, liquors, and/or other sodas, juices, or ingredients. There are seven main liquors used as a basis for most cocktails:

Cocktail
Any combination of alcohols. Aka mixed drink.

Vodka

- ▶ Most popular
- ▶ **Main ingredient:** grain-based
- ▶ **Process:** distillation, un-aged
- ▶ **Appearance:** clear
- ▶ **Taste:** no distinct flavor itself, but may be flavored with other ingredients
- ▶ **Popular brands:** Absolut, Stolichnaya, Smirnoff, Grey Goose, Chopin, Skyy, Ciroc

Gin

- ▶ **Main ingredient:** grain-based
- ▶ **Process:** distillation, un-aged
- ▶ **Appearance:** clear
- ▶ **Taste:** no distinct flavor itself, flavored with juniper berries
- ▶ **Popular brands:** Beefeater, Bombay, Gilbey's, Gordon's, Seagram's, Tanqueray

View of Speed Rack Behind Bar
© BrandonKleinVideo/Shutterstock.com

Rum

- ▶ **Main ingredient:** sugarcane, also beets or molasses
- ▶ **Process:** distillation
- ▶ **Appearance:** light to dark in color
- ▶ **Taste:** rounded, the darker the sweeter
- ▶ **Popular brands:** Bacardi, Havana Club, Captain Morgan
- ▶ **Other:** produced everywhere but originated in the Caribbean

Tequila

- ▶ A product of Mexico
- ▶ **Main ingredient:** agave plant
- ▶ **Appearance:** clear
- ▶ **Taste:** typically biting
- ▶ **Process:** distillation
- ▶ **Popular brands:** Jose Cuervo, Sauza, Patron, Herradura

Whiskey

- ▶ Main ingredient: grain mash
- ▶ **Process:** fermented and distilled, aged in oak barrels
- ▶ **Appearance:** medium golden-brown
- ▶ **Taste:** aromatic, oaky, bold
- ▶ **Popular Brands:** Jack Daniel's, Crown Royal, Jim Beam, Maker's Mark
- ▶ **Bourbon:** American whiskey from Bourbon County, KY (Wild Turkey, Jim Beam, Maker's Mark, Knob Creek)
- ▶ Canadian Wiskey (Black Velvet, Canadian Club, Seagram's 7, VO, Crown Royal)
- ▶ Irish Whiskey (Bushmill's, Jameson's, Tullamore)
- ▶ Scotch Whiskey—Single malts that aren't blended (Dewar's, Johnnie Walker, Chivas Regal, Cutty Sark, J & B)

View of Bottles
© monticello/Shutterstock.com

Brandy

- ▶ **Main ingredient:** distilled grapes or other fruit
- ▶ The saying goes, all Cognac is brandy but all brandy is not Cognac. This is because Cognac must come from the Cognac Region of France. Similar definitions occur with Champagne and Bourbon.
- ▶ **Cognac** is brandy from the Cognac Region of France
- ▶ **Armagnac** is brandy from the Armagnac Region of France
- ▶ **Calvados** is apple brandy from Normandy
- ▶ **Grappa** is Italian brandy

Cordials

- ▶ Aka liqueurs, flavored or sweetened
- ▶ *Cordials* are flavored or sweetened alcohols. They typically have a lower proof than spirits. They are alone or mixed. Familiarize yourself with the major brands and their flavors:
  - ☐ **Almond:** Ameretto
  - ☐ **Anise:** Sambuca
  - ☐ **Cherry:** Kirsch
  - ☐ **Citrus:** Cointreau
  - ☐ **Coffee:** Kahlua
  - ☐ **Hazelnut:** Frangelico
  - ☐ **Herbal:** Galliano
  - ☐ **Honey:** Irish Mist
  - ☐ **Melon:** Midori

View of Bottles Typical in a Full Bar Assortment
© cdrin/Shutterstock.com

View Behind a Bar With Speed Rack on the Right
© solepsizm/Shutterstock.com

Liquors are typically sorted and priced according to quality. Three main categories are well, call, and premium. They are also called other names and are ranked from lowest to highest, respectively. Full bars stock all levels and types. Party or banquet bars may only stock just a limited selection of the most popular brands.

Speed Rack

An assortment of alcoholic bottles most commonly poured. The rack is strategically placed in the most accessible area for easy reach of the bartender. Typically in a certain order, or light to dark, but varies: vodka, gin, rum, tequila, triple sec whiskey.

▶ **Well:** the lowest-quality alcohol of a type on the premise. Usually in the **speed rack**. Aka "pour."
▶ **Call:** a high-quality alcohol referred to by its specific brand name instead of type.
▶ **Premium:** the highest and most expensive brands of alcohol, above "call," aka top shelf
▶ **Cordial:** aka liqueur; any flavored, sweetened alcohol
▶ **Digestif:** alcohol served after a meal

COCKTAIL ORDERING TERMINOLOGY

Cocktails are ordered in many different styles. Most are chilled with ice. If so, it may be ordered as "*on the rocks*," or just presumed. If chilled with ice and strained, it is ordered as "*straight up.*" If preferred at room temperature, it is ordered, "*neat.*" "*With a twist*" is a request for a twist of a lemon or lime rind to be added as a garnish.

Alcoholic beverage

A general term referring to any beverage containing alcohol including beers, wines, liquors, liqueurs, spirits, and cordials.

▶ **Neat:** Alcohol at room temperature, without ice
▶ **On the rocks:** A drink with ice
▶ **Proof:** The amount of alcohol in a beverage. Twice the percentage of alcohol.
▶ **Straight Up:** Aka "up" an **alcoholic beverage** that is chilled, then strained to remove the ice.

Assorted Cocktails
© AnnaMorozova/Shutterstock.com

► **Tall:** Served in a highball or Collins glass, usually with a larger amount of mixer.
► **Twist:** Served with a twist of a lemon or lime peel and rind.

✧ KNOWING BEER

There are two main groups of beers: lagers and ales. While lagers offer a crisp, clean taste, ales offer a more complex taste.

► **Lagers:** Budweiser, Miller, Coors, Pilsners, and Bocks are varieties of lagers
► **Ales:** India Pale Ale, Stout, Porter, served at a slightly higher temperature (55° F)

Beer Service

► Serving: serve immediately after pouring.
► Foam head, tilt the glass at a 45° angle and pour onto the side of the glass to control the head. Slowly turn the glass upright as it fills. If bottle, twist slightly as you finish the pour to prevent dripping. Lagers 1″; ales, slightly less.

View of Several Draft Beers Being Poured
© Master1305/Shutterstock.com

► Numerous craft beers are now dominating the market. It is important to learn the names of at least a few mainstream as well as regional favorite beers along flavor profiles.
► Bar service for events: open bar, closed bar, tickets.

Coffee and Tea on a Rectangular Saucer
© pattavikorn ployprasert/Shutterstock.com

KNOWING COFFEES AND TEAS

Coffees and teas are an important part of beverage service. While not alcoholic, they are still quite special and essential to nearly every operation.

Coffee Service

- It is often made to order. If brewed by the pot, it should be made fresh and not held for more than 30 minutes.
- Pods should be kept sealed and refrigerated.
- Coffee is to be served black. It is to be accompanied with milk or cream and sweeteners.
- Have napkin in one hand to wipe the lip of the serving pot.
- Pour from the right with your right hand. Coffee handle in the 3:00 position. Pour from 1–2 inches above the cup to avoid splashing. Allow room for creamer and sweetener to be mixed in. Place teaspoon to the right of the cup. Also OK on the saucer. Place cup on saucer first.
- Usually refilled for free.

Specialty Coffees

Specialty coffees have been quite popular in the US and are now considered mainstream. There are three main drinks that you should be familiar with:

- **Espresso:** dark, deep-roasted, finely-ground type of coffee. A slight foam forms on top, served black but offer with sugar and lemon twist.
- **Cappuccino:** 1 part coffee, 1 part steamed whole milk, and 1 part foamed whole milk; other non-fat milk or non-dairy milks may be substituted. May be served with cinnamon, cocoa, or chocolate.
- **Latte:** espresso with steamed milk.

Tea Service

Fine tea service is an art form. There are many aspects of tea to be considered. Most tea is presented with hot water in a teapot with a choice of assorted tea bags. Then it is essentially up to the guest to prepare the tea to their liking. Tea is occasionally brewed in a pot and served generically. As a general guideline, tea can be divided into types and is available bagged and loose leaf. Tea portions vary and are typically revived with 8 ounces of hot water. Adding the hot water to the tea is referred to as steeping. The water temperature varies between types of teas. The table below is a guideline to show the basic difference. Personal preferences may dictate leaving the tea in contact with the water longer for a stronger tea or less time for a weaker tea.

White Teas—Flavored	1 minute	175° F
White Teas—Blooming	5 minutes	180° F
Green Teas	1 minute	175° F
Oolong Teas	3 minutes	195° F
Black Teas	2 minutes	195° F
Herbal Teas	4 minutes	208° F

Creamer and a variety of sweeteners are served with teas and left to the guests' preference.

Water Service

- ▶ Still non–sparkling, non-carbonated—tap or bottled.
- ▶ Sparkling—carbonated, naturally or through carbon dioxide.
- ▶ Pour for them.
- ▶ Ask first for preferences.
- ▶ Delivered on a beverage tray.
- ▶ Don't touch inside of glasses or with pitcher.
- ▶ Some pour from the side.
- ▶ Chilled ice-water temperature.
- ▶ Water glasses or goblets placed above guest's knife.

☀ CORKAGE FEE

Corkage fee is a fee paid to bring your own bottle into a restaurant. This is only legal is some states. Guests may bring in a bottle to enjoy with their meal. It is opened and poured by the server. Since profit is lost from the sale of the beverage, and glassware and labor is involved, many restaurants decide to charge a fee per bottle to "un-cork" and cover these costs. Fees can range from a few to several dollars by cork or bottle. Occasionally fees are waived, but typically range from $10–$20 and can be as high as $75 or more!

Note: Responsible Alcohol Service: Laws and regulations vary between states, certifications are encouraged if not mandatory.

Corkage Fee

A fee charged to uncork and serve bottles brought in by the customers.

Conclusion

Beverages are just as important as the food. Alcohol service is psychologically hospitable. It welcomes the guests, even though they know they are paying. Our culture expects it promptly when seated. Knowledge of the beverages and their service is crucial to effectively serving the guests. It is an integral part and art form of hospitality with deep-rooted traditions that has evolved over the years.

❖ CHAPTER REVIEW QUESTIONS

1. What is the difference between a Cognac and an Armagnac?
2. What is sparkling wine from Italy called?
3. List the steps in presenting and pouring a bottle of wine.
4. What flavor liqueur is Kahlua?
5. What are the general differences between Old World and New World wines?
6. List three common white wine varieties and three common red wine varieties.
7. What is the difference between Espresso and Latte?
8. What do Cognac, Armagnac, Calvados, and Grappa all have in common?
9. What is the ideal maximum length of time that coffee should be held?
10. Describe the position of a Sommelier.

CASE STUDIES

A Drink After Work

Lakeside Restaurant is your typical family restaurant. It is located beside Blue Lake where it enjoys a year-round draw of loyal clientele from the surrounding towns. It serves American cuisine in a casual environment. It is a popular place to enjoy a comfortable, affordable meal with the locals. The portions are always far too large to eat in one sitting. The bar is located on the side of the restaurant. It is a horseshoe-shaped bar in a recent addition. It has booths around the perimeter of the bar area with a half-wall and a fish tank separating it from the dining room area.

Lakeside has been in existence for longer than most people remember. It was originally smaller, but various owners have come and gone, each with different ideas. Over the last few years, it has grown to become a substantial and respectable establishment. The most recent owners have taken particular interest in growing the beverage sales. As a result, the bar area has become a thriving contributor to the overall success of Lakeside Restaurant.

The owners of Lakeside have always given the employees one free drink after the dinner shift as a token of their appreciation. This long-standing tradition has gone back further than anyone can recall. The employees look forward to this as a symbol of another shift completed. The owners or management are typically around and everyone debriefs the events of the evening.

The bar business continues to grow and the bar is quite full in the late evening. The employees, in their partially donned uniforms, are mixing in with the regular customers. Originally the customers liked this. They bought the staff drinks. The staff bought other staff members drinks and everyone bonded. Occasionally an employee would become intoxicated, but no real problems came of it.

Now that the bar business has increased, the bar is being overcrowded by its own staff. The customers are seeing this as more of a bother. The owners also believe that the bartender may be undercharging the employees for their second and third drinks. The owners want the employees to feel respected but are considering withdrawing this privilege and banning employees from the premise after shifts.

1. List the pros and cons of giving employees a free drink after the evening shift.
2. What are policies of other restaurants regarding employees on-premise after work?
3. How could this situation be best remedied?
4. How might the owners best go about banning employees from the bar?

Refusing Service

John is a regular at Cliff's 179 Pub. He is large in stature and presence, with a bold personality and a frame to accommodate it. He is well over 6 foot tall and 350+ pounds. He is very generous and has always tipped very well. He regularly brought business clients there for meetings and often buys a round of drinks for the entire bar. He owns his own construction company which has helped to renovate the bar and fix things for little or no cost over the past several years. He was a really nice guy and the owners feel greatly indebted to him. As a result, it was understood that John received whatever he wanted. Despite their tight controls on special orders and over-serving of alcohol, John has continued to push the limit. He would order items that weren't on the menu. He would order when the kitchen was closed, and, he occasionally drank more than he should have when driving. No one wanted to refuse John. He is their best customer.

Lately, John's homelife has been suffering and he has been spending more and more time drinking at the bar. While this is good for business, it is not good for John's health and the Cliff's 179 Pub's liability if John were to drive while intoxicated.

This one particular evening began like most others. John arrived around 6:00 p.m. He sat at the bar and consumed a few drinks. He ordered dinner, spoke to the other regulars, and watched a game on the television. He continued to drink until closing time. He was obviously intoxicated. He refused hints and demanded to be served even after the bar closed. John was accustomed to getting what he wanted and he didn't like being told to stop. At that point, John wanted to stay longer.

1. Describe the benefits of Cliff's.
2. What ethical liabilities does Cliff's owe to John?
3. What are the legal liabilities of this situation?
4. How should Cliff's handle the situation?

Rockwood Country Club

Peggy is a new hire at the Rockwood Country Club. She is a college student who was hired for the summer to work in their full-service restaurant. She has waited tables previous summers at a local cafe. She decided to work at the Rockwood Country Club (RCC) because her roommate works there and she heard the tips are great. Peggy is not accustomed to this higher level of service since she has only waitressed at a cafe, but she was able to bluff her way through the interview and the admission test with the help of her roommate. The RCC trains very little. Essentially, they hire experienced waitstaff who follow others for a few shifts until they are comfortable. They give them smaller stations with fewer tables until the Dining Room Supervisor feels they can handle more. Peggy has been working there 2 weeks and has done a fine job in the slower pre-season. Tonight is Peggy's first night on her own. In the beginning things are going quite well. Peggy has a sense of confidence that is quite admirable. About halfway through the night a couple at a table points to the wine list and says, "a bottle of Pinot, please." It suddenly occurs to Peggy that she has never actually served a bottle of wine. Regardless, she appears unslighted, trying to recall witnessing many bottles opened when out to dinner with her parents.

Peggy submits the order to the computer system and it is routed to the bar. The bottle is brought to the service bar for pick up. Peggy places the bottle and two wine glasses on her beverage tray. She then smiles and asks the bartender if he could open the bottle for her. He looks at her oddly and says, "It's not a bottle of beer. You open it at the table." Hearing this, Peggy immediately picks up the tray and brings it out to the table. The bartender is nervous from her reply and alerts the Dining Room Supervisor.

Peggy brings the tray over to the tray stand near the table and successfully opens the bottle. She pours both glasses on the tray and serves them to the couple. Immediately, the couple replies, "We ordered the Pinot. What is this red wine?" Peggy looks down at the bottle as she replies, "It is. It's Pinot Noir." The man says, "I pointed to the Pinot Gricio on the list. And we are having the Fish Special. Why would we order a red wine?"

Peggy apologizes and quickly returns with the correct bottle. This time, the man at the table asks if he could first see the bottle. He looks at it. It is the bottle they ordered. Peggy begins to open it, but the cork breaks. She continues to fumble with it, blaming the corkscrew, hoping to make it work but unsure what to do. At this point the Dining Room Supervisor comes over to the table to see if everything is okay. Peggy confidently replies that everything is fine, but the cheap wine key broke the cork. The Supervisor interrupts and tells her to quickly bring out another bottle. The Supervisor apologizes and assures them it will only be a minute. He then tends to other duties nearby. A few more minutes pass and Peggy reappears with a new bottle of Pinot Gricio. This time she shows it to them right away. Peggy then opens it as quickly as possible and pours both glasses to save time. As she is walking away from the table, they each take a sip and immediately sense there is something incorrect with the taste of the wine. It does not taste right. The Supervisor who has remained close by is called over and confirms the bottle has gone bad, or turned. At this point, no food has been ordered, they have been at the table 45 minutes, and everyone involved is frustrated.

1. What are the problems at RCC? List the issues of the case.
2. List the procedures for wine service.
3. What steps in this process did Peggy fail to do?
4. What could not have been avoided?
5. What could have been avoided?
6. How could RCC avoid this occurring in the future?

A Sommelier or Not?

"LiLi's Wine Bar and Kitchen—All Are Welcome" is a rather long name. This is a name of a sheik, upscale restaurant and bar that welcomes everyone. Its premise is to welcome diversity and shun pretentiousness. It is the brainchild of entrepreneur and activist, Linsey LiLi. She wants to fuse the elements of sophistication and intimacy with a hint of Asia into the downtown area, but in an atmosphere that makes everyone feel welcomed. Food will be equally as important as the wine, and no dress code is required. She envisions two entire walls and a ceiling filled with wines celebrating wines from all over the world. The menu will be equally as eclectic. She wants her servers to be prompt and educated, while being as casual and open-minded as possible. She envisions this as being a great success. In developing a staffing plan, Linsey cannot determine whether or not to employ a sommelier. She realizes that wine is important, but doesn't want to intimidate the customers by the presence of a sommelier. Other places have separate beverage bills to ensure proper tipping and she isn't sure that she wants to place such emphasis on this position. She would like her staff to have vast food and wine knowledge but realizes this isn't always possible with so many different foods and wines. Chris, her chef, friend, and adviser, tells her that the classic idea of sommeliers have changed. They are no longer the stuffy, intimidating man with reading glasses. They are now often younger, knowledgeable, and make great efforts to make everyone feel comfortable with their choice of a beverage.

1. Describe the service concept of Lili's Wine Bar and Kitchen—All Are Welcome.
2. Describe the position of a sommelier as it relates to guest service, in the past and now.
3. List the benefits and disadvantages of employing a sommelier.
4. In your opinion, should Linsey employ a sommelier? If so, under what circumstances? If not, how else should she handle beverage service?

Chapter 6

The Guest Service of Lodging

CHAPTER OBJECTIVES

After reading this chapter, you should be able to:

► Describe the common procedures for checking in and checking out a guest.
► Identify and describe common guest service issues and provide solutions for resolving them.
► Identify the primary guest service positions within a typical hotel.
► Describe the typical procedures associated with walking a guest.
► Explain the different meal plans common to hotels.
► Recognize and understand terminology common to the guest service experience.

TERMINOLOGY

Amenities
American Plan (AP)
Authorization
Bleisure
Block
Book
Bucket
Centralized Reservation
    System (CRS)
Charge Record
Check-In
Checkout

City Account
Continental Plan
Day Rate
Did Not Stay/Show (DNS)
European Plan (EP)
Folio
Full House
Gratuity
Guaranteed Late Arrival
Guest History File
Hospitality Suite
House Count

Incidentals
Modified American
    Plan (MAP)
Night Audit
Post
Property Management
    System (PMS)
Rate
Rooming List
Stay Over
Walking a Guest

Service Positions

BELLMAN

This position is also known as a porter or a bellhop. They are typically the first contact of the hotel. Although seemingly simplistic, they can be many different things to the hotel:

- ► Greeter of the property and door holder
- ► Security as the first line of defense
- ► Gatekeeper
- ► Transporting/storing/receiving luggage
- ► Directing crowd flow
- ► Concierge/problem-solver
- ► Valet
- ► Direct cabs

Bellmen encounter everyone. They must be great with people. They must instantly gauge the guest and their needs. They must be able to handle laborious work with ease and tact.

Bellman Removing Luggage From Car
© SARYMSAKOV ANDREY/Shutterstock.com

Luxury Hotel Lobby
© MrPhotoMania/Shutterstock.com

BACK OFFICE

The back office is a part of the hotel that is typically directly in back of the front desk. It is the support area for guest services. Management also typically resides there. Entry and mid-level managers are directly involved with guest service. Upper-level management periodically greet guests, but primarily concentrate on oversight.

CONCIERGE

A concierge is a person that assists guests with both hotel- and non-hotel-related matters. This involves everything from making dinner reservations in the local area to directions to a shopping center. A concierge has full knowledge of the hotel services as well as the local area. They assess the needs of the guest and make appropriate suggestions. They "pull strings" and make the guest experience extra special through their advice and services.

HOUSEKEEPING

The housekeeping department is the heart of the hotel. While all departments must work together, housekeeping is vital. To the guest, it is an invisible department until something goes wrong. Like other facets of hospitality, the departments do not always work well together. The management's job is to ensure they do.

Housekeeping Trolley With Supplies
© lunopark/Shutterstock.com

A popular trend in this area is greening. All but the most formal hotels have instituted green policies for re-using and recycling. Another trend is the issue of bed bugs. Housekeepers are being asked to extend their typical duties to meet these guest demands.

Turndown Service

To add a special touch of service to a guest's stay, a great feature is turndown service. It is the process of preparing a room for sleeping by making it warm and inviting for the guests. This is usually done between 6:00–9:00 p.m. This is popular or mandated in exclusive and 4–5 Star hotels. Some automatically offer turndown service while others are upon request. It typically involves:

- ▶ Closing of draperies.
- ▶ Turning down the lights.
- ▶ Playing of softer music or other music specified in the guest's profile.
- ▶ Folding the top corner of the bedspread away from pillow.
- ▶ Placing chocolates or mints on the bed.
- ▶ If children are present, teddy bears might be tucked in and books are often set out.

Turndown Service
© fivepointsix/Shutterstock.com

DND (Do Not Disturb) Issue

A DND sign is hung on the door when a guest prefers privacy. This means they do not want the housekeeping to enter the room. When this happens, record time the guest refused service on your report. Note: many reports are turning electronic to increase communication between housekeeping and the front desk.

When you have finished all other rooms, return to the DND room. If the DND sign is still on, most hotels have a "Privacy Card" that is slid under the door reading, "We respect your privacy. If you would like your room to be made, please call . . ."

Do Not Disturb and Please Make up the Room Door Hangers
© ZASIMOV YURII/Shutterstock.com

FRONT DESK

The importance of the front desk cannot be undermined. Most everyone must come in contact with them. They are the main contact during the entire stay.

The front desk is also a catch-all for issues. Consequently, they handle a multitude of issues such as:

- impolite guests
- missed guests' needs
- could not find reservation they made but they did in fact make it
- wrong key
- key doesn't work
- room occupied
- lines too long
- missed something held for guest
- credit card not verified
- luggage sent to wrong room
- rates don't match or not available
- room is not what they expected
- wrong information regarding area or hotel
- uncleaned room
- room deficiencies

Customer Receiving a Key Card at Front Desk
© Monkey Business Images/Shutterstock.com

Luxury Hotel Room Bed
© Kanyapak Lim/Shutterstock.com

Rates

Rates are usually the first question of a guest. Some hotels have meals included in their rates. The packages are as follows:

- **American Plan** (AP) a plan in a hotel that all meals included in rate: breakfast, lunch, and dinner.
- **Continental Plan** (CP): room plan that includes only continental breakfast. A continental breakfast is a very light breakfast offering.
- **Modified American Plan** (MAP) aka Demi-pension. A room package including breakfast and one other meal, typically dinner.
- **European Plan** (EP): room rate with no meals included.

The trend in the US is now heavy toward the EP or the CP. AP and MAP are still present in resorts.

CHECKING IN A GUEST

Every property varies with their check-in procedures, but the basics are essentially the same.

- Greet the guest. Smile, warm welcome.
- Ask if they have a reservation. If so, verify name and check identification.
- Ask them to fill out guest registration form or ask the questions: number of people, type of room, length of stay?

Couple Checking Into a Hotel Using Digital Tablet
© Monkey Business Images/Shutterstock.com

▶ Establish form of payment—give quote.

▶ Ask preferences.

▶ Ask for a credit card for incidentals.

▶ Inform of policies (checkout, deposits, cards . . .).

▶ Verify length of stay and preferences.

▶ Assign their room.

▶ Write down the room number on card with their room keys and present it to them.

Couple Receiving Information From Concierge
© Bignai/Shutterstock.com

☀ CHECKING OUT

Checking out a guest may be automatic, but the manual procedure is essentially as follows:

▶ Greet with a warm welcome.

▶ Ask the room number.

▶ Ensure everything is posted to the folio.

▶ Ask if there were any recent charges that may not have been posted.

▶ Ask how everything was during their stay.

▶ Be as brief as possible. People typically want to get somewhere.

▶ Present charges—many place under door after night audit.

▶ Verify how to pay. This is typically on credit card that is being held.

▶ Collect the keys.

▶ Thank them. Ask them to return at a later date.

▶ Ask if they need directions or assistance with bags, etc.

OTHER TERMS TO SERVING GUESTS AT HOTELS

Amenities: extra items provided in addition to basic essentials. There may be an additional charge. Examples could be a pool or extra personal items.

Authorization: permission from credit card company to make a charge.

Bleisure: a portmanteau of business and leisure travel combined.

Block: a group of rooms placed on a temporary hold for a group.

Book: to sell or reserve a room or space.

Bucket: a file holder for guest folios and other reserved material kept behind front desk.

Check-In: a procedure of receiving guests and completing the guest registration process.

Checkout: a procedure of closing a guest folio upon which the guest departs.

Charge Record: a list of all transactions specific to a department or account.

Centralized Reservation System (CRS): a central system for multiple properties. Often accessed internally and externally.

City Account: an account for non-guests.

Day Rate: a lower rate charged to guests that do not occupy the room overnight. Typically between 10:00 a.m. and 4:00 p.m.

DNS: did not stay—guest who checks in and quickly returns to the desk without having occupied the room.

Folio: aka guest account.

Full House: hotel in which all rooms are occupied.

Gratuity: aka tip; typically money given or charged for service.

Guaranteed Late Arrival: assurance that a room will not be sold if guest arrives late.

Guest History File: record of guest's previous transactions.

Hospitality Suite: room for a group to greet or entertain.

House Count: record of the total number of recorded hotel guests.

Incidentals: minor, miscellaneous expenditures.

M.O.D.: Manager on Duty. Department Manager assigned to oversee all operations while others are off or not present.

Night Audit: daily reconciliation of all accounts receivables, performed at night.

Post: to make an entry on an account.

Property Management System (PMS): a computer system that records and integrates many systems throughout the hotel. Useful in tabulating, reporting, and predicting.

Rate: price charged for a room night. Also combined within best available rate (BAR) and lowest available rate (LAR).

Rooming List: a roster of guests and their lodging needs given to a hotel by a group prior to a meeting.

Stay Over: guests who opt to remain at a hotel past the departure date.

Podiums or Pods

Podiums or pods are a relatively new way of accommodating guests. It breaks down the barriers between the guests and the front desk agents. It is also easier for the handicapped guests. Pods can also be used in addition to the front desk or auxiliary areas.

DEALING WITH FRONT DESK ISSUES

Through the process of customer service, inevitably there will be issues that arise. How well you deal with these issues makes or breaks the level of customer service.

If Busy

Call for backup help. Most hotels have a system with a buzzer to the back office or a telephone. Be sure to use it. Stay calm, and work quickly and efficiently, but still give guests their deserved attention. Acknowledge the other guests waiting. Let the other guests know that someone will be with them shortly.

SERVICE INSIGHT

Grandma Is Visiting

Consider this approach to customer service: consider that your grandmother is visiting you for a couple of days. What would you do? Would you clean more than usual before she arrived? Would you welcome her with a sincere smile? Would you give her the bedroom instead of the couch? Would you cancel your other appointments to give grandma your full attention? Would you show her out when she leaves? Would you help her to the bus or the train or carry her bags out to her car? Would you even do a follow-up call? Yes, of course you would do all of these things. Of course you would.

In hotels, there is a strong correlation between your grandmother and the guest. You are compelled to do this for both your grandmother and the guest. You do this for your grandmother out of love and you do this for the guest out of a sincere concern to serve them. You should give the guest a warm welcome and a sincere smile. You should clean even better than normal. You should give them the best accommodations that you have and provide them with your full attention while they stay at your property. When they leave you show them out, wish them farewell, and even do a follow-up.

Courtesy of Aziz Bandriss—Rooms Division Manager—Central Park Ritz Carlton, NYC.

Couple Checking Into Hotel at a Pod Reception Desk
© Africa Studio/Shutterstock.com

Declined Credit Cards

This is typically a sensitive issue. When this occurs, be sincere, understanding, and direct. In a soft voice, apologize and inform them of the decline. Ask for another form of payment.

Missing Reservations

It can be quite bothersome when a guest calls or arrives at the desk and you cannot find the reservation. Ask them again to verify spelling and confirm the dates and search again. Ask for other ways to retrieve information such as their confirmation number, company name, or their telephone number. Ask when they made the reservation because all systems don't instantly update. Tactfully inquire if they could have made the reservation at another property. If possible, call the other property to assist them. If you have availability, apologize, and suggest a new reservation and give a quote.

Walking a Guest

Walking a Guest

When the guest has a reservation that the hotel cannot honor because they are over capacity. Usually due to overbooking. The guest is transferred to another hotel.

Walking a guest means that the property has overcommitted by accepting more reservations than they could supply. Either guests have overstayed, they booked too many foreseeing cancellations that haven't occurred, or rooms have been unavailable for repair. In any case, the guests have made a reservation but the hotel does not have an available room. Consider the following steps:

Realize that some higher-level guests should not be walked. High priority members may be entitled to cash bonuses. Other considerations: length of stay, business affiliation, comped?

Guest Paying With Credit Card
© Monkey Business Images/Shutterstock.com

Know what other properties are open for rooms; try to do it earlier in the evening; make it as easy on them as you can.

- Apologize, have the manager apologize, have a letter of apology prepared.
- Ask/think—what can you do to help them? Calls? . . .
- See if they care?
- Provide transportation.
- Be as brief as possible.
- Have car ready.
- Refund or comp the room if policy dictates.
- Tell their concierge.
- Call over to ensure things are good.
- See if you can have them come back if multiple-night stay.
- Send to a nicer place.
- Send a gift to their room?
- Record the incident.

Giving Information

Regarding the property or the local area, try to use the following guidelines:

- Begin from your current location or a closer location they are aware of.
- Stick with the most basic, simplest path.
- Use street names and give landmarks.
- Point with entire hand open.

Surveying the Stay

Ask guests how their stay was. Empower your staff to also randomly ask. It is everyone's job. The Lateral Service Principle states a staff member must assist if they see a guest need, regardless of whether or not it is within their job description. They must stop whatever else they are doing and help the guest.

Technological Changes

Technology is changing quality guest service in hotels and resorts. It is changing the types of services that we provide, the way that we communicate with guests, and the way that the guest experiences the services. When coordinated and managed properly, it is a spectacular display of meeting and exceeding guest expectations.

CHANGING DELIVERY OF SERVICES

Technology is changing the way that it delivers services to the guests. Traditional staff positions are being supported or even replaced by mobile booking, automated check-in, checkout, and mobile payment. The Millennials Generation is becoming a large segment of the guests and they are comfortable with texting or self-service. In fact, they often prefer it to calling and are embracing these trends and their advantages. For example, concierges are immediately available from anywhere via text even before or after the stay.

To further accommodate this need for automation, new techniques are being refined for near-seamless guest identification. Guest recognition software can identify guests through IFRD, Bluetooth, facial recognition, finger prints, and even retina scanning. This can be used for recognition to enter floors, unlocking rooms, and even check-in/checkout.

Another new type of technology is the term Internet of Things (IoT). This relates to connecting the Internet to many common items like the HVAC and

---

SERVICE INSIGHT

Making Magic Happen

The hotel has learned that a couple is checking in and the man is going to propose to the woman. The couple is given a room with a view of the park and a telescope in the window. The man goes to the window and sights in telescope at a predetermined time. He finds a hotel staff member that is sent out into the park to hold up a sign that reads, "Will you marry me?" If the woman says yes, the door is opened and employees rush in and fill the room with champagne and strawberries.

Courtesy of Aziz Bandriss—Rooms Division Manager— Central Park Rtiz Carlton, NYC

© lenisecalleja.photography/Shutterstock.com

appliances. The Internet collects data and communicates or interacts with these devices over a network. For example, a smart HVAC system could regulate the temperature when you are present and conserve electricity when you are not. It could sense the presence of sunlight and dim lights during the day. These technologies turn previously unintelligent devices into "smart" devices, which could be made semi- or even fully autonomous.

Robot Butler at a Hotel
© MONOPOLY919/Shutterstock.com

CHANGING COMMUNICATIONS

Technology is also changing the way that hotels communicate with their current and perspective guests. New means, or channels, such as social media have been popularized. Customers have the ability to research and understand their hotel options before making a decision. Because of this, hotels can communicate their offerings in a soft-sell to browsing customers.

Existing guests also have the ability to communicate directly with the hotel in a number of ways. Because of this, the hotel has new opportunities to understand and relate to guests more meaningfully, providing a chance to strengthen guest relationships. For example, a guest posts a review in a social network. A manager responds. These interactions help guests to feel heard. Everyone sees it and it makes a difference. JD Power data shows that responding to social feedback with a problem resolution doubles the percentage of people who will recommend the hotel to others. It also increases customer loyalty to a property or brand.

Other technologies include chatbots and artificial intelligence (AI) that are taking the place of a concierge. Chatbots understand simple questions and provide answers. AI is also used for data analysis. Guests can now receive immediate responses through a variety of channels which might be nearly impossible without the assistance of chatbots and AI.

Another communication technology is Smart Speakers. Marriott International has begun to offer Echo Smart Speakers by Alexa in some of their properties. These Echos perform many of the tasks performed by calling the front desk. Eventually, guests will be able to sync their own Amazon account to the hotel devices.

CHANGING GUEST EXPERIENCES

Lastly, technology is changing how the guest experiences service. Many of the traditional services are still provided, but now enhanced through the use of technology.

Virtual Reality (VR) technology can provide a 360° imaging experience of a product. It can showcase the property and show rooms to help set expectations when guests decide to book a room. This technology can also offer local attractions and other games for entertainment purposes.

Another type of augmentation to service are robots. One of the first well-known robots was Connie. This was developed for Hilton Hotels using IBM's

SERVICE INSIGHT

Who Might See the Guest?

The front desk typically sees the guest, but who else might come into contact? The housekeepers in the hallway. More hotels are training their housekeepers to make contact with the guests by acknowledging them and asking how their stay is. When was the last time that a housekeeper asked what else they could do to make your stay better? It is a powerful guest service technique!

Robotic Front Desk at Hotel With Robot Assistant
©MONOPOLY919 /Shutterstock.com

Watson supercomputer. It was popularized on the television show *Jeopardy*. It was one of the first to utilize speech recognition and AI to respond to queries from customers and intelligently learn from interactions. As innovative as it was, it still had limitations with its vocal interactions with guests. Since Connie, AI and robots have developed immensely. Grocery stores now have robot porters. Knightscope robots are being deployed in some airports for security purposes. Hilton is working on refining a robot concierge program. And, perhaps the most progressive example of robots is The Henn-na Hotel in Japan. It is known as the world's first robot-staffed hotel. This property uses robots as front desk staff, customer information assistants, and as luggage porters. Robotic guest service is still in its infancy, but predictions show that they could become mainstream by 2030. Already they are replacing low-level line jobs in hospitality as they have been in other industries since the invention of the first machine.

❖ CHAPTER REVIEW QUESTIONS

1. How does the concierge help the guest service experience?
2. List and provide solutions for three common front desk issues.
3. Describe the responsibilities of a bellman.
4. List the procedures common to checking out a guest.
5. What is the difference between EP, AP, and MAP?
6. Why might it be helpful to consider your grandmother visiting when relating to hotels?
7. Should housekeepers acknowledge the guest?
8. How is technology changing the way the hotels deliver service?

CASE STUDIES

Walking the Guest

There is a phrase in the hotel business, "Heads in beds." Hotels must fill each room each night. Lost revenue from an unsold room can never be made up. Each night, a small percentage of reservations are either canceled at the last minute or simply deemed "no-shows." This leaves hotels in a predicament because they may have refused others earlier, or simply did not try to sell the room. As a result, many hotels overbook by a small margin. Some properties have taken to securing the first night on a credit card to be paid in advance. To make things worse, some guests stay longer and hotels have rooms that are unexpectedly unavailable pending repair. When the calculations do not add up, and too many reservations show, the result is that the hotel honors the reservation at another hotel. This is referred to as "walking a guest." Hopefully this happens very infrequently. When a hotel is too overcommitted and overbooks to the point that it ends up walking people on a regular basis, it stands to lose many customers and much money. Business customers may have meetings scheduled at the hotel. Conference attendees may have an event at the hotel. This may change their travel plans, making it quite bothersome. There are also initial monetary losses. The hotel loses revenue of the guest, and pays for their room at the competitor's property. They lose the time transporting them to another property, writing a letter of apology, and so on.

1. What is walking a guest?
2. Why do hotels walk a guest?
3. How much does it really cost a hotel to walk a guest? (Consider costs of losing a future customer as well.)

Basics Hotel

The Basics Hotel is a generic, no-frills hotel that provides only the essential accommodations for a very reasonable price. The Basics Hotel brand strives to lead the economy sector by only providing the basics. Its motto is phrased with humor stating, "Basic rooms and basic service, at a basic price." It offers no restaurant, no spa, no business center, and no lounge. The rooms are basic, with few amenities. The beds are reasonably comfortable and the bathrooms offer just the essentials. The rooms offer a television, lamp, bed, a desk, and chair. Guest interaction is kept to a minimum. The front desk has a sign on it that humorously reads, "Basic Hotel Service." Guests are encouraged to check in and check out at a kiosk. No concierge desk is provided, but the guests can ask the front desk "basic questions." A series of vending machines has a sign over it that reads, "Basic Essentials." It provides solutions to most needs offering snacks, toiletries, ice, and beverages. The Basics Hotel also offers an app for smartphones that serves as a concierge and can automate the entire check-in and checkout process if guests wish.

After the stay, guests are electronically sent a basic survey. The technology and price are the two highest scores of the returned surveys. Guests receive basic service and accommodations at The Basics Hotel.

1. Describe The Basics Hotel's customer service concept.
2. How high are the customer expectations at The Basics Hotel?
3. Do you believe that the "The Basics Hotel meets customer expectations"?
4. In your opinion, do you believe this a good thing?
5. Do you believe that guests really mind this at the Basics Hotel?

The Green Earth Hotel

The Green Earth Hotel is a concept that offers lodging in a sustainable manner, while striving to offer as high of a level of service as possible. They offer such common sustainable features as:

- ► LEED Certified construction
- ► Paperless front desks
- ► Air driers in place of hand towels
- ► Options for changing sheets on beds and towels
- ► Water-saving devices
- ► Optimal use of natural lighting
- ► Energy efficient light bulbs

These earth-friendly features have been a major selling point to the guests. It has also reduced labor and utility costs. In addition to being earth-friendly, however, they also want to deliver the highest level of guest satisfaction possible. Because they are paperless, they collect comments from their guests verbally and electronically. Recent guest surveys have shown that guests at the Green Earth Hotel have considered the level of service to be lacking. The compost pile out back smells in the summer months and is attracting many pests. There have been several comments regarding the use of gray water in the toilets. Some guests are not accustomed to this and consider it to lessen their experience. The management is dedicated to providing a sustainable experience, but they also want the guests to feel appreciative to their cause and enjoy their experience.

1. Rate the guest experience at The Green Earth Hotel.
2. Is it possible to be both earth-friendly and guest-friendly?
3. What changes could the hotel make to improve guest satisfaction?
4. What do you believe is the future of balancing these two qualities?

REFERENCES

Interview with Rick Garlick, Global Travel and Hospitality Lead at JD Power. https://www.hotelmanagement.net/text-messages-chat-are-new-ways-to-communicate

Chapter 7

The Guest Service of Events

CHAPTER OBJECTIVES

After reading this chapter, you should be able to:

► Apply the six stages of ensuring customer service to an event.
► Identify and explain the different types of meetings and events, and the specific challenges related to customer service.
► Identify and explain the different types of customers or attendees and their specific challenges as related to customer service.
► Describe how to ensure quality service during pre-event, event, and post-event activities.

TERMINOLOGY

Air Walls	Dead Man
Apron	Exhibition
Auditorium Seating	Forum
Banquet Event Order (BEO)	Hollow Square Seating
Banquet Round	Horseshoe Seating
Blackout Periods	Lecture
Break-Out Rooms	Load In/Load Out
Chevron Seating	Logistics
Classroom Seating	Pipe and Drape
Clinic	Pre-Convention (Pre-Con)
Conference	Request for Proposal (RFP)
Convention	Retreat
Crisis Management Plan (CMP)	Rider

Risers
Seminar
Serpentine Setup
Skirting
SMERF
Stakeholder
Stanchions

SWOT Analysis
Touch Points
Trade Show
Traffic Flow
Transcript
Walk-Through

Introduction: Special Pressure From Events

The coordination of an event is very demanding. Even the seasoned professional has intense stress placed upon them. Mostly, they thrive on it. They have the weight of the world and they can handle it. When planning or working an event, it is crucial to place yourself in the role of the attendee. With so many things to coordinate, true event professionals never lose sight of walking in the shoes of their guests. Consider the following:

- ► Nearly everyone is emotionally invested.
- ► This could be a once-in-a-lifetime event for the participants.
- ► Tens or hundreds of thousands of dollars or more will go into this event.
- ► It is on display for everyone to see.
- ► It typically happens once and cannot be re-done.
- ► People's health and safety are at risk.
- ► Staff intensely plans for several months to over a year.
- ► All of the work will commence within a few hours to a few days.

In order to have a great event, there may be thousands of variables needed to come together. A formula for delivering quality service at events can help to ensure your guests leave satisfied with the event. A structure for managing these variables is to:

- ► Assess the Environment
- ► Predict the Outcomes
- ► Plan the Success
- ► Monitor the Weaknesses, and
- ► Assess the Quality.

Components of Event Management
© Trueffelpix/Shutterstock.com

Grand Dinner Show Event Setup in Large Auditorium With Stage
© Jade ThaiCatwalk/Shutterstock.com

Pre-Event Services: Setting up the Event

There are five steps to consider when setting up an event:

1. Assess the Environment
2. Predict Outcomes
3. Plan Success
4. Monitor Weaknesses
5. Assess Quality

ASSESS THE ENVIRONMENT

Types of Meetings

It is important to determine the venue. This is often proposed by the company or organization, and a title is everything. It sets the expectations of the event. There are many types of meetings and events, each with a different name that will inspire a distinct tone in the minds of the attendees. Their tone may be formal or informal. They may be informational, educational, or even entertaining. The size may be small or tens of thousands. It may be hosted by an association, corporation, or a social group. One of the first steps is to determine and name the type or function of the event. Below is a list of common meeting or event types:

► **Lecture:** formal, structured, speaker
► **Forum:** multiple speakers, moderator, open to Q&A with audience
► **Retreat:** less formal, typically smaller in size and at a remote location, great for planning
► **Convention:** meeting of delegates, cyclical scheduling, general sessions for all attendees and breakouts for smaller subgroups, may be in conjunction with exhibition
► **Clinic:** specialize training
► **Exhibition:** vendors display, in conjunction with another type of meeting, built-in audience
► **Conference:** meeting, typically for specialty area to display advances
► **Seminar:** smaller groups, leader, work on problems
► **Trade show:** vendors display goods and services of a specific trade, open only to specific trade

Types of Special Events

► Children's
► Cultural
► Group
► Professional
► Sporting
► Themed

Wedding Event Table Setting
© Ruslan Iefremov/Shutterstock.com

- ▶ Tours
- ▶ VIPs
- ▶ Music productions
- ▶ Spousal events

⚜ TYPES OF ROOM SETUPS

Auditorium Seating: chairs in rows, facing stage/speaker, also known as Theater Style Seating.

Break-Out Rooms: smaller rooms used to divide up larger groups into subgroups.

Chevron Seating: chairs in rows forming a V-shape facing stage/speaker, also known as V-Shape or Herringbone.

Classroom Seating: tables in rows with chairs, facing the stage/speaker, also known as Schoolroom Seating.

Hollow Square Seating: tables arranged in a square shape, with chairs around the perimeter of the square.

Horseshoe Seating: tables arranged in a U-shape, with chairs typically on the outside of the U.

Serpentine Setup: tables set together forming a curvy line. This setup is often used for food.

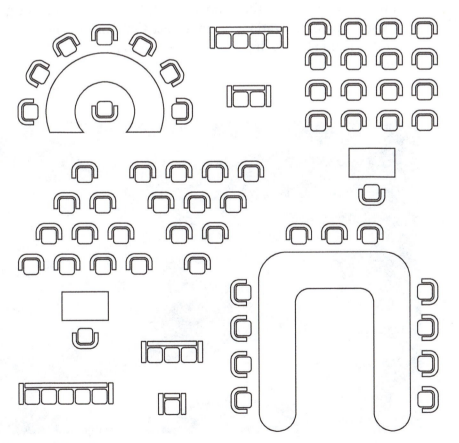

Diagram of Room Setups
© darsi/Shutterstock.com

TYPES OF ATTENDEES

There are many types of attendees. Below is a list of the primary categories. Each type of attendee has its own special set of needs and expectations:

- ▶ Corporate
- ▶ Associations
- ▶ General Public
- ▶ **Social, Military, Educational, Religious, Fraternal (SMERF)**

Social, Military, Educational, Religious, Fraternal (SMERF)

A type of customer group that combines Social, Military, Educational, Religious, and Fraternal Organizations.

Each type of attendee comes with its distinct set of qualities, making each a very different experience. Within each of these is also a great variance of formality, skill, assumptions, and decorum. It is important to predict but not prejudge a type of attendee because of past dealings with the market. Many event professionals have been surprised at how different groups act. Also, groups change leadership and direction from event to event.

MANAGING TOUCH POINTS

Touch Points

Each time that a guest has an experience with your organization, a representative of it, or an aspect the organization planned.

One great way to assess the environment is to look at things through the eyes of the guests. The Moment of Truth scenario by Jan Carlson holds true to events. Think of an event as many smaller events, in a series, and some simultaneously. Now break down each of those smaller events into each time the guest has contact with you, your organization, or an aspect that you planned. We call these **touch points**. Managing by touch points allows you to plan, troubleshoot, and best serve the guest.

Classroom Business Meeting Setup
© Setta Sornnoi/Shutterstock.com

A **SWOT Analysis** is another great way of assessing the environment. A SWOT Analysis is a survey of the things that you control and the things that you do not control. It lists the good and the bad of each.

> ► Strengths: the positive attributes of the organization.
> ► Weaknesses: the negative attributes of the organization.
> ► Opportunities: the positive outcomes that may occur beyond the control of the organization.
> ► Threats: the negative outcomes that may occur beyond the control of the organization.

To perform an initial SWOT analysis, begin by making a bulleted list within these categories:

To do this, begin by asking the following questions. (Typical examples of answers follow.)

> ► **Strengths:**
> Q: Of the things that you control, which are positive?
> A: Volunteers? Special content/product knowledge?
>
> ► **Weaknesses:**
> Q: Of the things that you control, which are negative?
> A: You do not have a specialty in this area.
>
> ► **Opportunities:**
> Q: Of the things outside of your control, which can positively affect you?
> A: New change in the market. Competitor now out of market.
>
> ► **Threats:**
> Q: Of the things outside of your control, which can negatively affect you?
> A: Competition, poor press, weather.

WHAT ARE YOU OFFERING?

To continue to assess the environment and expand on the idea of a SWOT analysis, it is important to realize that you are offering both goods and services to your customers. An example of this is:

Goods

> ► rooms
> ► pipe and drape
> ► food
> ► beverage
> ► temperature
> ► lighting
> ► A.V.

SWOT Analysis
A survey of strengths, weaknesses, opportunities, and threats.

Elegant Chinese-Style Dinner Setup
© kornnphoto/Shutterstock.com

Services

- ► planning
- ► support
- ► information
- ► advice
- ► safety

As you realize what it is that you are offering, you will then want to begin to monitor and control it. Too many organizations take these things for granted. Also, the customer needs to be informed of your offerings so they can appropriately set their expectations, and you can meet them. The old adage holds true: What gets monitored, gets controlled, and gets improved upon.

ROOM-RELATED TERMS

Air Walls: folding, moveable panels used to divide a larger room into sections for smaller, individual events; somewhat sound-proof.

Apron: portion of a stage visible to audience when curtain is closed.

Banquet Round: a folding round table, various sizes, seats between 6–12 guests.

Dead Man: beam or post used to support an overhead structure; usually temporary.

Risers: temporary platforms used to make a stage.

Skirting: linen that attaches to the side of tables or stages; helps to hide underneath or behind.

Stanchions: posts used to attach ropes to form lines or block off an area.

Predict the Outcomes

After assessing the environment, predicting the outcomes is the next step. This can be done for good and for bad. You must have desired outcomes of the event, even if they are obvious or implied. This can be expressed in a few ways:

► Mission of the parent company
► In the event description
► In theme

These points will be monitored and evaluated in a later section.

It is also important to realize and plan for the bad so that it can be reduced. This is referred to as risk management. There are professionals and entire companies that specialize in this area. Other times, it is done in-house. This is a way of assessing the "what-ifs." Below is a three-step model for achieving the objective.

☀ RISK MANAGEMENT

1. Identify the Issues

What are the possible risks? History is a great indicator, but also be sure to consider current conditions. The risks come from many areas within and outside of your control. Also see the weaknesses and threats from your SWOT analysis.

Elegant Evening Wedding Table Setup
© Contimis Works/Shutterstock.com

Typical survey risk areas to identify are:

- ► Technological
- ► Legal
- ► Financial
- ► Natural disasters
- ► Safety
- ► Suppliers
- ► Entertainment
- ► Attendees

2. Identify the Likeliness

This may be more difficult to do. It is often a hunch, or intuition. It will likely be based on a blend of:

- ► Past events of this type
- ► Current conditions
- ► Inside information
- ► Published reports
- ► Unpublished reports

3. Identify the Potential

What are the implications of this occurrence? To what degree would it impact the event? Would it be inconvenient, substantial, or devastating? Something may occur relatively often, but if it is of little or no consequence, then it may not be a huge priority. Consider rating the potential as low, medium, or high for initial categorization. Also be sure to ask if these issues interfere with other things, creating a larger potential.

PLAN SUCCESS

Now that the environment has been surveyed, and the outcomes are established, the true planning can begin. Quality guest service is about meeting or exceeding guests' expectations. To do this, the first step is to set their expectations.

SETTING THE EXPECTATIONS

The guests at an event have expectations. There are many things that have established this. It is crucial not to oversell, while not drastically underselling. If oversold, the expectations were too high and the attendee feels slighted. If undersold,

Event Planning Collage
© Kheng Guan Toh/Shutterstock.com

you will over-deliver, but attendance may be low because you didn't accurately portray what the event was about. To take this a step further, you are planning and selling expectations.

The customer service experience is about meeting or exceeding the expectations. How do you set the expectations? Expectations are established from a well-orchestrated culmination of:

- ► Marketing efforts
- ► Past performances
- ► Word of mouth
- ► Meetings
- ► Location
- ► Price

Most larger events are planned years in advance. When designing the event you set their expectations by establishing and setting up:

- ► Theme
- ► Site selection
- ► Site inspections
- ► Layout
- ► Suppliers
- ► Technicalities
- ► Catering and services
- ► Audience
- ► Financial

▶ Well-established program guideline to work from

Example: Timing/Schedule

- ☐ mealtimes
- ☐ event times
- ☐ free times
- ☐ transition times

▶ Regulation compliance

▶ Registration

▶ Confirmations

▶ Badges

Forms and Charges

▶ **Banquet Event Order** (BEO): also called a Function Sheet, detailed document with specific instructions pertaining to running a single event.

▶ **Request for Proposal** (RFP): request made by an organization, intended for potential contractors, soliciting a bid or quotes to perform a job or other request.

▶ **Rider**: amendment added to a contract for something extra needed after the fact, or outside of the standard.

▶ **Transcript**: also known as transcription, a typed storyline of the proceedings of the event complete with directions and speeches.

Logistics

▶ **Blackout Periods**: times when rooms, tickets, or some prices are unavailable. This could be due to high season, holidays, or previously booked events.

▶ **Load In/Load Out**: a specific time for loading/unloading of equipment, props, and other event-related items into or out of the building or premise.

▶ **Pipe and Drape**: pipes of tubing that is covered with a draped fabric; this is used to make walls and petitions at trade shows.

▶ **Pre-Convention** (Pre-con): a meeting between the planner and facility staff to review details of the conference or event.

▶ **Traffic Flow**: the pattern of guests through an event area.

▶ **Walk-Through**: organizers of the event inspect the facility prior to the event to ensure setups and finalize details.

PROMOTIONS MARKETING

Promotions marketing is the main communication used to establish expectations and attract attendees. You must let them know what it is about. You build anticipation. In order to market effectively, you must be able to answer the following questions:

- ▶ What is the product?
- ▶ Who are the customers?
- ▶ What are their needs and expectations?

Novel experience? Learning? Excited? Scared? Purchase items? Entertain? Get away?

Once this is established, you can begin to tailor your promotions campaign to achieve your goals. The answers are mostly intuitive and all of your promotions should be geared toward it.

❖ ESTABLISHING JOB DESCRIPTIONS

As planning continues, it is important that everyone has a clear definition of their roles. Due to the ever-changing nature of events, roles are not uniform as in other parts of the hospitality industry. Many of the staff members will experience at least something new or different in each event. Despite this, clear roles and responsibilities must be established. There are keys to maintaining order, and hence, customer service. There are similarities between roles from event to event, particularly if they are on-premise.

Does everyone have:

- ▶ their job descriptions?
- ▶ an appropriate line of communication?
- ▶ established procedures? (as much as possible)
- ▶ checklists?

Do they know:

- ▶ their responsibilities?
- ▶ the chain of command?
- ▶ what is acceptable?

There are key skills that each role requires. Do they have:

- ▶ problem-solving strategies?
- ▶ essential computer skills?
- ▶ organizational skills?
- ▶ clear descriptions of their areas of responsibility, even if the role may vary?
- ▶ support to complete the expectations?

Positions common to events that require these would be:

- ▶ Speakers and entertainers
- ▶ Question desk, point person
- ▶ Sales
- ▶ Community relations
- ▶ Box office
- ▶ Registration personnel
- ▶ Event supervisor
- ▶ Exhibition manager

- ► Operations manager
- ► Ushers
- ► Safety and security
- ► Concessions and catering
- ► Merchandising
- ► Facilities
- ► Intermediaries
- ► Volunteers

CRISIS MANAGEMENT PLAN

In a past section, the outcomes of a risk assessment have been established. At this point, it is time to construct a plan. The first goal is to reduce their likelihood of occurrence. For the instances that cannot be avoided, you can still plan to reduce the potential impact of their occurrence. You should be ready for almost everything:

- ► Plan.
- ► Have a backup plan.
- ► Have a backup plan for your backup plan.

A **Crisis Management Plan (CMP)** is a detailed guide describing the procedures in the event of an emergency. Typically, a CMP is assembled with a Crisis Management Team (CMT). This team consists of trained professionals in all possible areas. Ideally, many are on-staff. Some may be on an on-call basis. They should have a system of communication in place with a basic plan for almost anything including:

- ► Fire
- ► Bomb threat
- ► Evacuation
- ► Catastrophe

Crisis Management Plan (CMP)

Crisis Management Team. A specialized staff that responds to a crisis or catastrophe.

Crisis Management Collage
© Kheng Guan Toh/Shutterstock.com

EVENT SERVICES

The surveying, forecasting, and planning are done. The guests are arriving. Everyone feels it in the air. The band is warming up. A thousand things race through your mind. It is now or never. It is now show time!

As you plan, work, or wrap up an event, issues will inevitably arise. Even the best-laid plans need monitoring and tweaking to be successful.

Monitoring the Weaknesses

Assess the Environment → Predict Outcomes → Plan Success → Monitor Weaknesses → Assess Quality

ATTENDEE NEEDS

Guest service is about taking care of the attendees! The needs of the attendees can be overwhelming. Tending to the attendee needs are resource-intensive. They require planning, manpower, facilities, capital, patients, and time. To begin, consider all the things they need. Anticipation based upon the past is a great start. Next, let them know; communicate through signage, announcements, staff posted at stations, and electronically. Send them early mailings. Address areas such as:

- ► Schedule of events
- ► Special events
- ► Weather and climate
- ► Dress/attire
- ► Lodging
- ► Dining, special diets
- ► Special needs
- ► Changes
- ► Payment options
- ► Restrooms, floor maps, emergency care
- ► Surrounding area information
- ► Transportation
- ► Location services offered
  - ☐ valet, parking, spa, handicapped, special allergies, pets, interpreters, child care

WORKING WITH VOLUNTEERS

Volunteers are essential to most events. Without them, the labor costs would make the event cost prohibitive. They provide extra service and care that makes the event a success. They may serve in high-level positions. Some event managers are volunteers, although it is likely not a full-time event position. Volunteers primarily serve in lower and mid-level positions such as:

- ► Ushers
- ► Door holders
- ► Referees
- ► Security
- ► First aid
- ► Information
- ► Customer relations
- ► Traffic control

When managing volunteers, they should be seen as coworkers, despite their lack of monetary compensation. This means that they should be given responsibility and held accountable for their actions as if they were paid employees. Tell them that you expect:

- ► As much as a paid worker, not less
- ► Enthusiasm/belief in the organization/project/event

Remember, most of the patrons don't realize they are volunteers. In doing so, consider the following points:

- ► Make positions clear
- ► Make expectations clear
- ► Offer promotions within jobs
- ► Provide support
- ► Give suitable tools or materials
- ► Offer to open two-way communication
- ► Treat them with respect
- ► Give them a token of appreciation, or involve them in a token-reward activity

In giving of their time and expertise, remember that volunteers are compensated in other ways. While not paid, they do receive many things in return. They receive:

- ► Social contact
- ► Feelings of usefulness
- ► Feeling a part of something larger, a camaraderie
- ► Satisfaction in helping an organization they believe in
- ► The opportunity to help in something worthwhile
- ► A token of appreciation

❖ POST-EVENT SERVICES

There may be congratulations, celebration, or even a sigh of relief once an event is over, but the work is certainly not done. This is when the finishing touches are placed on the service provided.

Assessing the Quality

| Assess the Environment | Predict Outcomes | Plan Success | Monitor Weaknesses | Assess Quality |

SURVEYING THE EVENT

Many events are surveyed. Guests are often asked opinions and many feel overwhelmed with the requests and filter the surveys without second thought. The surveys tend to be long, and they lose interest. They can be a nuisance to complete, and the guests wonder if anyone even reads their responses. As a result, many people will not fill out a survey. A majority of those who complete the surveys do so because they are upset. Consequently, the responses do not accurately represent the general population. So, the question begs, what will you assess? Who will you assess? How will you assess? And, what will you do with the information?

Content: What will be assessed?

- ▶ Does the event or the organization have a mission/purpose statement to check it against?
- ▶ Who do we need to please?
- ▶ Is their image upheld?
- ▶ More than "how was it"?
- ▶ What are the take-away points from this event?
- ▶ What were the goals/objectives? Were they met?
- ▶ Are the sponsors pleased?
- ▶ Are the guests pleased?
- ▶ Is the parent organization pleased?

Population: Who will be assessed?

To begin to answer this task, you must first determine the stakeholders. A stakeholder can be described as anyone who has interest in the event. It could be anyone who would be affected if the event were to cease to exist.

After the list of stakeholders is established, the groups become evident. Potential stakeholders may be:

- ▶ Attendees
- ▶ Spouses
- ▶ Parent organizations
- ▶ Sponsors
- ▶ Purveyors

> **Stakeholder**
> Any person or group that would be affected if the event, company, or situation were to cease to exist.

Medium: How will you assess it?

This can be a formal survey, printed survey, mailed, electronic, or telephoned. It can be on a comment card or even at an on-site portal. Each medium has its own advantages and disadvantages. The qualities or characteristics should drive the decision of the medium. Here are some general tips:

- ► Make it easy to complete.
  - ☐ Encourage respondents to complete.
  - ☐ Reward?
  - ☐ Send follow-ups?
  - ☐ Meet and ask them personally?
- ► Let them know how and why it counts.
- ► Avoid boilerplate or standard phrases such as "your comments are important to us" or "we value your input." Be original and fitting to the group and the event.

Interpretation: What will you do with it?

Evaluation is crucial, but is not the only piece of the puzzle. Ideally, monitoring and evaluation occurs before and during the event. As a result, findings should not be a surprise. They should be informative, validating, but seldom ever shocking. Findings should be taken in context, and not disproportionately. A handful of poor comments is not great, but it does not mean that the entire event was a failure. Consider the bad with the good. When reviewing, consider:

- ► Who will look at it?
- ► To whom will it matter?
- ► What went right?
- ► What went wrong?
- ► What is at the root of the problem?
- ► What are the possible costs or damages?
- ► What can you fix?
- ► What will you do differently next time?
- ► What will you do the same next time?
- ► What are the list of take-away lessons?
- ► What are the immediate actions, or to-do's as a result?

In closing, the meetings and event industry is a vital part of the hospitality industry. There is much that goes into effectively serving the guests. However, if handled with professionalism, planning, and appropriate response to their needs, the events are likely to be a success.

CHAPTER REVIEW QUESTIONS

1. Describe why there is special pressure to perform well in events.
2. List and briefly describe three different types of meetings or events that are especially designed for smaller groups.
3. Why is it important to identify the importance of an issue when conducting Risk Analysis?
4. List and describe four ways that you can set the expectations of guests.
5. Explain the concept of managing touch points.
6. In events, you offer the customer both goods and services. Explain.
7. List at least five different room setups.
8. What is a CMP?
9. What benefits might volunteers receive?
10. List three ideas for making volunteers feel appreciated.

CASE STUDIES

Can You Deliver?

Sales representatives are crucial to events. When they sell events, they earn commissions. They tell about how great the event will be. Typically, they are honest and accurate. Occasionally, they promise more than they can deliver. In some cases they simply aren't aware, and in other cases they compromise to make sales quotas.

In this case, an event planning company is trying to enter into the market. Their goal is to gain 10% of the anticipated market share for the next year. This is an aggressive goal considering the market and larger, established competition. They hire Christina, a Sales Manager that worked for the competition prior to leaving the industry 5 years ago to raise her child. She was the top-grossing planner when she left, and now she wants to regain her former title. She still has some leads in the area and remembers all of her training. She recruits two sales assistants and is promised a bonus if they make the 10% goal. After a slow, rough start, the sales begin to roll in. The calendar begins filling all at once. The business is now off to a great start and back on track to meet the market share quota. Because of Christina serving as such a great front person, the business is excited. Problems begin to arise when the rest of the company doesn't perform as well as the sales staff claimed. In fact, they are having a difficult time meeting most of the sales contracts Christina is selling. Christina hears about this from her customers. She sensed there was trouble with the disconnect between the sales department and the operations department but had no idea it was to this extent. Furthermore, she learns that the field support is very upset at her "for promising the impossible." She is terribly upset because she believed that she didn't make any promises that were unreasonable. In fact, she believes the field staff are overreacting and incompetent.

She stops by the director of operation's office to discuss the matter, but he is out in the field troubleshooting an event. Christina decides to devise a strategy for dealing with this based upon what she remembers from her past employer. She knows that she has to be tactful.

1. How important is it to deliver what is promised?
2. What are the discrepancies between the sales and the operations departments?
3. How should Christina approach the situation?
4. Outline ideas for assessing and improving the disconnect at the company.

Different Interests

Weddings are wonderful and joyous events. It is the perfect day for the bride. It is the day that she has dreamed of since she was a young girl. Everyone will look forward to it. It will be perfect. They will love it!

Now let's talk about the Mother of the Bride (MOB). The MOB is a very strong-willed woman. She was present at all of the planning meetings and is paying the bill for the wedding. The MOB was resistant to any suggestions and kept changing the plans without communicating it to others. "It's all about the bride. I just want it to be perfect for my baby," she says. Not really. In truth, it is all about the MOB taking control and intimidating everyone else. The bride-to-be (B2B) was mostly timid around her mother, although she would occasionally let others know that she didn't like her mother's choices. The groom is easy-going and non-confrontational. Even after hints and interventions from others, the MOB continued to be adamant and confrontational. Consequently, the MOB got precisely what she wanted.

The setting of the wedding was a tent in the yard at the private estate of the MOB. It was a beautiful setting with many great offerings. The MOB was insistent that there would not be alcohol on-premise at the event. She was a religious woman who was opposed to alcohol. The MOB was irate when it was revealed that the groom's family had brought alcohol and was drinking it in the lawn parking lot and out by the horse stables. She immediately went to the wedding planner and complained. She insisted the wedding planner go eradicate the alcohol immediately. The meeting planner wanted to keep everyone happy.

1. Is it possible to please everyone?
2. How do you please many guests with competing interests?
3. Who should the planner satisfy first?
4. Should the planner have stuck up for the bride during the planning?
5. How should the planner handle the alcohol situation?

Turf Battle

The All-Sport Arena is a multi-use facility that accommodates two minor league sports teams in addition to numerous other sporting events and functions. The arena is always busy and everyone must follow a strict schedule of when each team can and cannot be on the field.

One Friday afternoon the two minor-league teams were both scheduled to be on the field for practice at the same time. They had inadvertently double-booked the field. Typically, this type of conflict is settled with the arena director. A few game changes and practice shifts, combined with the director leaving early with a stomach bug, caused the situation to occur and flare out of control. To add, the assistant director was on vacation and no one else in a position of authority was available.

At this point, the two teams are at the facility at once. Both have rights to it. Only counter staff is present. No one else in management can be reached. The coaches have figured it out in the past, but this time neither would back down. There had been some field changes in the past with both teams and the cold-war was on. Both coaches felt as if the other was pushing them. Both teams were backing their coach and the mood was quickly escalating. Both sides claimed to have rights to it and they both refused to share the field. The direct line of control cannot be established. Fans were issued special passes to watch one of the teams practice. The other team had the press on-site for promotion and interviews of the upcoming game.

1. How did the problem occur?
2. What happens if the direct line of control is unavailable?
3. What could have been done to avoid this problem?
4. What could be done at this point?

Backstage Pass

Freak-3K, a popular European band, was giving a concert at the Gen-Z Center. Kenson was a friend of the band who was invited to attend the show and discuss other promotional opportunities while touring in the US. A meeting was scheduled backstage after the show. Kenson was given a VIP pass and lanyard. This was a big opportunity for him, since he had just begun his own music promotion company.

The night of the concert, Kenson went to the Gen-Z Center and flashed his VIP pass. He was escorted to a VIP box overlooking the arena. He was served complimentary snacks, wine, and beer. Kenson enjoyed the show immensely. After the show, Kenson asked for directions to the backstage area. Things seemed to be going well until he approached a security guard standing in front of the entrance to the backstage area. Kenson smiled and flashed his VIP pass. The security guard told Kenson that no one was permitted backstage without a backstage pass. Kenson began to explain that the VIP pass is what he was given and that he was scheduled to have a very important meeting with the band backstage after the concert. The guard told Kenson the director of security told all guards that he would terminate any of his security staff that admitted someone without a back-stage pass. He added that due to enhanced security it was imperative that everyone had proper credentialing and the director fired other guards who breached orders. It was zero-tolerance, no questions asked.

Kenson explained his situation again. The guard politely replied that he had no knowledge of this and reiterated that he could be terminated if he admitted him. Kenson pleaded for the guard to call the band or manager or anyone and verify his story. The guard then replied that people say all kinds of things to get backstage and that he wasn't going to call the band every time someone requests. Meanwhile the band wonders where Kenson is.

1. Was the security guard correct to disallow Kenson to gain backstage access?
2. What could be done to salvage the situation at this point?
3. How could this have been avoided?

Chapter 8

The Guest Service of Travel and Tourism

CHAPTER OBJECTIVES

After reading this chapter, you should be able to:

- ▶ Apply guest service principles to the tourism industry.
- ▶ Identify and describe types of travel.
- ▶ Explain the specific wants and service needs of the travelers in each of the major travel segments.
- ▶ Identify and explain the dynamics of the external environment of tourism.
- ▶ Explain recent changes in tourism and detail how it affects the service of the guests.

TERMINOLOGY

Accommodation
All-Inclusive Tour
Carbon Footprint
Charter
Code Sharing
Conservation
Convention and Visitor Bureau (CVB)
Destination Management Company (DMC)
Destination Management Organization (DMO)

Eco-Tourism
Excursion
High Season
Hub and Spoke
Incentive Tour
Low Season
Niche-Travel
Open Jaw
Pension
Tourism
Yield Management

Introduction

Travel may be essential for business; it may be for fun, or even life-enriching. A professional in the field of travel and tourism must realize what they are offering in an effort to best serve the guests. Consider the following statements:

- ▶ You are selling the world.
- ▶ You are selling memories.
- ▶ You are selling bragging rights.
- ▶ You are competing against every other memory and experience they have ever had.

Definition of Tourism: The World

The product of tourism has always been the world so it cannot be easily defined. An official definition of **tourism** is everything associated with the traveling of more than 50 miles from home.

To expand, tourism includes all activities in a complex system involving everything that goes into awareness, searching, traveling, accommodations, activities, and post-travel experiences. With such a broad definition, it makes tourism very difficult to quantify.

Tourism

Everything associated with traveling more than 50 miles from home, typically for leisure.

Miami Skyline at Night
© fotomak/Shutterstock.com

Travel and tourism is the service industry, so relating service management is natural. Controlling it for a favorable outcome is much more difficult. Much is demanded of you, and you must always be vigilant of vulnerabilities that are largely outside of your direct control. This chapter relates delivering quality service management in travel and tourism to four main points:

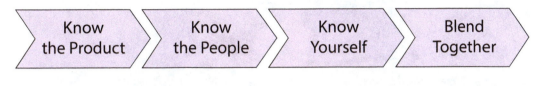

1. Know the product.
2. Know the people.
3. Know yourself.
4. Blend the three together to best meet the desired goals of all.

STEP 1: KNOW THE PRODUCT

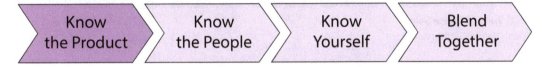

This first step is unlike marketing where you must first know your customer. In most aspects of travel, you must know the product first, then match people to your product. The most difficult part of this is that your product is the endless possibilities of the world. You must be able to calculate the odds of success with many variables that are out of your control. To begin, the variables outside of your control are:

- The people
- Transport
- Cycles of rates
- Crowd flows
- Calendars
- Health factors
- Social climates
- Personal safety
- Pricing strategies
- Major players
- Cultures
- Governance
- Societal norms
- Laws, grading
- Classifications
- Lodging

Aerial View of Cruise Ship
© Denis Beltsky/Shutterstock.com

These are all aspects to consider when encountering the product. Remember, although these are outside of your control, they are predictable. With experience, you will get better at working with your predictions.

> ▶ **Low Season:** The time of year when travel to a property or destination is at its lowest and prices typically decline to attract customers.
> ▶ **High Season:** Time of year when travel to an area or property is most active and rates are at their highest, also known as the Peak Season.

Types of Travel and Tourism

There are many types of travel but the main two most common categories are business travel and leisure travel. Each of them have many subcategories and each tend to balance each other out depending upon day of the week, season, and venue. For example, a hotel may cater to business travelers during the week and leisure travelers on the weekends.

1. **Business Travel:** business functions, development, incentive.
2. **Leisure Travel:** adventure, cruise, golf, honeymoons, eco, family, luxury, spa, special lifestyle, winery.

Businesses that want to recognize their best staff for exceptional results are likely to arrange an **incentive** tour for them. These trips are usually **all-inclusive**, or, include all costs, so the employee can enjoy the trip without worrying about having to pay for small, incidental costs. Arrangements are usually to a very desirable location. Spouses are usually able to accompany the award-winners.

Incentive travel
A reward tour, typically given to an employee by the organization for outstanding achievement. Typically a festive environment. Spouses typically accompany.

All-inclusive tour
Sold for a total price, including rooms, food, taxes, and usually most or all incidentals.

All-Inclusive Island Image
© Happy ants studio/Shutterstock.com

An **excursion** is when travelers decide to take a short, alternative trip, either from home or from a hotel, ship, or other point of reference during their stay.

Niche-travel is becoming popular as a way to satisfy the traveler who wants something different. These are small, unique tours. There are many types ranging from odd to entertaining. The Age of Communication has brought a new light to these tours, making them easily referenced and, hence, widely known.

It is also common to **charter** the transportation. This is when a bulk purchase is made on any mode of transportation. It may be purchased by the time, distance, head count, or even a combination of these variables. This guarantees availability and secures a lower negotiated price than could be had through other means. Tourists appreciate the dedication and price of the transit.

Airlines also work together to provide customer service. **Code sharing** is an agreement that permits two or more airlines to share, view, and book on a system of another. Customers really appreciate this option when being re-routed.

Yield management is a valuable technique that allows airlines and hotels to vary prices depending on supply and demand. This balances supply and demand with prices to optimize the profitability of the operations. This is established through highly-secretive formulas that continually change to adjust to the market conditions. Many variables are present and it is impossible to know precisely what will occur when predicting prices. Travel agents, websites, and novices alike all have ideas on "cracking the code" to obtain the best price. Many myths exist on saving money. Information is the key, and travel agents tend to have the most at hand. The others are lucky, at best. These fluctuations most impact the leisure market. Less impacted by this is the business traveler who "must" travel at certain times, on certain days. Lately, however, companies are pressuring business travelers to conserve their travel budgets, resulting in an elevated level of price sensitivity.

Hub and spoke is a term describing the configuration of airports and air routes. When viewed on a map, it resembles a hub and a spoke of a wheel with the center hub being the main airport and the spokes leading out to smaller cities or other hubs. This configuration optimizes connections across the country. Learning which airlines dominate which hubs is important for availability and pricing.

Excursion

A small trip, typically less than a day.

Niche-travel

A small, unique area of specialty or special interest.

Charter

Bulk purchase of a boat, plane, auto, or bus carrier. Sold by time, distance, count, or a combination of those and other variables.

Code sharing

Agreement between two or more airlines which permits use of viewing and booking on a system of another.

Yield management

Pricing structure common to air and hotel companies. The goal is to optimize profit while balancing supply and demand.

Hub and spoke

A configuration of air travel resembling a wheel with a center hub being the main airport with spokes leading out of it connecting to smaller cities or other hubs.

Open Jaw

A flight where passenger arrives at one point and departs from another, making an outline of an open jaw on the map.

Accommodations

Typically a room for bedding, but also food, services, or anything needed during a trip.

Pension

French term meaning guesthouse or boardinghouse or the payment for. It is essentially a lesser lodging establishment with or without meals.

An **open jaw** is an industry term that describes a passenger's flight pattern. It resembles an open jaw on the map and involves three airports where a passenger departs from one city and then departs from another.

Accommodations are involved in most travels. At its core, accommodations involve lodging, but may also include food, services, and anything else needed during the trip.

Pension is a French term meaning guesthouse or a boarding house. It is typically associated with a more basic property. It may involve meals. It is also used to describe payment for accommodations.

Qualities of Travel and Tourism

Like service in general, travel and tourism falls victim to the intangibility of its product. This is called intangibility. It cannot be sampled or held before consumed, you must provide them with a vision of what it would be. There are many ways to do this:

- ▶ Websites
- ▶ Posters
- ▶ Family tour
- ▶ Personal experiences
- ▶ Ratings
- ▶ Reviews

An experience is unique to all. This is called heterogeneity. It depends on the individual. Two people can experience the same service with extremely different outcomes, or perceptions of service. You must know the person and the product in order to match. It is an art. This is what makes or breaks customer service.

Robot Adviser at Airport Concept
© MONOPOLY919/Shutterstock.com

Changes in Travel and Tourism

The age of technology resulting in the age of communication has made tourism a manic field. Communication has allowed reviews and the like to proliferate. Some are legitimate, while others need to be taken in context.

Guests have much different expectations than in the past. Since airline and hotel commissions have diminished, the agents need to charge service fees. This added expense changes guests' expectations. While the service fee is often saved in ticket prices and expert advice, the customers expect more than in the past, and they second-guess with secondhand advice via the Internet. The guests are aware of many different options now like never before. This includes sales, searching, and the like.

Below are some common terms related to guest service with airlines:

GUEST SERVICES RELATED TO AIRLINE SERVICE

Itinerary: schedule of a visit or the route of a tour

Cancellation Clause: part of a contract that summarizes penalties, if cancellation occurs

EDT: Estimated Departure Time

ETA: Estimated Time of Arrival

Ground Operator: local transportation company; this may include shuttles, taxis, and land tours

Skycap: airport staff member position that assists passengers with their baggage

---

Quite often travelers are planning domestic travel on their own. While this has certainly taken routine travel arrangements out of the hands of the traveler agents, the detailed arrangements are still entrusted to the professionals.

The External Environment

Tourism has many variables that lie in the external, macro environment. Travelers and travel professionals alike are dependent upon them. Agents are a "broker of things that are beyond their control." Travel professionals have little or no control over these variables. They include:

- ▶ Accommodations
- ▶ Transport
- ▶ Food and beverage
- ▶ Destinations and events
- ▶ Vendor services
- ▶ Environmental, cultural, demographic

With this in mind, providing quality service means calculating the likelihood of success of many variables outside of your direct control. This is done a number of ways. Once again, knowledge, combined with insight, is the key to control. Below is a list of areas that the travel professional should be knowledgeable of:

- ▶ Business-related
  - ☐ Knowledge of services provided
    - ▶ Services and amenities
    - ▶ Staffing
    - ▶ Hours, frequency, patterns
    - ▶ Capacity
    - ▶ Billing
    - ▶ Availability
    - ▶ Communication, key representatives
    - ▶ Terminology, coding
  - ☐ Past performance
    - ▶ Ratings
    - ▶ Evaluations
    - ▶ Credibility and reputation
  - ☐ Backup plans in case of failure

So, knowing everything that you can about what you are selling is imperative. If you don't fit this with the needs of the client, or if you misjudge the product, it will likely reflect poorly on you and your company. It would be great if all of your products were easily assessed and consistent is their performance, but that is hardly ever true. Management, staff, and processes change making it a constantly evolving course to navigate. It is likened to a minefield of mishaps, that you are trusted to lead the tourist through safely.

STEP 2: KNOW THE CLIENT—UNDERSTANDING THE GUEST

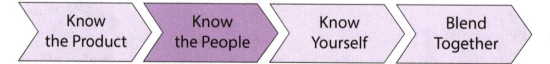

The clients are a mystery. They are not always as they appear. They can be unsure or absolutely certain, then change their minds.

Develop Relationships

A key to knowing their needs is to develop a relationship with them. It can take over five times the amount to gain a new customer than to retain a current one, so return customers are the key to success! This can be achieved through:

- ▶ Remembering names
- ▶ Keeping profiles
- ▶ Taking a few extra minutes to listen to them

► Sharing in something a bit personal
► Sending newsletters

Learn Their Motivations

Before a traveler embarks on a tour, it is important to realize their motive. Learning the motivations of travel helps you to be able to best meet their needs. Customers may not even be aware of their underlying motivations, and even sometimes hesitant to admit them.

This may seem obvious. For example, they might state it is to attend a class reunion, to go to Walt Disney World, or to take a cruise to the Bahamas. This motive is the obvious motive, but there is usually a second, underlying motive in mind. They probably want something else:

Greetings in Different Languages
© Cienpies Design/Shutterstock.com

► A sense of completion, having been able to say they went somewhere
► A sense of identity
► An escape from the usual
► An escape from reality
► To learn more about a culture
► To impress former classmates
► To have bragging rights

Travelers on Train Enjoying Mountain View
© Poh Smith/Shutterstock.com

SERVICE INSIGHT

Acute Amateur Authorities

Because of the age of communication, the guests are educated in areas like never before. They have, in a sense, become "content experts" in micro areas. This leads to advantages and disadvantages:

Advantages:

► Confidence . . .

Disadvantages:

► Arrogance . . .

► Limited knowledge . . .

They are able to book their own flights, but have no knowledge how to change their flight without absorbing high costs.

These goals may be entertaining, educational, security, economical, or even a blend.

As another example, a business meeting seems standard. But there are many variables. Do they want to impress, just show up? Are they anxious to return home? If so, flights and layovers with possible delays make a huge difference. Is cost the issue? At what sacrifice? They probably do not know all of the options available. It is up to you to determine and assist. Sometimes they don't even want to admit their second, or, ulterior motive.

Glamping (Glamorous Camping)
© Moise Sebastian/Shutterstock.com

As you explore these possibilities, you begin to ask questions:

- ► Do they basically want to escape from something by going to something else?
- ► How much of a change would they prefer?
- ► How much of their rituals do they want to maintain for comfort?
- ► Without certain rituals, many people feel too far out of their element so you must determine how many new components they really want and for what purpose.

STEP 3: KNOW YOURSELF–THE TRAVEL PROFESSIONAL

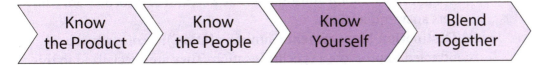

Know the Product → Know the People → Know Yourself → Blend Together

Essential Qualities of Travel Professionals

You must attain and project the skills, knowledge, and abilities of a travel professional. You must also apply the knowledge effectively and tactfully.

To begin, you need to collect as much information as you can about your customers. You need to determine their desired behavior before, during, and after the trip.

You also need to know how you will react to their stance. We all have conditioned responses to set behaviors. These are gathered from our past experiences. We constantly hone and refine these reactions. This will gauge how you apply your customer-service strategy.

You need to be able to relate to different people from different parts of the world. Some of the characteristics include:

- ► Language
- ► Culture
- ► Empathy

You need to eliminate negative cues, or anything that detracts from the desired customer service. This may be:

- ► Greetings
- ► Responses
- ► Gestures
- ► Facial expressions
- ► Eye contact

Some of the typical positions in the Travel and Tourism Industry are:

- **Tour Operators:** work with the guests at the first-line. They must be able to discern, inform, advise, and direct travel arrangements for the clients. They primarily book air, hotel, rental cars, tours, cruises, and railways of which they typically earn a commission in addition to charging a small service charge. They are able to provide a tour at a price equal to or less than what the public could find on their own. They may be associated with tour packages run through the agency. Used synonymously with tour operator are tour agent and travel agent.

- **Tour Guides:** the individuals that operate tours. They should have extensive knowledge regarding the area. They must gauge the tourists and anticipate their actions. They must ensure that the tourists have a safe and fun day. Some must memorize a wealth of information, while others answer questions.

- **A Destination Management Company (DMC):** a company that is contracted to promote a specific location. They are specialized in this area and typically handle all aspects from planning and coordination to execution of advertising.

- **Destination Management Operator (DMO):** represent a company that has extensive local knowledge of an area. They arrange ground transportation and other services. They are able to purchase in bulk at a lower rate and pass along the savings to the tourists.

- **Convention and Visitor Bureau (CVB):** provide destination marketing information for the city, county, and state. Most are

Destination Management Organization (DMO)

A company that leads and promotes the marketing of a destination.

CVBs (Convention and Visitor Bureau)

Organization that provides destination information regarding an area. It is financed through bed-tax.

Guided Bus Tour, Marmaris, Turkey
© KELENY/Shutterstock.com

non-profit organizations that are financed through bed-tax collected whenever a hotel room is sold. CVBs provide visitors with information about an area. They are a first stop in most things hospitality. They list hotels, restaurants, events, and activities. Their goal is to promote the area. Some offer tours, incentives, and other information to inform and attract tourists. They serve as a wealth of information for the area. The local businesses work closely with the CVBs to provide them with updated information. In turn, the CVB is a resource for both visitors and businesses.

STEP 4: BLEND THE GOALS TO BEST MEET THE DESIRED GOALS OF ALL

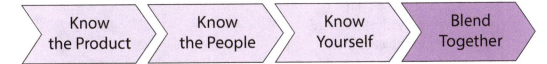

Know the Product → Know the People → Know Yourself → Blend Together

Whose Goals Are We Meeting?

There are no distinct lines between the goals of everyone involved in travel and tourism. Hopefully the goals will cross over into each other. This point of intersection or overlapping of goals is the key to please the customers. It will surface and plague the customer-service system if any single other entity is left.

Guided Boat Trip at Khao Sok National Park, Thailand
© Ggamies/Shutterstock.com

Customers' Goals

The goals of the customer should always be placed first. Phrases such as "the customer always comes first" proliferate the literature in nearly every industry. The idea of focusing everything around the customer is referred to as customer-centric. While the goals of the customer are certainly important, it would be unwise to consider only them without taking everything else into consideration. Thus, a common ground should be established. Let's understand the customer goals and find the common areas that are easily shared with the other constituents.

Understanding customer goals requires an understanding of what motivates them.

What are their true goals? Once understood, the next step is to prepare the customer. This is done both logistically and psychologically.

- ► Understand the goals
    - ☐ What motivates them?
- ► Preparing the customer
    - ☐ Logistically
        - ► Itinerary
    - ☐ Psychologically
        - ► Setting the appropriate expectations
        - ► Making tangible the venue (websites, pictures, essential readings, etc.)

Organizational Goals

Without meeting the organizational goals, you will go out of business very quickly. To blend this into the equation is essential. The profits cannot be eroded. Fees must be collected. Too many comps will eat away at profits and should be monitored. Labor costs must be scrutinized. Some services require immediate attention, while others can wait. Prioritization and automation are key.

Personal Goals

All too often this lies in an imbalance. Either it is all about the customer, the business, or all about the employee.

If a position is too demanding:

- ► What are the labor-intensive components? Can they be altered?
- ► Is it a certain customer or profile? Can they be altered?
- ► What is the true value of their business?
- ► Are they worth the disproportionate allocation of resource?

Can you work off-premise during certain hours?

You must satisfy you own realistic needs in order to be truly happy and naturally be able to please others. If you are not happy, it will show. Of course, there will be times when you simply need to endure, but those times should be few and the rest should be a flow. If not, the customer will know long before anyone else even realizes it.

Industry Goals

Every industry sets up guidelines. The travel and tourism industry is no different.

The World Travel and Tourism Council (WTTC) establishes guidelines to promote and protect responsible travel and tourism growth throughout the world. There are several other

Guided Segway Tour, Germany
© Kzenon/Shutterstock.com

organizations that have similar goals uniting the industry through research and collaboration of their members. Ethics, greening, and sustainability are particularly large topics of the industry. All travel professionals should be involved and current with industry associations such as the WTTC to unite and help perpetuate the industry that so many depend on.

Environmental Goals

Environmentally conscious travel is a huge trend throughout the travel industry. **Eco-tourism** is a term describing the travel to, or promotion of, environmentally-conscious actions in tourism. It implies **conservation**, or the reasonable and responsible use of resources in the environment to insure optimal current and future appreciation. Another term that follows this is **carbon footprint**, which is the effect of one's carbon dioxide produced into the atmosphere. It is also used in a general fashion as being synonymous with being environmentally conscious. All of these terms together are generalized under the term "green" or "greening." Without consideration of greening, there would not be a future.

The key to meeting the goals of all is understanding them and concentrating on the areas where they overlap. Realize where all are coming from and try to find a common ground.

- ► **Prepare** the customers,
- ► **Understand** that business must be conducted,
- ► **Take care** of yourself,
- ► **Align with** the industry, and
- ► **Protect** the environment.

This is how customer service is delivered in the Travel and Tourism Industry.

Eco-tourism

Travel to, or promoting, environmentally-conscious actions, typically based around awe-inspiring natural resources.

Conservation

Reasonable and responsible use of natural resources in the environment which insures optimal current and future appreciation.

Carbon footprint

A person's effect on the amount of carbon dioxide produced into the atmosphere. Also used in more general terms as being environmentally-friendly.

Booking a Reservation on Computer
© REDPIXEL.PL/Shutterstock.com

Online Travel Agents (OTAs)

OTA's are companies that aggregate accommodations and transportation data. They offer real-time, automated inventory of this data. They allow the general public to choose one and book many components of their trip based on price or other incentives.

In 2015, Expedia acquired Travelocity for $280 million, merging two of the world's largest travel-reservation (OTA) companies. Expedia now owns Hotels.com, Orbitz, Hotwire, Trivago, and Travelocity brands among others. It also owns HomeAway, Pillow, and ApartmentJet short-term rental technology services.

CHAPTER REVIEW QUESTIONS

1. List at least five variables of the external environment of which travel professionals have little or no control.
2. Why is eco-tourism good for a community?
3. Describe the difference between a tour operator and a tour guide.
4. Why is tourism so difficult to define?
5. List and briefly describe five types of leisure travel.
6. How does intangibility and heterogeneity of services apply to travel and tourism?
7. What is niche-travel and how can it be an effective means of pleasing your client?
8. How has the field of travel and tourism changed in the past few years?
9. What are some of the essential qualities of a Travel Professional?
10. What is an OTA and how are they changing the tourism industry?

CASE STUDIES

Offering a Service

Travel agencies have undergone many hardships in the past few years. The advance of technology has placed the power of travel arrangements into the hands of the consumer. Anyone with a computer or a smartphone can locate and compare fares, availability, and predictability. Travel agencies have lost the power of exclusivity in travel arrangements.

It is now about more than price. The leisure traveler is typically shopping for the lowest price but also needs the service that accompanies it. It is a balance act with trade-offs that some customers make mistakes.

As travel professionals witness this change, many have done more than complain. They have begun to alter their marketing efforts. They have begun a challenge of retraining the general public on what they can still offer.

When a traveler plans a trip, things don't always go as planned.

Travel professionals assist people with their knowledge of what works and what does not. They are more familiar with rates, airlines, charters, and many other logistics that can make or break a trip.

1. What has happened to travel agencies in the past few years?
2. How are some agencies changing their marketing tactics?
3. How is service a distinguishing factor?
4. List ideas of how a travel professional can use this as an advantage.

Establishing Bus Protocol

Garrison Bus Lines offers several different types of tours. Many of these are assisted travel trips aboard their buses. They offer transportation to many different venues from ski trips to casinos, to theatres, to ballgames. They are an older, established transit company with a pricing strategy that offers a real value.

Occasionally, the guides encounter issues on the bus. Often, they can resolve it well. Lately, the guides have been having more trouble and the old-school styles of being strict are simply not working. The owners wonder if this can be attributed to the changing demographics of the clients. The guides attribute it to the lower prices of the chartered trips. The owners want the guides to be kind to the patrons and let them have fun, but fear that some are inconveniencing others.

As a solution, they have hired a college student on internship to help them develop a protocol for preventing and handling customer service scenarios. The deliverables are a training program for the guides and a small set of demonstrations accompanying each type of incident.

The company has several logs from the drivers and incident reports from the tour agents. From those, a list of the most popular and difficult guest service situations have been produced. The list is as follows:

- ► Late passengers
- ► Misinformed passengers

- ► Vaping
- ► Intoxicated guests
- ► Inebriated, high passengers
- ► Unusual items aboard the bus

1. Devise tips for avoiding these scenarios.
2. Devise methods for dealing with these scenarios after they have occurred.

Glowing Algae and Other Surprises

Many tourists come to the Bahamas for sun and relaxation. They also dine, shop, and snorkel by day. At night, comes more dining, parties, and perhaps gambling. As an excursion, a segment of the tourists want a unique experience. A niche tour for those who want to experience a wonder of nature is a guided kayaking tour through the glowing algae. It has an intriguing allure to tourists and many inquire about it.

In order to do this, tourists are shuttled to a remote spot near the beach around 9:00 p.m. They watch a small instructional film and demonstration. Then, they are given gear and kayaks. They carry or drag the kayaks down to the beach, get in the water and get acquainted with the boats and paddles. Once everyone is in and adjusted, they paddle together out to the reef. This paddling takes about 45 minutes and is done in the near total darkness.

Finally, they reach the glowing algae and, for most, it all seems extremely worthwhile. It lights up and glows as the kayaks pass over the top of them, causing the water movement. The bio-luminescent awe is tranquil.

As great as it is, the experience is not for the weak and the tour company receives several complaints. It seems that people either love it or hate it. Despite stating upon making reservations that it is a kayak tour and tourists should be in very good physical shape, not everyone is prepared for the tour. Occasionally, paddlers tire and need to be towed or assisted. Some tire from just dragging the kayaks down to the water.

Occasionally the tide is strong and water is rough. Sometimes a storm blows in unexpected rains, making it miserable. On rare occasion sharks are spotted, although no attacks have ever been reported, it makes the tourists rather scared.

1. List the inherent issues with Glowing Algae tours.
2. What is outside of their control?
3. What is within their control?
4. How could the company reduce the number of guest complaints?

Chapter 9

The Guest Service of Casinos

CHAPTER OBJECTIVES

After reading this chapter, you should be able to:

- ► Identify and describe types of casinos.
- ► Identify and describe types of floor positions typical to casinos.
- ► Describe the unique characteristics of providing guest service at a casino property.
- ► Explain and apply the concept of guest service to various casino guests.

TERMINOLOGY

Booth Cashiers	Low Rollers
Change Attendants	Player Tracking Systems
Comps	Shift Manager
Firing	Slot Manager
Fish	Slot Mechanic
Floorperson	VIPs
George	Wales
Junket	

Introduction

Casinos are unlike any other facet of the hospitality industry. For the average guest, they will lose more than they will win. How then, do you make them leave happy and want to return? It is the experience! The casino experience is very difficult to replicate outside of a casino. The guest is provided with some of the best services available. The more they spend, and lose, the better the services. The lights, the energy, the spirit behind it can be a real thrill. Guests crave this experience. It is up to the casino professionals to make it happen.

Casino Collage
© Kheng Guan Toh/Shutterstock.com

Las Vegas Strip
© Dominic Gentilcore/Shutterstock.com

Macau at Night
© Zen S Prarom/Shutterstock.com

TYPES OF CASINOS

Casinos offer much more to guests than gaming. Many casinos offer a full range of services because once you leave the property, you stop spending money.

Casinos may be freestanding or on a riverboat, but quite often they are part of a larger entity. Many casinos are within hotels. Some of these are even hotel-resorts with many other attractions. Casinos are linked to hotels, food and beverage operations, meetings and convention halls, entertainment arenas, golf courses, and even cruise ships. Gaming is typically considered the money-maker and other offerings are support to the casinos. Their hope of the extra amenities is to contain the spending within the property by offering them everything they need. Once they leave, the money goes with them.

Friends Looking at Menu and Ordering at Casino
© antoniodiaz/Shutterstock.com

FROM CRIMINAL TO RESPECTABLE

Casinos are now very respectable. In the past, casinos were viewed as a criminal enterprise. Now they are owned by major companies and are highly regulated. Anyone who wants to own part of a casino can simply buy shares in their stock.

Casinos also have interest in responsible gambling. They have made great progress in helping guests who indulge with compulsive gambling behaviors. Many work with agencies like the National Center for Responsible Gaming and the Responsible Gaming Council.

Tradeshow at Mandalay Bay, Las Vegas
© Scott Prokop/Shutterstock.com

COMPLEX ENTITIES

Because casinos are typically not stand-alone units, they are part of a larger offering of services and amenities, making their existence quite complex and altering the typical operations of the other department. The environment, the views toward profitability, and the customer profiles are all unique to this entity.

Floor Positions

Front of House (FOH) casino games are typically split into two primary divisions: slot machines and table games. Table games require much more support. Typically everyone on the floor must be state licensed. Table games are:

- ► Blackjack (21)
- ► Roulette
- ► Craps
- ► Baccarat
- ► Poker

A dealer runs the table. He or she is given table responsibility for an individual table. Several tables together in an area are referred to as a pit. Floorpersons oversee a group of games within a pit. Pit Managers oversee all of the groups of games with the pit. Shift Managers oversee most or all of the pits, and a Games Manager is in charge of all games.

Dealers get the most guest interaction. They must be completely fair and honest with no prejudice. Dealers cannot give advice. People are typically friendly and talkative, but they have a job to do. They are highly scrutinized. They have pit bosses and cameras observing every move. It may seem exciting, but most of their actions are routine. They must keep up the pace and deal a certain number of hands or spin a certain number in order to keep the game moving and earn the casino a profit. They are constantly pressing to keep going and some of the players may not.

Roulette Table
© Nejron Photo/Shutterstock.com

Blackjack Table at Casino
© Nejron Photo/Shutterstock.com

Common Back of House (BOH) casino departments that support customer service may include:

- ► Accounting
- ► Cashier's station/cage
- ► Countroom
- ► Bookkeepers
- ► Surveillance
- ► Security

Most money is tracked using electronic cards. When money is moved, teams of three people are common.

Slot machines have staff positions as well:

Woman Playing on Slot Machine
© Maridav/Shutterstock.com

- ► **Slot manager:** overall management
- ► **Shift manager:** responsibility for slots on a given shift
- ► **Slot mechanic:** repair and maintenance of slots
- ► **Floorperson:** verifies payouts, hopper fills, supervises change attendants
- ► **Change attendants:** make change
- ► **Booth cashiers:** complete payment of payouts, make change, may also be called "the cage" because it is protected.

The front office is staffed with bell staff and reservations. The administrative staff houses the sales and marketing department. The housekeeping, maintenance, security, and room service staff also play key roles in customer service.

Slot Machine Floor
© Pe Dra/Shutterstock.com

Unique Environmental Characteristics

⋎ MAIN GOAL

The primary goal of a casino is like any other business. They must earn a profit. In order to do that, the casino must provide a service and retain the customer. Once they leave the property, they are no longer spending money. Much goes into keeping the casino customer. Consequently, many casinos have evolved to become everything to the customer. They offer food and accommodations without ever leaving the property.

⋎ HIGH-TECH TRENDS

Customers of casinos demand technology. Competition pushes casinos to embrace the latest technologies. Consequently, they must have the cutting edge of everything from lighting, to entertainment, to communications. For example, all players are tracked on **player tracking systems** through reward cards. Customers are rated. **Comps**, or free food, beverage, lodging, or prizes are given to those according to the amount they gamble. Comps may be done with a point system. Casinos can also share information with each other regarding profiles.

Player Tracking Systems

A system that monitors the frequency and usage of gamblers. Used to give rewards or comps.

Comps

Free compensation for food, beverage, rooms, or other gratuities to reward guests.

It isn't just one person that has knowledge, it is a team equipped with Customer Relation Management (CRM) and database technologies.

OTHER DEFINITIONS

Firing: a guest betting large amounts at money games.

Fish: player that is losing money.

George: generous tipper.

Junket: trips for the highest spending players. Usually everything is included. Players agree to play/pay minimum advanced deposit to the casino. Also may be used to describe small souvenirs.

FREE DRINKS

It is customary for drinks to be offered free of charge on the casino floor. This keeps customers there longer so they don't have to leave for a drink. This also helps them to feel welcomed and as if they are valued and receiving something, even if they may be losing at the tables.

FOOD AND BEVERAGE

Meals are offered in all styles so that the customer does not have to leave the property. Some eat quick meals so that they can get back to a "hot" slot machine they

Snow Crab Legs at Casino on Promotional Placemat to Remind Customers
© 1000Photography/Shutterstock.com

believe is "paying out soon." Other restaurants give them a chance to relax and enjoy before returning to the games. Originally, restaurants were "loss leaders" meaning they were only there to support the gaming function. They offered $2.95 prime rib dinners as an attraction. The food and beverage operations lost money that was quickly regained through the casino. Things have changed and while the food is still considered a support, it is now considered to earn a profit. It is also nowadays common to have every possible type of food outlet. Some may offer as many as 20–30 or more while smaller casinos may only have a handful. Some are chains and others are celebrity-named. A wide variety brings in the gamblers and meets the demands of the rest of the players. The restaurants see different traffic patterns, increased comps, and different demographics than non-casino operations, but quickly learn to adjust and accommodate to the overall plan.

ROOMS

Casino hotels are some of the largest in the country and the world.

Some have 3,000–4,000 and even 6,000 rooms. A casino hotel is for VIPS, frequent players, and tourists. It also supports conferences and conventions. A casino hotel operates as a lodging facility, but is intended to facilitate the casino. Many comps are given. It is not uncommon for as much as 90% of the rooms to be comped. Busy patterns may also be different than other hotels. The casino hotel is not designed for the locals unless they are medium or high rollers. The hotel keeps players on-premise. Once they leave, they spend dollars elsewhere and they may not return. Free rooms or "comps" are given to the frequent players and VIPs to draw in and maintain these crowds. Upgrades are also common. These are billed directly to marketing. These demographics can be very demanding, so the hotel has to be ready to consistently deliver a high level of guest service. Since it is a festive environment, wild vents can occur. People are celebrating and some are less than scrupulous. As with other great hotels, it is also common for a few guests to take permanent residence at the casinos.

Example of a VIP Gold Card
© robertindiana/Shutterstock.com

VIPS

Very Important People (VIPs) are celebrities, high-profile people, or high rollers (very high rollers are also known as **Wales**). They are crucial to most properties, because they represent a high percentage of total gaming revenues as they tend to wager very large amounts, particularly the medium and high rollers which can spend in the millions.

Entire departments may be dedicated to the care of them. Interpreters, concierges, chefs, and the like are at their immediate disposal. They have all of their personal needs met. Whatever it takes is done for them. They want for nothing. They are provided with privacy and given special areas to gamble. Casinos keep rooms set aside for unexpected VIPs. They are given large suites on separate floors

VIPs

Celebrities, high-profile, or high rollers who receive special attention and services from the casino.

Wales

Gamblers who spend very large amounts gambling. They are accustomed to receiving very high levels of service.

Shopping Mall Within a Casino, Marina Bay Sands, Singapore
© joyfull/Shutterstock.com

with many extras and have personal attendants dedicated to them. Their suites may have separate bedrooms and a dining room so they can invite guests and entertain. All of these things create overall value. The player feels appreciated with the comps.

ATMOSPHERE

Casinos appeal to the sense. Every casino is a party. No matter what day or time of day that you are there, it is a festive atmosphere. Lights of all colors and sounds of bells fill the air. It looks very similar despite the time of day or the weather, and most casinos do not display clocks so it is very easy to lose track of the outside world. All of this helps to provide an escape into a fantasyland where fun is the theme. Guests feed off of this energy. It fills the senses.

OTHER ACTIVITIES

Some casinos are even resorts with golf, spas, shopping, shows, and many other activities. They offer alternative activities for gamblers to spend or to occupy the non-gamblers in the party. Like the restaurants, medium and luxury brand names have been lured to open shops, making the overall offerings very attractive.

SECURITY

Security in casinos is much higher a level than at other hospitality operations. Surveillance is very big. Everything is monitored on video. Cameras cover nearly

Security Room at a Casino
© Gorodenkoff/Shutterstock.com

every angle and every square foot. You literally cannot go anywhere without being on camera from many views. Profiles are established. Customer levels are monitored. Facial recognition is in place. Cheater information is available and shared to track them globally. The casinos work with each other so that information can be shared anywhere.

Security officers are visible; they control access, cash drop and counts, and all physical assets. A Director of Surveillance oversees the surveillance department, games, compliance, and conduct.

Meetings and Events

Many casinos are tied to meetings, trade shows, exhibitions, and conference centers. This makes a great draw to attendance when hosting meetings. Meetings and events attract new customers to the casinos. In fact, Las Vegas is considered a conference city. Without conferences, the city could not support itself on individual gamblers. Conference attendees are compelled to stay there because of the conference. While they are there, they typically patronize the property, including food, beverage, shows, and gambling. When they stay and eat they pay nearly full price. There are few comps with these crowds. Some even gamble when they are supposed to be in the conference meetings.

Casino shows attract many different types of people. It is not uncommon to see a rodeo, a computer trade show, and a business meeting all being held simultaneously. Lately, sports teams are being integrated into shows, bringing yet another type of new crowd. Meeting the needs of this crowd is very different because their primary goal is different than typical gamblers. They may be non-gamblers or very **low rollers** who spend very little gambling. Casinos are an extra perk for them.

Low Rollers
Guests who spend very little gambling.

They can be enticed into loosening up their purse strings if they feel the need for adventure or a splurge. These attractions bring in business during the week when the casino might be slow, so they are advantageous to the property.

OUT-OF-TOWN GAMBLERS VERSUS LOCAL GAMBLERS

When visiting a casino, the valet or doorman are the first to assess and welcome the guests. You have a culmination of people. When people are traveling and are out of their element, they tend to spend more per person. It might be a special occasion or a vacation getaway chance to splurge. It doesn't happen often, so expectations are specifically unknown but high.

The local gambler isn't as impacted by the glitz and the glare of the casino atmosphere. They have become accustomed to it. They avoid the places that do not work specifically for them for one reason or another. It could be small things like parking or clientele. A casino quickly learns if it is attracting local gamblers. This crowd has different and lower, quirky expectations. It likely isn't a special occasion for them, just casual entertainment. They spend less but make up for it in frequency.

CHAPTER REVIEW QUESTIONS

1. How have casinos changed from criminal to respectable?
2. Why does a casino hotel give most of its rooms away?
3. Why do casinos typically serve free drinks?
4. Explain how food and beverage is different at a casino.
5. How are conference attendees different from typical casino guests?
6. Why do casino hotels give so many comps to high rollers?
7. List at least five different floor positions.
8. How important is casino security?
9. Why do casinos offer so many services to the guests?
10. How are the guest service offerings different for a high roller than a low roller?

CASE STUDIES

Catering to the Low Rollers

Casinos have much competition. The smaller, older properties cannot compete with the other newer, bigger properties. Some decide to go after the low roller market and take the fast-food approach by catering decreasing costs and sales per customer, but increasing customer counts.

The High-Stepper Casino is one of the oldest properties in the area. It has been renamed a couple of times and has seen a few different owners and management companies over the years. Originally in a great location, the area had once seen a boom of business, then lost out to downturn in the local gaming community. Over the past 10–15 years, it has seen a rather steady growth of new entrants into the market, but they are building in an area about a mile away from this location, making it less likely to be visited.

The Management of the High-Stepper is trying to determine a new direction. The Management must report this new idea to the Board of Directors and the Asset Managers in a formal presentation next month.

After looking at what the casino has to offer, they decide to be a casino that accommodates to the low rollers and the medium rollers. Basically, they want to make all new gamblers feel at home. They want to be there for the guests who don't have as much to spend. They believe they attract local traffic. They also want to cater to the medium rollers making them feel like high rollers.

1. Evaluate what the High Stepper has to offer to its customers.
2. Will the new strategy work?
3. What will they have to change at the property to better serve their target guests?
4. What would you change about the strategy?

Spain, Inc.

Spain, Inc. is an upscale dining chain. They have several free-standing units. They run a tight operation, with strict operations protocol. They train their managers to operate the business in the Spain, Inc. manner. They adhere specifically to the methods of customer service that have served them well for many years. As a result, they are known for their old-world hospitality. From the food and décor, to the staff and customer service, they provide a consistent and exceptional experience.

As they continue to grow, the corporate office development team has decided to assume an open slip in a full-scale hotel, casino, and resort. They will be one of 35 food service operations on-premise. They believe this move will further the exposure of Spain, Inc. and provide the company with much additional revenue.

Jason is a Spain, Inc. store manager who has been with the company since he graduated from college. He has been through all of the strict training. He has advanced from waiter to dining room manager, to assistant manager and finally to store manager. He won an award for best new store manager this last year. His operation runs well, but is relatively small and has limited bonus potential. Jason accepted an offer to become store manager of the new unit located within the casino.

As they open the new Spain, Inc., Jason soon learns that his restaurant within a casino is very different. Everything from the employees, to the customers, to the hours are different from those restaurants on the outside.

One of the first things that Jason notices is that his recruitment efforts have been attracting a different type of employee. Next, he is caught off guard by the peak and non-peak hours. His customer counts had always varied depending on the weather. Now, things are different. His outside seating is really inside the huge, climate-controlled building. It is as if they had brought the outside inside with a perfect climate. It never too hot nor is it too cold. His deck is now the preferred seating. He also noticed the busy days aren't the same. The new place followed the typical Friday and Saturday nights, but also saw strong counts on other days and whenever there were special events held at the casino.

He also saw a change in the wants and the needs of the guests. As a result, many of his former customer service strategies were not working. Many of the guests were receiving comps. Jason quickly noticed that customers don't behave the same when their meal is free. Many order differently, so their menu mix has been very atypical. It seems like people are either extravagant or cheap. To add, they either took a long time with their meal, or wanted it quick, so they could get back to an event, or gambling, or shopping, or their room.

Spain, Inc. typically hosted many special occasions such as birthdays. It was something that people made reservations for, and the restaurant was ready to accommodate them. These demands had decreased in this unit. Jason also noticed that parties arrived together instead of waiting for the rest of their party to join them. Also, the groups were smaller, and many didn't have a reservation.

Jason also noticed that more of the customers desired to be respected and receive special accommodations. The Casino's VIP Team would frequently accompany these people behind the scenes to ensure their needs were met. Jason had never before experienced this type of intervention into his operation. He also witnessed some wild and crazy characters that were very atypical to Spain, Inc. patrons.

All of these changes came as a surprise to Jason. Much of what Spain, Inc. had done in the past had ceased to apply in a casino operation. His comment cards were lower from anything that he saw in his former store. He tried to make small adjustments, but his standard operating procedures were not ready for this drastic change. The staff wasn't ready, and Jason was becoming frustrated. Jason's district manager was aware of the situation and decided to visit Jason along with the director of operations.

1. How might operating a food service establishment within a casino be different?
2. Why wasn't Spain, Inc.'s customer service training working?
3. What questions should be asked at the meeting?
4. What should Jason do differently to accommodate these changes?

Meeting the Needs of Meetings

Skytop Hotel and Casino is an established, older property. It has offered gambling, accommodations, food and beverage, and meeting space to patrons for many years. Most recently, the hotel has decided to gain additional revenue by revamping its meetings and events. Its hope is that it could bring new groups to benefit the entire property. It has undergone a recent change in the Director of Sales (DOS) who has turned over the sales staff and implemented an additional profit-sharing incentive system. Everyone must work together to fill the hotel, the casino, the restaurants, and the meeting space. If all are successful, the sales staff will receive an additional profit-sharing bonus.

Generally, this has worked out quite well. The entire property has been quite busy. One of the new strategies was to develop a pursuit for the SMERF (social, military, education, religious, fraternal) market resulting in a few new groups booked at the property. With it, a couple of religious and educational groups brought in very different customer profiles. In short, they were frugal and didn't like gambling. They didn't spend as much at the restaurants. They went off-property to eat for less. Many would not even enter the casino. They did not patronize the shows unless they were free and some voiced that they were offended at the content. To add, most did not drink and the bars were empty. In fact, some of the people from the groups scoffed at other casino guests. The employees wondered why or how these groups were even booked at a casino property if they didn't like to gamble. Consequently, the groups, the employees, and the other patrons were upset.

The Director of Operations (DOO) met with the DOS and the Food and Beverage Director (FBD) to understand and solve the situation. The FBD explained that food and beverage sales were down, except for banquet food. The DOS explained that the sales staff made their sales quotas. The DOO explained that as a result, the property now had new groups that they did not know how to service. The FBD admitted that they could provide different options. The DOS admitted that they needed a new system for sales quotas. The DOO admitted that they needed a new way to serve these new groups.

1. How are these groups different from their typical meeting groups?
2. Can non-gambling groups attend meetings at casinos?
3. Can a casino property still earn a profit from these groups?
4. How can the property best accommodate their needs?

The Glitz and the Glamour

Ron is an employee at a casino on the local strip. He grew up in a nearby town and had always aspired to be part of the limelight associated with casinos. He always found gambling to be an interesting hobby. He enjoyed the casinos on the strip as fun places to visit. The action never stopped, 24-7. There was always an event with people and lights and everything else that filled all of the senses.

When it became evident that his other job did not have a future, Ron decided to make a career shift. Looking to gain more enjoyment and satisfaction from future employment, he decided that a job working with people topped his wish list. He also considered his hobbies, and how he spent his spare time. Finally, he listed local businesses in his general area that were hiring and most closely matched his newly developed career profile. Casinos quickly climbed to the top of the resulting list.

Ron began in the back of the house as part-time support staff. After his state qualifications were met, he began working the casino floor. He enjoyed helping people. He enjoyed the atmosphere and the steady pay. He learned to deal cards and became a dealer at one of the blackjack tables. He began getting regular shifts and regular customers. Tips quickly grew and then became consistent. He enjoyed his job.

Now, after a few months, the glitz and the glamour is beginning to wear off. Despite the fun casino atmosphere and the pay, it is a regular job with some downsides. He always liked to please people. Some of the players aren't happy unless they win. A few people have obvious gambling issues. By policy, he cannot even give them advice. He has to stand there and watch people gamble away more than they should. He can report it, but his involvement ends there. The glitz and glamour of a 24-7 environment isn't as glamorous when you occasionally have to rotate through the night shifts and holidays. Gaming isn't turning out to be nearly as attractive as the movies led him to think. It is a regular job, with good points and bad points, ups and downs.

Ron's personal life has also been impacted. He is working more than before, and his hours vary at times, compromising his social life. He is finding it difficult to sleep and is watching more television than ever on his time off.

All of this has had an impact on his work. Ron's pit boss realizes that he hasn't been as cheerful as he was when he first began. He doesn't seem to be as welcoming to his regular customers. Ron was even warned once about his attitude. He thought that he would enjoy this job at a place that he loved, but working in his field of hobby is very different than enjoying his hobby.

1. What were the original expectations of Ron? Were they realistic?
2. Was Ron a good fit for the job?
3. What should the casino do to help Ron stay motivated and best serve customers?
4. What can the casino do to motivate Ron and others like him?
5. What can Ron do to motivate himself?

The Riverboat

The Riverboat is a riverboat casino on the Mississippi River. It has enjoyed years of a loyal, local following. The staff and management has been in place for many years. It ran a great operation, but recently its revenues have been falling. It has witnessed 5 consecutive years of 1 to 2% declining revenues. Although this is a slight decline each year, the trend continues. The owners of the boat visit occasionally and are obviously beginning to get nervous. The management company that runs operations is also very concerned. The future is unsure. Many of the employees have rumored that the management company needs to turn business around within the next year or the owners will not renew its contract. Overtime hours and customer comps have been eliminated and the company is tightly monitoring the other expenses. Employee and customer morale has diminished, and is evident in the service. Employees and lower-level management are nervous and trying to do the best they can.

One day the new district manager of the management company came aboard for a visit. Everyone knew she was there and tried to perform at their best. She spent the day on the Riverboat observing and talking to as many employees and customers as possible. After a series of informal discussions, she meets with the boat management and a plan is devised to conduct research to determine the issue behind lost revenue and seek a solution.

1. Did the new district manager begin the process correctly?
2. Outline the next research steps that the Riverboat should take.

Assessments and Planning

Chapter 10

Strategic Planning for Service

CHAPTER OBJECTIVES

After reading this chapter, you should be able to:

► Define and apply strategy as it applies to a service operation.
► Outline and apply the three main facets of strategy.
► Implement four parts of a Strategic Service System.
► Analyze the internal and external aspects of a service organization in a SWOT Analysis.
► Understand Vision, Mission, and Statements of Purpose as they relate to service.

TERMINOLOGY

Champion
Change Theory
Continuous Improvement
Co-Production
Credo
Customer Centric
Direct Competition
General Competition
Indirect Competition
Mission
Objective
Problem Statement

Process Reengineering
Resource Viewpoint
Service Guarantee
Service Mission/Service Vision
Service Process Implementation
Service Strategy
Silo
Strategic Service System
Strategy
SWOT Analysis
Vision

Failing to plan is planning to fail.

Service doesn't just happen; it must be planned. You need a strategy.

Introduction to Service Strategy

This chapter focuses on strategic planning for service. It is divided into three parts:

- ▶ Introduction to Strategy
- ▶ Evaluation for Strategy
- ▶ Implementation of Strategy

In section one, the premise of strategy is introduced as it relates to hospitality management and a foundation is established. Section two discusses the internal and external evaluations of the SWOT Analysis in an effort to analyze the position and the market environment. Section three covers writing objectives and implementation of the strategy.

☀ STRATEGY DEFINED

The science of strategy can be quite complex. Numerous books, courses, and even college majors are devoted to this subject. Consultants and professionals devote entire careers to the study of the topic. As complex as it may be, it is also a very basic concept at its roots. Simply put, a **strategy** is a calculated plan to achieve a common, chosen objective. This definition sounds deceptively simple. However, each word and phrase has distinct meaning. Let's dig more deeply into the three main facets of strategy:

Strategy

A calculated plan to achieve a common, chosen objective.

Calculated Plan

We aim to develop it through methodical means, to structure a well-thought plan with direction. This is anything but ad-hoc. It involves self-analysis and external input to make the best possible plan with the information available. It will appear as a seemingly linear process, but will also require intuition and creativity to form the plan. Any and all progress will be monitored and revised as needed. As a result, a strategy must also be flexible to accommodate for unforeseen issues that commonly arise. We assume that things will be reasonably stable and predictable, but environmental factors and other intervening variables will bring a need for on-going adjustments. This is not seen as a deviation from the calculated plan, but instead as a normal part of the process. It is, "calculated flexibility." This agility will follow for changes to be made along the way and prevent pitfalls.

Common

The framework is agreed upon and supported at all levels of the business. Everyone is made aware of the plan, the direction, and the commitment involved to get there. Upper-level management supports low-level management and line staff in all of their efforts. Everyone is working together.

Objective

The desired outcome may vary greatly in nature and scope based on the organization and the goals, but it is always present. Objectives ultimately help you to achieve goals. Most **objectives** involve a plan for improvement. Some examples of aggressive objectives include being known as having the absolute best service or gaining market share. Others are to develop a unique characteristic, in order to create a distinction from the rest of the competition. In bad economic times, a few strategies enable a business to merely survive a forecasted, unstable economic period. In the end, everyone is working together, with a plan, in an effort to reach a common goal or objective.

Objective
individual, specific intents aimed at reaching goals.

❖ STRATEGY IS NATURAL

Strategy is a natural way of thinking. We are all programmed to think strategically about many things in our lives. We have a want or a need (objective and goal). Formal or not, we perform research and decide how we will achieve it (plan). We, and others, agree to follow, support, and monitor the plan and direction (common, chosen).

For example, a student in this course has an objective to complete it and other courses so they can graduate from college. The goal is to obtain a job, position, or career. The objectives (graduation) are part of a plan to help them reach the goal (job). They did the research and decided on a college, which courses to take, which professors to take, when to take the courses, and how to balance other priorities to obtain a degree. They allocated the resources (time, money, effort) and made a plan to make it happen. The objective is graduation. The goal is a job. The plan makes it happen.

❖ IMPORTANCE OF STRATEGY

Strategy creates many benefits to the organization. Strategy is the underlying premise to delivering quality guest service. Every Fortune 500 company utilizes strategy. Below are some of the benefits:

- ▶ Increased Communication
  - ☐ Planning and monitoring facilitates communication.
  - ☐ Everyone hears and knows what is happening.
  - ☐ Grapevines and rumors are minimized.
- ▶ Increased Understanding
  - ☐ Promotes a deeper understanding between departments.
- ▶ Establish Common Direction
  - ☐ Everyone is working the same way toward the same goal.
- ▶ Increased Efficiency and Productivity

- ► Ease in Decision-Making
    - ☐ It provides a basis for making decisions.
- ► Increased Commitment
    - ☐ All are committed to a common purpose.
- ► Reduction of Stress
- ► Reduction of Anxiety
- ► Awareness of cCompetition
- ► Awareness of Market Place
- ► Awareness of Internal Operations

✦ LACK OF STRATEGY

Failing to plan is planning to fail.

- ► Crisis management: a great manager can fix problems as they arise.
- ► Optimistic management: just do the best that you can.
- ► Mental management: it is all in my head.

Strategy has many pitfalls. The wrong approach or lacking in just one aspect could spell disaster. Some may have a direction, but are not in agreement on how to proceed. The intents may not be well-communicated. Some only have an idea in their head and don't see value in outward planning. Some have a plan but are monitoring progress in their head. Some are reasonably pleased with the current situation and become complacent. Others see a need for a plan but lack knowledge on how to proceed. Or, worse yet, some are simply burnt out or lazy. Whatever the reason, a business that fails to plan is planning to fail.

✦ STRATEGY APPLIED TO THE CUSTOMER MINDSET

Consider this. You have a strategy. It leads you to objectives and goals. Your intentions are well-constructed in the procedures and processes. Conflicts arise when processes and procedures don't meet the demands of the customers. Suppose the customer arrives at 9:00 a.m., exhausted from an international flight. They only have sleep on their mind. You follow the process. You tell them that check-in is at 3:00 p.m. and offer to hold their bags. Now you have a process and they have a process. Their timing isn't always your timing. Why should the customer have to pay you to accommodate to your ways? If you truly care about the customer, a process should accommodate these instances if at all possible. This doesn't mean giving away the hotel, but processes shouldn't be so formal that they conflict with the customers.

Continuous Improvement

A premise of instituting quality through a cycle of planning, monitoring, interpreting, and revising.

✦ CONTINUOUS IMPROVEMENT

Continuous improvement is an essential premise of instituting quality. It is a cycle of planning, monitoring, interpreting, and revising in a constant effort to improve something. The hospitality industry is very dynamic—technology changes,

Continuous Improvement Icons
© HowLettery/Shutterstock.com

expectations change, economic conditions change, and the marketplace changes, so companies must always be on their toes and be ready to identify areas in need of improvement or change. As these areas are outlined, care must be taken to prioritize objectives. In order to maximize the return on available resources, there should be a structure in place for planning, executing, and monitoring, then revising, executing, and monitoring again. It is an unending cycle. It is an adaptation process in a continually evolving environment.

Continuous improvement is analogized in the common idea that *quality service is a journey, not a destination.*

Change Theory

> It is not the strongest of the species that survives, nor the most intelligent, but the ones most responsive to change.
>
> —Charles Darwin

Change theory is the idea that there is a science behind change. Several theories exist and Organizational Behavioral Professionals dedicate careers to specializing in helping businesses succeed through transitional periods.

There are many things that make instituting changes difficult. Preconceptions, habits, insecurities, past practices, fear of failure, and jumping to conclusions all effect instituting change.

There is an analogy of change management as being periods of frozen, thawing, white water, and re-freezing, as shown in figures. The initial frozen state is the status quo, the usual, the expected, or the norm. It is the way that we have always done things.

Change Theory

A science behind helping businesses transition through changes.

Change Analogy 1
© Yeti studio/Shutterstock.com; © Yeti studio/Shutterstock.com; © StudioSmart/Shutterstock.com

Changes will come in many forms. Change will continue throughout your career. It is said that "the only thing consistent is change itself." The change may be a new technology system, a new service procedure, new management, or a myriad of other things. It is important to realize that change may take many shapes and forms. When change occurs, a period of un-freezing occurs. To extend the analogy, this may even seem like a splash of water or even white water. It will be very problematic. Stress and disorganization will likely occur. Everything is unsettled.

Then, eventually, the change will calm, and it will again re-freeze. Things will also settle in the workplace. It will not freeze the same as before. In fact, it will probably be much different, but things will settle down. Then it will again become a new definition of the term "frozen."

These changes with unsettling middle points and different end results will continue to cycle throughout life. During these times, reinforce, give compliments, motivate, reassure, remain optimistic but realistic and address and admit failures. The cycle times of these unsettling periods may be a few weeks to several months, and even a few years, but they will eventually form a "new normal."

People specialize in smoothing these transitions, but just realizing the cycle and the current stage helps you to see it and manage it more effectively.

Similar to the prior unfreezing–refreezing analogy, a change may be in the form of something interjected that is considered very foreign to your operation. Within this type of change cycle:

▶ you are accustomed to the "new normal."
▶ a radical idea is interjected into your operation.
▶ it re-freezes but in a very awkward state. The change was not initially successful, even after things settled down.
▶ then additional changes are needed to restructure, rearrange, or develop in order to make it work much better.

Change Analogy 1: When Something New Is Added to the Refreeze
© StudioSmart/Shutterstock.com; next 3 images © Yeti Studio/Shutterstock.com

Resisting change is normal. Most people are hesitant and do not have an automatic predisposition to change. This is a built-in safety mechanism. We always assess new situations for danger. This feeling is very natural and this feeling varies with each person and each situation. The change could be presented as an opportunity, which some people will welcome, but trust must also be established. If people trust others, the initial leap of faith will seem less threatening.

Analyzing Position and Market

Does your business have a current strategy? If so, what is it? If not stated, where is the company currently headed? What would a silent observer guess is the strategy? In other words, what does the writing on the wall tell you? Follow your intuition. That is probably the strategy, by design or by accident. It is likely focused on objectives such as:

- ▶ Sales
- ▶ Fixing or avoiding an error
- ▶ Reducing a cost
- ▶ Forming an alliance
- ▶ Adjusting staffing levels
- ▶ Retraining or retooling

This will help you to develop a **problem statement**. This is the underlying reason why something is occurring. Often this is made clear through the SWOT Analysis, described below.

It may have come from the top administration or from the line staff. It may be based on feedback from return customers, perceptions of new customers, a desire to outpace the competition, or developing new sales opportunities. A lack of communication could be a result of a **silo**, a metaphor for departments and groups within the company that do not communicate well with each other. Instead, they all work in their specific areas instead of working together. There could be multiple or overlapping reasons. In any event, it is important to know where your business stands.

Problem Statement

The root problem or fundamental cause of why something is happening. Often the results of both internal and external analysis.

Silo

A metaphor used to describe the separate departments of an organization that work independently and fail to communicate with each other, thus replicating processes, working inefficiently, and causing frustration.

Illustration of Silo Metaphor
© Aleutie/Shutterstock.com

❖ SWOT ANALYSIS

A **SWOT Analysis** is a valuable tool commonly used to establish a starting point in strategic development. It evaluates both internal and external attributes of a business and is very useful for observing the big picture or macro view.

It allows you to know where your company stands, where the competition stands, and how the outside variables influence your business. The letters of the SWOT stand for:

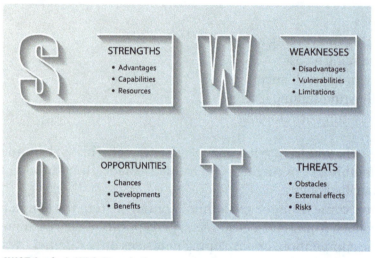

SWOT Analysis With Descriptions
© prizma/Shutterstock.com

The SWOT Analysis has two primary components: Internal and External. The strengths and weaknesses make up the internal analysis and the opportunities and threats make up the external analysis. The internal components represent the areas of the operation that are within the direct control of the business such as operations, marketing, staffing, management, and finances. The external components represent the areas of the business the business has little or no control over, such as competition, economic conditions, and changing technologies.

The attributes are sorted as:

- ▶ Internal = within their control = good = Strength
- ▶ Internal = within their control = bad = Weakness
- ▶ External = outside of their control = good = Opportunity
- ▶ External = outside of their control = bad = Threat

Although the business has no direct control over the external influences, it can only adjust to them.

A SWOT Analysis reviews each of these areas. A statement within your control is internal and is either good or bad. If it is good it is a strength, and if it is bad it is a weakness. If it is not within your control it is external and your *response* to it is either good or bad. If your response is good it is known as an opportunity, and if your response is bad it is known as a threat.

Other tools such as the Internal Factor Evaluation Matrix (IFE) and the External Factor Evaluation Matrix (EFE) rates and assigns points to the categories for comparison.

Below are questions to ask as a starting point of SWOT analysis:

Internal		Strength	Weakness
Operations	What standards do you have in place?		
	How are the costs of operations compared to industry standards?		
Finance	How strong are your financial ratios?		
Marketing	Can you make your service tangible?		
	Do you have a strong brand image?		
	Are you different?		
	Do you want to be different?		
Staffing	Do your employees know the strategy?		
Management	How does your business support this strategy?		
Research & Development	Are they innovative with new products and services?		
Management Information Systems	How strong is your ability to gather, control, and manage information?		

External		Opportunities	Threats
Culture	How has the mindset of the population changed?		
Market—Customers	What are the growing demographics in your marketplace?		
	What does the market look like?		
	How do the customers perceive you?		
	How do they perceive the competition?		
	What are their needs?		
	Why do the customers come to your business as opposed to the competitor?		
	Do your customers know the strategy?		
Technology	How is the technology changing?		
	Have you leveraged the available technologies?		
Competition	What is the competition doing?		
	Are you a leader or are you catching up?		
	Barriers to entry? What prevents new entrants into the market?		
	Benchmark?—looking at best-practice methods. Observing the best-in-class at methods, or products, or services.		
	Retaliation?—how will they respond to your changes?		
Economy	Unemployment rate, G.D.P., inflation rate?		
Legal—Politically	Any new laws that will affect your business process?		

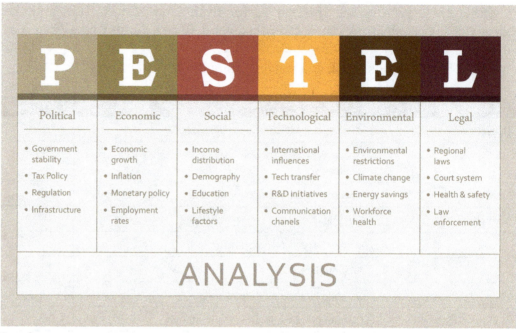

Pestel
© prizma/Shutterstock.com

Sometimes this external macro list is more easily remembered as PESTEL:

Political

Economic

Social

Technological

Environmental

Legal

IDENTIFYING YOUR COMPETITION

Determining your competition is highly subjective and often misunderstood. In one sense, your business is unique in what it offers to its customers in at least one way. It is either unique by location, by marketing, by service, by product, or by delivery. In another sense, it shares many of the same qualities as other businesses and competes with those businesses on one or more levels.

Direct Competition

An interesting planning exercise is to ask a small business owner to name his competition. He will typically come up with a handful of competitors in the same geographic area delivering similar products and services to the same customers. He is naming what we refer to as **direct competition**.

Direct Competition

Other businesses who compete for the same clientele, in the same industry, delivering similar goods and services.

Indirect Competition

If you were to ask the same small business owner about businesses that provide a slightly different product the owner might claim, "He doesn't touch me. He isn't my competition at all." In one sense he is correct, but in every other sense he is terribly wrong. Other businesses may be delivering a different product or service, but they are still competition. A business offering slightly different products to the same markets is an example of indirect competition.

Here is another thought. Have you ever been on your way to go out to dinner at a nice restaurant and decided to eat at a quick-service restaurant instead? How about the opposite? What changed your mind? What were the other options?

Indirect competition is still competition. In poor economic times, fine dining lost customers to upscale-casual dining. Upscale-casual dining lost customers to casual dining, who lost customers to limited service who lost to quick-service. Some customers jump two or three levels on a whim.

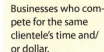

Indirect Competition

Other businesses who compete for the same clientele, delivering related, but not identical, products and services.

General Competition

Also, consider a getaway destination package for $299.00. You would love to go. You may even have the time, but you don't have the money. Where was it spent? Who else was competing for your time or your dollar? In general competition, businesses compete for the same time and/or dollar of the clientele, but with very different products and services. It may not be directly related, but it still hurts the bottom line.

General Competition

Businesses who compete for the same clientele's time and/or dollar.

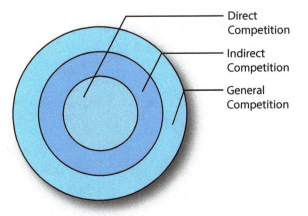

Interorganizational Partnerships

Instead of competing, businesses can also join together and form interorganizational partnerships which can serve even larger interests. These coalitions could help the community, the industry, or the environment. Companies working with suppliers could provide feedback and lead to problem-solving and greater efficiencies.

Integration: Implementing a Service Strategy

> You need to have everyone on the bus is only part of it. It needs to be the right bus, headed in the right direction, and the right people need to be in the correct seats.

> —Adapted from Jim Collins, *Good to Great*

There is much to this quote:

▶ Having everyone on "the right bus" means that you need to have the company together in a united effort.

▶ The right bus means that it needs to be the right, proper, or most suitable objectives.

▶ The right direction means that the bus (strategy) needs to be properly implemented.

And everyone in their correct seats means that you need the right people in the right places. This may mean moving, retraining, or even replacing people.

Good intentions are not enough. Plans are great, but implementation and follow-up are crucial to even the best-laid plans. The employees are the resource that is key to making service happen. Employees and management must share the same values.

Implementation is the process. It is the art of transforming plans and potential into practice. It needs to go from paper into practice, from a service strategy to actual service. All of this is part of the Strategic Service System.

✦ THE STRATEGIC SERVICE SYSTEM: PURPOSE, PRODUCT, PLAN, PEOPLE

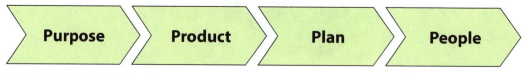

The Strategic Service System

> **Strategic Service System**
>
> A four-part system that involves purpose, product, plan, and people.

The **Strategic Service System** involves four main components: purpose, product, plan, and people. All are prerequisites, all must exist simultaneously, and all are equally important in the strategic process. Each will be discussed in more depth later in the chapter.

Purpose

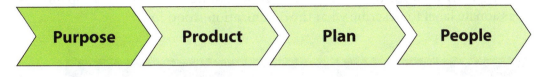

> Our mission statement about treating people with respect and dignity is not just words but a creed we live by every day. You can't expect your employees to exceed the expectations of your customers if you don't exceed the employees' expectations of management.
>
> —Howard Schultz, CEO, Starbucks Coffee

What do you stand for? What do you want to change? What do you want to focus on? Customer-centric is an idea that the business should focus every decision with the customer as the main priority, outranking all others. While this view may seem drastic, the customer should certainly be a consideration in decisions.

In defining the purpose, objectives will likely follow. Objectives come from having a well-developed purpose. These tools are known as mission and vision statements. Other objectives come from similar statements such as a credo.

A mission statement for the overall business typically answers the question: why are we in business? A **service mission and service vision** are similar but are targeted toward service. The service mission is also known as the service concept.

> **Service Mission/ Service Vision Statement**
> Similar to a traditional vision and mission statement but targeted toward service.

Customer–centric

The premise of placing the customer first in all that a company does. Focusing on pleasing the customer and organizing the company with that as a primary goal.

Mission

A statement that explains the purpose of your business. It is usually a paragraph and states the core purpose of the organization. It should be the origin and foundation of all other decisions for the business. They are written for the customers and employees. It is helpful when evaluating the direction of the company. Topics typically mentioned in mission statements are:

- ▶ Products or services
- ▶ Markets
- ▶ Technology
- ▶ Profit/growth
- ▶ Philosophy
- ▶ Employees
- ▶ Customers

Vision

A statement, usually a sentence or two that explains where a business is striving to go or be in the future. Typically inspirational and sometimes a bit lofty, is used in strategic planning.

Credo

Originally used for professing religious beliefs, was adopted by companies as a passionate label to describe what the organization stood for.

SERVICE INSIGHT

MGM Resorts Mission Statement and Core Beliefs

Our Las Vegas roots are a proud part of our history and a signature element of everything we create, wherever we may go. In our eyes, entertainment is not extracurricular—it's a fundamental human need. Therefore, we exist to ENTERTAIN THE HUMAN RACE.

We accomplish this goal every day through four core beliefs that have long remained tenants of our strategy and operating philosophy:

▶ Develop and create extraordinary experiences.

▶ Provide consistent and outstanding guest service.

▶ Build and sustain the communities in which we work and live.

▶ Be respectful, inclusive, and responsible in all we do.

https://www.mgmresorts.com/en/company.html#/Mission%20and%20Core%20Beliefs

SERVICE INSIGHT

Tyson

Tyson Strategy: Sustainably Feed the World With the Fastest Growing Protein Brands

How they will achieve their strategy is found at this link:

https://www.tysonfoods.com/who-we-are/our-story/purpose-values

SERVICE INSIGHT

Ritz Carlton Credo

Ritz Carlton's Credo can be found at the below link:

http://www.ritzcarlton.com/en/about/gold-standards

A **Service Strategy** is a formula for delivering a service. It is a plan that defines the practical interpretation of service. A strategy is a means of obtaining an objective to fulfill goals. General business strategies are classified by function. Service strategies are more focused on achieving a specific service objective or goal so they are primarily geared toward better serving the customer. Service strategies and general business strategies should complement each other. Both are important in hospitality. Below is an example of a service strategy:

We are committed to delivering superior customer service that meets the needs of the customers in a consistent manner of professionalism. Our commitment to our guests is **SERVICE**:

Satisfaction
Ethical
Respectful
Versatile
Innovative
Communication
Empathy

Service Strategy

Formula for delivering a service that defines the practical interpretation.

Product

In many instances of service, the product is a service. By changing the staff and the systems, you are, in a sense, changing the product. In other situations, better seats, larger screens, better amenities may be needed.

Many businesses offer service guarantees. A **service guarantee** is a promise of satisfaction for your products and services. This is something the customers will see. The staff will be required to memorize it and it will probably be posted somewhere obvious. Examples of this are:

▶ "We will meet the expressed and unexpressed wishes of customers."
▶ "Total customer satisfaction, guaranteed."
▶ "If you're not happy, we'll fix it."
▶ "If you are not 100% satisfied, bring back the unused portion and proof of purchase and we will gladly refund your purchase price."

Cartoon Deciding on Customer Guarantee
© Cartoon Resource/Shutterstock.com

Service Guarantee

A promise of satisfaction for your products and services.

While for many others it is implied that something will be done if the customer is not satisfied with the product and/or the service provided. This usually involves management and a negotiation. A service guarantee is a great gesture.

Is a service guarantee the primary goal of the business? Is that their reason for existence? When developing or evaluating a service guarantee, criteria should be established. Recommendations involve making it believable and easy to comprehend for both customers and employees, and making it easy to invoke without fear. Should it be unconditional? Many would argue that it should at least be appropriate. While a service guarantee will, at times, present difficulties, it should be seen as a tool for improvement. Deming would argue that you should be thanking the customer for bringing to your attention instead of simply leaving disgruntled. Documentation and follow-ups will help to refine your service systems to use these as training topics with the eventual goal of reducing your overall errors.

Plan

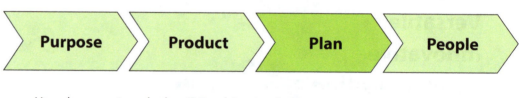

How do you eat an elephant? One bite at a time.

—Bill Hogan, Lluimna Press 2004

How does it meet the objective? The same principle applies; you break it down and begin. It has been said that every great journey begins with a single step.

A plan is filled with thought and good intentions, but is never a sure thing. Instead of thinking of a plan as a "must," think of it as trying to shoot an arrow at a target on a windy day. Conditions keep changing, and you need to adjust as you go.

Service process implementation is the overall mechanics of implementing actual standards in the guest service process. It might be a customer relations plan, how guests will be served, or the actual changes the employees make.

When developing a plan, you must first break it down into pieces. It must be based on the desired objectives and fit with the overall service strategy. It must have guidelines, a timeline, leadership, and clarity.

Timeline

All plans must have a timeline. Each procedure should be calculated and an order of completion clearly stated. It should be realistic, and provide for a margin of error.

Communication

How will everyone know? Everyone must be able to recognize and comprehend the goal. Progress toward objectives cannot be monitored, measured, and achieved if there is a lack of comprehension. Have a slogan. Make it identifiable. Hold a contest or a campaign. Report the status.

Service Process Implementation

The overall mechanics of implementing actual standards in the guest service process.

Guidelines

Revise the employee policies. Ensure that all are aware.

Leadershi

Develop task force. Have a champion. Make it all internal and all line staff and all management or make it cross-functional.

Measurable

You must have some way of measuring outcomes. It can be speed of service, or comment card averages, or a reduction in the number of complaints.

Relatable

The objectives should relate to the service mission.

Obtainable

It must be possible to achieve the goal. Target points set too high can cause the staff and management to become disheartened and frustrated. This leads to a reduction in motivation.

Challenging

Too easy a goal is inefficient, wasting staff and management's full potential. The total cost of the objective should be within reach.

Reengineering

When a process fails to the point at which it should no longer be patched, engineering could be a great alternative in developing a plan. Consider this story. A student cannot afford a car and rides his bicycle to school every day. It has been very rainy lately, so he purchases a raincoat. His pants kept getting wet so he buys fenders for the bike. His backpack still gets wet so he waterproofs it with a trash bag. With process reengineering, he looks at his goal: to get to school. He realizes that he can sell his bicycle and take the bus.

SERVICE INSIGHT

We Have Changed Our Services

Occasionally, businesses will have to change the way that they offer services. Changing employees is difficult enough, and you pay them! Changing the way that customers transact is even more difficult. Most customers can be placed into three different groups:

- ► Customers that mind little or not at all.
- ► Customers that need assistance with the change.
- ► Customers who want it the old way.

Every change is different. Some are smooth and some create a big headache for all. Some businesses incur so much grief that they revert back to the old way. It is trial and error.

What seems obvious to you may not be obvious to others. No matter the change, whether it is self-check-in, a new rule, or a different pattern, customer service representatives should always be readily available for assistance. Don't assume signage and mailings regarding the change will be noticed or understood.

Process reengineering

Process reengineering follows the mantra that making radical changes can have the most impact on achieving the goals.

People

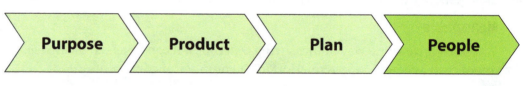

Training

They must have the proper skill sets. Training or retraining is often needed with changes. Many successful organizations promote ongoing employee enrichment.

Attitude

A service culture must be evident. Evoke passion, emotion, and a sense of belonging.

Cultivate in them a feeling of importance. Let them know how their job supports the overall quest to fulfill the objective. Let them know where the business would be without them. Only admit those who instill a sense of pride in their work and take a sense of ownership. Do they call it "theirs"? Do they refer to it as "their hotel"?

Build their confidence. Train, monitor, and reinforce it.

When a staff member is given personal responsibility for achieving a specific goal, they are referred to as a **champion**, or service champion. They would be responsible for organizing all of the efforts to achieve the goal.

Motivation

What are the motivators to change? Incentive? Performance? Bonus? It's your job?

Encourage and support employees to do their job. They must be empowered. Make sure they buy in to the service strategy. They must see a need.

Customers

Don't forget about your customers in this process. How much are they involved in the service process? Some customers prefer to control their service experience. When they are substantially involved, as in the case of self-service, this is referred to as **co-production**. For this to occur, customers themselves need to be comfortable with this process. They must be trained and aware.

❧ WAITING SYSTEMS

Since service is something that cannot be prepared and stored ahead of time, every business experiences service capacity constraints which result in the customers waiting. At best, waiting is perceived by the customer as part of the customer service experience. There is an entire subfield dedicated to the science of

Frustrated Waiting Customer
© CREATISTA/Shutterstock.com

waiting. How we manage the wait will determine the outcome of the overall service experience.

To begin, establish the minimum and maximum allowances for waiting. Ask:

- ▶ How long is too long? Increased value means they will wait longer.
- ▶ Is it socially acceptable? Waiting to get into clubs or restaurants without reservations on a Saturday evening may be considered acceptable, while in other situations it is not.

Depending on your service system, there are many options available:
- ▶ —Single or multiple queue,
- ▶ —take a number queue,
- ▶ —text notifications,
- ▶ —go to the bar,
- ▶ —wait in the lounge,
- ▶ —experience a pre-show,
- ▶ —experience games, snacks, or appetizers . . .

To help assist the waiting experience, below are common tips worth integrating:

- ▶ Occupy them. Occupied time feels shorter than unoccupied time.
- ▶ Reduce anxiety and make them comfortable. Anxiety makes waits seem longer.
- ▶ Groups are better than solo waits.

- Provide known wait times. Uncertain waits are longer than known waits.
- Provide knowledge of the waiting system. Explain or communicate the process so they understand the system. Unfair waits appear longer than equitable waits.
- Can they pre-order?
- Benchmark others to see what they do well. Learn the industry standard. What other industries or sectors have wait solutions that you can adopt?
- Surprise them. Give them something extra/unexpected.

RESOURCE VIEWPOINT

A resource is something that can be tapped into and worked with to create something even more valuable. Consider crude oil in the ground. It is worth marginal value per barrel, but if you refined it you can do so many more things with it. It can become diesel fuel, gasoline, jet fuel, or even a multitude of plastics and other petroleum-based products.

Resources in business and hospitality are the same way. The **resource viewpoint** states that every hospitality business has three main resources:

> **Resource Viewpoint**
>
> The idea that every business has three resources upon which to work with and use to their benefit.

- Human Resources
- Financial Resources
- Physical Resources

Human resources is the most important resource of all. It is also the most variable, the least controllable, and the least efficient.

Financial resources are the dollars that move through the business. They are the most closely regulated. Bank deposits are made daily. Financial Accountants and Revenue Managers precisely calculate, predict, and control every facet of the stream of revenue through a business.

Physical Resources consist of all of the tables, seats, beds, planes, rooms, buildings, screens, monitors, and technology in a business. They are controlled and monitored to produce optimal efficiency while balancing costs and demand.

Every decision involves the allocation of resources in some sense. In a way, the manager is constantly managing and balancing resources. Increasing guest service is not free. It involves retraining and monitoring. Sometimes, an increase in staff is necessary. It usually involves a demand in physical resources for nicer seats or infrastructure, which in turn places a greater demand on financial resources. Ideally, the manager should be working with each of the three main resources to build them up just as you would refine crude oil to make other more valuable products.

❧ CHAPTER REVIEW QUESTIONS

1. List the three components of strategy.
2. Explain why strategy is both important but natural.
3. Outline the basic concept of continuous improvement.
4. What is the strategic service system?
5. What are the three resources common to most all businesses?
6. List at least three tips for developing waiting systems.
7. What is the benefit of conducting a SWOT analysis?
8. List and explain three different levels of competition.
9. List and describe four elements included in developing service process implementation."
10. What is the best advice that you could provide for a property about to experience a renovation?

CASE STUDIES

Emily's Farm House Chicken

Emily's is a small restaurant located in the Midwest. It features fried chicken in an old farmhouse. Locals and those from the surrounding area patronize Emily's for homemade chicken and dumplings. White gravy is a specialty. Emily's has a very limited menu, but it has worked well in the past. People that were fortunate enough to get in to the small dining room/living room are served family-style, all-you-can-eat chicken for one low price. Places like Emily's populated the Midwest and South for many decades. They were successful until cities developed and chain restaurants offered many more choices at competitive prices. While Emily's still holds a loyal clientele, the experience of eating homemade cooking in a small, old farmhouse is slowly beginning to lose the interest of some patrons. Carol, Emily's daughter and long-time employee of Emily's, noticed this change. She mentioned it to Emily who told her, "Don't fix it if it ain't broken." Carol tried to explain that it was beginning to be broken and that if you don't look toward the future now, it will soon be too late.

1. Evaluate Carol's mindset.
2. Was Carol thinking strategically? Explain.
3. At this rate, predict the future of Emily's in 10 years.

Sheila's Spa

You could say that Sheila's whole life was about spas. Her mother owned one when she was younger. Sheila had always worked at spas since high school. She went to a local college and took classes on Spa Management. She delighted in traveling to destination spas for vacations, and now she finally has her chance at owning and operating her very own spa.

She has spent countless hours exploring the options. She wanted just the right everything! She kept a journal detailing her experiences at various spas around the world. She had saved all of her plans from her class projects at college. She went to the bookstore and bought every book available on spas. She even found a few computer programs that allowed her to play spa simulations. It was a labor of love. Everything would be perfect!

Sheila decided to begin the interview process, so she set up a series of interviews. She interviewed all candidates at least twice. She used a behavioral interview for the finalists, then went to their past employers and clients to verify firsthand. Some candidates had as many as six interviews.

She went to shows and warehouses and shopped online, observing literally every product on the market relating to spas.

She used a computer program to lay out the spa and projected her earnings for her business plan. Her banker asked her when she planned to open. Although her financial situation was still in great standing, Sheila told him that she did not yet want to open until everything was perfect. She believed that if you open and it isn't perfect, then customers will not return. During the next few weeks, a few of her new hires took positions at competing spas. Things were very close to opening, but Sheila feared they weren't quite perfect.

1. Assess Sheila's planning technique.
2. What issues do you foresee in Sheila's planning?
3. What advice would you provide for Sheila?

Rusty's Emporium

Russell (Rusty) Donovan loved having fun. He scraped together enough money to buy an old factory and begin Rusty's Emporium 15 years ago when he was in his 20s. Rusty's motto has always been, "Have fun." Rusty's Emporium is an entertainment center. Over the years, Rusty had filled his Emporium with a multitude of attractions. He went to auctions and acquired many items. Some are displayed and used, while others are sitting out back with large blue tarps over them.

Rusty began with laser tag and an arcade, but has grown to include a skateboard park, paintball, trampolines, rock climbing, a pool with a slide, four hot tubs, miniature golf, a foam pit, a carousel, and a snack bar. Most recently, he began hosting kids' birthday parties.

Things have become busy with the parties and all of the other attractions but the growth has also brought problems. Very different crowds of people attend the different attractions and they don't always blend. He is having difficulty maintaining the different attractions, and they often spill over from one to another. He can no longer oversee the Emporium himself, so he has had to hire more staff and incur more expense. It is difficult to predict what attraction will be busy so staffing has become difficult. His revenue has increased, but is becoming overshadowed by his costs. This was originally a fun place that Rusty enjoyed and now it is a disorganized mess.

1. Evaluate Rusty's strategic plan.
2. What has Rusty done correctly?
3. What advice could you provide for Rusty at this point?

Hal's Diner

Hal is a veteran of the food service industry. He is self-taught, beginning his career washing dishes at age 9 in his father's diner. Everyone knew this because he told them about it nearly every day. Hal recently opened Hal's Diner with his own savings. He served typical diner Greek food that he had always served. He knew it all very well. A few other diners also scraped out a meager existence within the downtown area, but Hal believed that his would somehow be the best.

Jason was hired as a waiter. He waited tables, but was much more than a waiter. Jason was studying to be a food service manager in college and was a very bright and talented young man. He was working his way through school and took on night shifts to make ends meet. Late one evening when things were slow, Hal struck up a conversation with Jason. He asked him if they ever taught anything like this at his school. Jason wasn't sure what to say because Hal was very outspoken. Hal pressed further, "I see you watching everything. How do you think I am doing?"

Jason decided to speak his mind. "Hal, you are a veteran of the industry and I respect that, but times are changing and you have to have a plan for it. Customer service and monitoring the competition are important. You cannot simply think that you are somehow unique with what you are doing."

Hal's face turned bright red and his fists clinched. "I have been doing this for 53 years. You kids think that you know so much. The competition has nothing on me and the customers who don't like it can go down the road."

1. Who was correct, Jason or Hal?
2. Assess Hal's Diner compared to the competition.
3. What can be done to help Hal?

❖ EXERCISES

Exercise 1: SWOT Analysis

Directions: Choose a local hospitality company and complete the SWOT Information Chart below.

Company Name: _____

Internal Components	Strength or Weakness?	Substantiation
Operations		
Marketing		
Employees		
Management		
Research & Development		
Market—Customers		
Technology		
Competition		
Economy		
Legal—Politically		

Exercise 2: Vision/Mission Review

Directions: For the purpose of this exercise, use the vision, mission, credo, and any other motto that the company publishes. Choose a hospitality company that interests you. Review their Vision/Mission Statements and attach them to the back of this assignment. Complete the questions below.

Company Name: _____

1. What is the one line that sums up what the company stands for?
2. What is the main priority of the company?
3. How many times is customer/guest service mentioned?
4. What would you change, remove, or add to the statements?

Exercise 3: The Strategic Service System

Directions: Relate the Strategic Service System to a business in the local area. Outline your responses below:

Business Name: _____

Type of Business: _____

1. Purpose:
2. Product:
3. Plan:
4. People:

Chapter 11

Quality Tools

CHAPTER OBJECTIVES

After reading this chapter, you should be able to:

► Identify the basic procedures of research methodology.
► Identify and apply various quality research tools and techniques.
► Construct a research assessment utilizing appropriate quality tools and techniques.
► Assess and improve a process properly utilizing quality techniques.

TERMINOLOGY

Affinity Diagram
Baseline Measurements
Benchmarking
Brainstorming
Check Sheets
Control Chart
Cost-Benefit Analysis
Cost of Error
Delphi Method
Fishbone Analysis
Flowcharts Diagram

Focus Group
Force Field Analysis
Gantt Chart
Kano Model
Multi-Voting
Net Promoter
    Score (NPS)
Pareto Chart
Poka-Yoke
Process Reengineering
Pros-Cons Sheet

Quality Assessment Tools
    and Techniques
Risk Matrix
Root Cause Analysis/
    5 Why's
Scatter Diagram
Secret Shoppers
SERVQUAL
Six Sigma
Surveys

Introduction

In the management of service, you will have to do much research. It isn't usually formal and you probably won't be wearing a white lab coat. The term "research" means investigating, thinking about it logically, and determining a solution. Quality tools are the vehicles for doing just that. Tools are the keys to unlock the doors of mystery. They provide organization, logic, clarity, and insight well past what the mind could do on its own.

In quality research it is often more than seeking a conclusion to a question or problem. You may want to investigate an issue, you might want to perform a scientific study, or you might want to learn about the effectiveness of procedures and tools.

This chapter is divided into three main sections. The first section discusses the foundations of performing research. The second section discusses the use of tools and techniques used in the service industry. The third section covers external awards and certifications common to the hospitality industry.

Setting up for Research

Research is anything but haphazard. It is a formal process. It is scientific. It follows a set of steps that allow it to be standardized and critiqued for validity. In setting up for research, there are criteria that need to be established to ensure a successful experiment. We can refer to these casually as the why, what, who, and how of research experiments. Their more formal labels and explanations are listed below.

☆ WHY: COLLECT BACKGROUND INFORMATION

Collecting background information is crucial to any research. It identifies areas of concerns which help to establish a starting point and build a case for the direction of future investigation. Without it, you are shooting in the dark.

You can begin an analysis by asking questions such as:

- ► Are you providing wants and needs?
- ► What's involved in your service?
- ► What is good, what is bad, and what can be changed?
- ► How consistent can you be?
- ► What are the newest trends?

Baseline Measurements

"Before" measurements that describe a situation or condition prior to intervention.

You should also take **baseline measurements**. These are "before" measurements that describe a situation or condition prior to intervention. Baseline measurements are helpful in monitoring growth or change after you make changes.

Another source of background information could be from your customer complaints. It could be helpful to turn each one into just one word or a few short words.

You could also hold a focus group or simply just listen to your staff because they probably have some great answers.

WHAT: DETERMINE WHAT TO MEASURE

The Who, What, When, Where, and How of Research
© Yabresse/Shutterstock.com

After background information has been conducted, the information must be sorted and analyzed. This is when the real direction takes place. The end product of this step is having the primary areas to measure. All suggestions should be considered in determining the primary areas.

Examples of this could be:

▶ Empowerment
▶ Customer service
▶ Communication
▶ Job security
▶ Price
▶ Wait times
▶ Speed of service
▶ Consistency
▶ Problem resolution

WHO: CHOOSE THE POPULATION

After you know what to measure, you need to determine who to measure. This may seem straightforward, but the details need to be considered and rules must be established. Something even as simple as measuring the customers may become an issue:

▶ Do you want former, current, and potential customers?
▶ Can you measure every customer every time?
▶ What if they are repeat customers?
▶ What if you cannot reach them or they refuse?
▶ What if they purchase a lot, or a little, or their transaction is voided?

As you are setting this up, you should also determine how the population will be divided. For example, it could be divided by demographic or psychographic:

▶ **Demographic:** Age, income, marital status, education, stage in family life cycle, home ownership, gender, zip code, occupation, household size and type, travel patterns, ethnicity, religion.

▶ **Psychographic:** Lifestyles, mode of living, needs, attitudes, reference groups, culture, class, family influences, hobbies, political affiliation.

HOW: CHOOSE THE METHOD AND MEASUREMENT

After laying the background work and determining what and who to measure, the rest of the experimental research typically follows a logical path. The "how" completes the classic research format. Meaning, research is typically conducted using this methodology. It has six steps and will take much diligence to complete, but will likely yield superior results.

1. Choose instrument type
   a. Tools
   b. Techniques
2. Adapt the tool or technique
3. Pilot-test
   a. Trial-run of your experiment
   b. On a smaller scale
4. Revise based on results of the pilot test
5. Administer the experiment
6. Interpret the data

Tools and Techniques

Quality Assessment Tools and Techniques

A research instrument used to target, analyze, develop, or evaluate a service system.

There are many **quality assessment tools and techniques**. These can be used in experiments and in every step of the quality service process.

Quality assessments, tools, and techniques can be divided into four main groups by their purpose. They are used for specific reasons depending upon your needs. The four main purposes are to:

1. Target an opportunity for improvement
2. Analyze the area targeted for improvement
3. Develop and implement improvements
4. Evaluate improvements

Primary Uses for Quality Assessment Tools and Techniques

Some tools can be used in more than one group.

Target an opportunity for improvement

▶ Define the process, identify and describe the problem

▶ These are tools that analyze processes or that determine current conditions

▶ They help to write a problem statement or specify areas for improvement. They help to prevent misunderstandings. This forms a foundation for objective analysis.

Analyze the area targeted for improvement

▶ Determine cause

▶ These are tools that assist understanding areas for improvement. They could also help to classify quality issues and analyze the preliminary data.

▶ They help to assess:
  ☐ Importance to guests
  ☐ Importance to management
  ☐ Importance to staff
  ☐ Control over the improvement area

Develop and implement improvements

▶ Determine and implement solutions

▶ These are tools that identify, select, and implement potential solutions

▶ They can help to develop an action plan that has:
  ☐ Acceptance by guests
  ☐ Acceptance by management
  ☐ Acceptance by staff
  ☐ Cost-effectiveness
  ☐ Timelines of implementation
  ☐ Practicality of implementation

Evaluate improvements

▶ Assess the changes

▶ These are tools that assist in evaluating the impact of the changes or solutions. They include many different sources of feedback to assess questions such as:
  ☐ Did the changes work?
  ☐ Am I asking the right questions?
  ☐ How do I know?
  ☐ Can I trust this information?

This next section will detail many of the quality assessment tools and techniques common to the quality service research process. There are still references in literature that detail the 7 Original Tools of Quality: check sheets, control charts, fishbones, flowcharts, histograms, Pareto Charts, and Scatter Diagrams. While these seven tools are covered in the section, they were not the original, nor are there only seven. In fact, there are many more than seven quality tools.

Quality Management Collage
© serato/Shutterstock.com

They are listed next in alphabetical order. A brief definition is provided followed by a display of their place in the research process along with tips of when they are most useful. Additionally, basic instructions are provided along with an example of most. This should help to place them into a context of how, where, and when they could be best used.

AFFINITY DIAGRAM

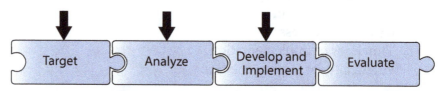

Definition: A process that sorts ideas into categories for further interpretation.

Helpful when: Analyzing verbal data or too many facts or ideas are in need of sorting.

Time	Cost	Labor	Difficulty
Low	Low	Medium	Low

Instructions:

1. Brainstorm, collect, or assemble different ideas for potential problems, causes, errors, or reasons.
2. Record each idea on a sticky note, on a whiteboard, or in a similar fashion.
3. Begin to place in groups. Look for relationships and commonalities.
4. Begin to develop and refine labels for groups. Look for primary and subgroups. Make duplicates if ideas belong in both groups.

Step 2: Record each idea on a sticky note, on a whiteboard, or in a similar fashion.
© REDPIXEL PL/Shutterstock.com

Step 3: Begin to place in groups. Look for relationships and commonalities.
© REDPIXEL PL/Shutterstock.com

Benchmarking Collage
© master_art/Shutterstock.com

BENCHMARKING

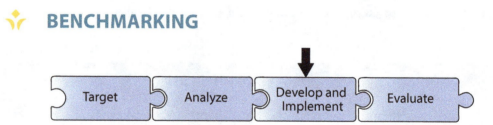

Definition: A comparison of best practice methods.

Helpful when: You need to find the best way that a process is performed.

Time	Cost	Labor	Difficulty
Medium	Medium	Medium	Medium

Instructions:

1. Determine process that needs improvement.
2. Determine who will be compared (benchmarked). This should ideally be with another business who is the "best-in-class" at this process. They may be a competitor or even in another industry.
3. Analyze what makes them best.
4. Adapt and adopt findings.

BRAINSTORMING

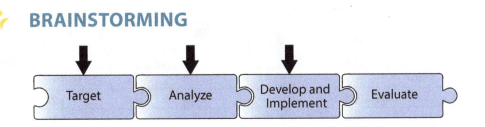

Definition: Free-form thinking to generate ideas.

Helpful when: Use when trying to obtain a wide range of ideas or options.

Time	Cost	Labor	Difficulty
Medium	Low	Medium	Low

Instructions:

1. Gather participants. Any size group will work, but larger is more difficult.
2. Present participants with issue for thought.
3. Give participants 2–5 minutes of silence to think and make notes.
4. Give everyone a chance to speak at least a few different times.
5. Accurately record all ideas on board without judgment.
6. Process answers by seeking trends, eliminating duplicates, and so on. Also see "Affinity Diagram."

CHECK SHEETS

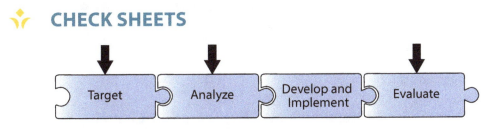

Definition: Tabulation of frequency for repeated data.

Helpful when: Collecting and analyzing repeated data like counting number of cars at the valet station every 5 minutes.

Time	Cost	Labor	Difficulty
Low	Low	Low	Low

Instructions:

1. Determine what data will be observed.
2. Determine how the data will be observed. It should be measured the same way at the same location, at appropriate and consistent times.
3. Trial test for measuring or methodology errors prior to actual use.

	Renovation Complaints					
	Day					
Reason	**Mon**	**Tue**	**Wed**	**Thurs**	**Fri**	**Total**
Noise	LIIIIII	III	II	L	0	12
Mess	LII	II	III	LIIIIII	II	17
Eyesore	LII	III	I	LIIIII	I	14
Congestion	LII	0	0	LII	0	6
Other	LI	0	0	LII	0	5
Total	17	8	6	20	3	54

❖ CONTROL CHART

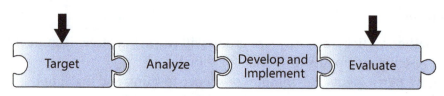

Definition: Measure of deviations of processes over a period of time. Other name: Statistical Process Control (SPC).

Helpful when: Looking at varying data over time.

Time	**Cost**	**Labor**	**Difficulty**
High	Low	Medium	Medium

Instructions:

1. Determine data to be measured.
2. Determine control (average or ideal) line.
3. Determine Upper Control Limit (UCL) and Lower Control Limit (LCL) that indicates when measurement is unacceptable or out-of-control.
4. Trial test for measuring or methodology errors prior to actual use.

Control Chart

Upper Control Limit

Lower Control Limit

Control Chart
© Dusit/Shutterstock.com

COST-BENEFIT ANALYSIS

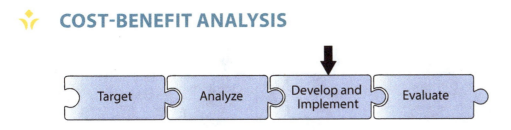

Target → Analyze → Develop and Implement → Evaluate

Definition: Used to decide whether an idea or project is cost-worthy.

Helpful when: Financial implications are a main priority. It answers whether it is worth it from a purely financial standpoint.

Time	Cost	Labor	Difficulty
Medium	Low	Low	Medium

Instructions:

1. Determine total costs associated with idea. Consider costs at all levels present and future. Some of these may be difficult to quantify, such as time and satisfaction.
2. Determine total benefits associated with idea. The same qualities apply to these as in costs. Some of these areas, such as frustration, may be difficult to quantify.
3. Compare the results of each total against each other. This can be done as a one-cost and savings or annual costs, or both.
4. When comparing, you will encounter a break-even point. You must decide what is acceptable. In the case below, it is just under 3 years, which is likely acceptable since the system has a projected life of 11+ years.

New Property Management System	
Costs:	
System	$25,000
Installation	$2,300
Training 200 staff hours @ $12/hour =	$2,400
Training 70 staff hours @ $20/hour =	$1,400
Trainers 15 hours @$45/hour =	$600
Ancillary costs $	$1,200
Total costs:	$32,900
Benefits:	
Reduction of incorrect orders voided	$5,000 / year
Improved inventory efficiency estimate	$2,000 / year
Improved ordering efficiency estimate	$3,000 / year
Reduction of system maintenance costs	$1,200 / year
Total Benefits:	$11,200 / year
Payback:	$32,900 / $11,200 = 2.9375 years

COST OF ERROR

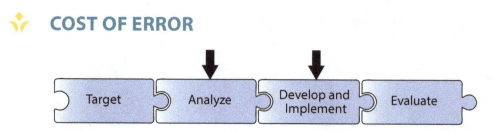

Definition: The total amount of costs associated with a customer service mistake or losing the customer.

Helpful when: Reviewing consequences of errors in processes.

Time	Cost	Labor	Difficulty
Medium	Low	Low	Medium

Discussion:

When you find a problem, simply locating it may not be enough. It is important to determine the extent to which a problem exists and costs. What are the true consequences? Consider the iceberg analogy. With icebergs, only a small portion of it might be visible above the water. There is often a huge amount of the iceberg just below the water. To add, as it erodes away in the water, an iceberg can suddenly flip over, causing your experience with the iceberg to change dramatically. To conclude, it is important to know the extent of the issue that you are dealing with because, while all problems are important, some may be worse than others.

Instructions:

1. Determine process to be measured.
2. Calculate amount of errors in set period of time.
3. Calculate total costs associated with error.

Example of Error

- ▶ Lines too long for customer to wait.
- ▶ Occurs to two patrons per night.
- ▶ 2 patrons × 315 days open per year = 630 lost customers per year.
- ▶ 630 × $15.38 check average per person = $9,689.40 per year.
- ▶ Other expenses that are more difficult to quantify: poor word of mouth, loss of tips.
- ▶ This can also be done in a hotel setting based on a percentage of error.

Cost of Error Example

- ▶ 0.5% customers leave because of a type of error.
- ▶ 0.5% × 400 rooms = 2 rooms per night per day.
- ▶ 2 rooms per night × 365 days = 730 nights
- ▶ 730 nights × 80 occupancy = 584 room nights per year
- ▶ 584 room nights × $89.65 average daily rate = $52,355.60 per year.

(Note: there are typically other expenses that are difficult to quantify such as loss of reputation.)

Additional Costs

- ► Lost time of workers
- ► Amenity/gift
- ► Add-space loss of revenue
- ► Percentage for loss of ancillary services that may have been consumed

Additional Non-Financial Costs

- ► Brand loss
- ► Frustrated employees that might leave or deliver less service to others

DELPHI METHOD

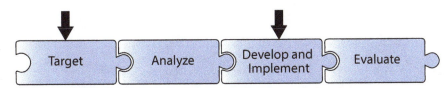

Definition: A method of gaining group consensus.

Helpful when: You need to get a group to make a decision. Members avoid having to publicly defend their decision and are free to change their minds after reading the responses of others.

Time	Cost	Labor	Difficulty
Medium	Low	Medium	Medium

Instructions:

1. Expert participants are selected and given a problem. They are asked to comment on it in bullet form and not share responses.
2. The results are collected, tabulated, then handed out anonymously and in summative form.
3. The participants consider the group responses and repeated for more bullet statements or rated on a devised scale.
4. The results are again shared with all.

Comment	Score (1 is low, 5 is high) [previous score in square brackets] (number is how many people scored in this column)				
	1	2	3	4	5
New logo has retro appeal		1[3]	5[3]	1[2]	2[1]
New logo has fresh look	1[2]	4[3]	2[1]	1[2]	
New logo mimics competitors	1[1]	5[5]	2[2]		

SERVICE INSIGHT

Group Consensus

Not everyone in a group will always get their first choice. When a group must make a decision, it is unlikely that everyone will agree on precisely the same choice. The idea of group consensus means that everyone doesn't have to believe a choice is perfect or that it is their top choice. Instead, they believe it is reasonable. They understand the group as a whole believes it is the best choice or blend. Consensus means they will support it and they will not stand in the way of the choice at this time or in the future. Sometimes, group consensus is the best that we can hope for.

FISHBONE ANALYSIS

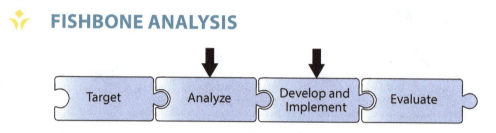

Definition: Identifies potential causes for a problem in categories. Other names: Ishikawa Diagram, Cause-and-effect diagram, Problem Analysis.

Helpful when: Identifying problems or causes for a multifaceted issue.

Time	Cost	Labor	Difficulty
Medium	Medium	Medium	Medium

Instructions:

1. Write down problem or effect.
2. Set up with generic headings as applicable to your situation. Make them branches from the main arrow (problem). Typical headings are: Methods, Materials, People, and Equipment. Measurement and Environment are also sometimes used as additional headings.
3. In each heading ask, "Why does this happen?" and record the reason.
4. Continue to ask, and broaden the branch as the reasons expand and deepen. The branches extend to indicate causal relationships.

Discussion:

The labels will be specific and unique to the operation and application. Below are some typical examples of Fishbone Analysis Labels:

4 P's for Service Industries

- ▶ Equipment
- ▶ People
- ▶ Procedures
- ▶ Materials

8 P's for Service Industries

- ▶ Physical evidence
- ▶ People
- ▶ Place
- ▶ Product/Service
- ▶ Productivity
- ▶ Process
- ▶ Promotion
- ▶ Price

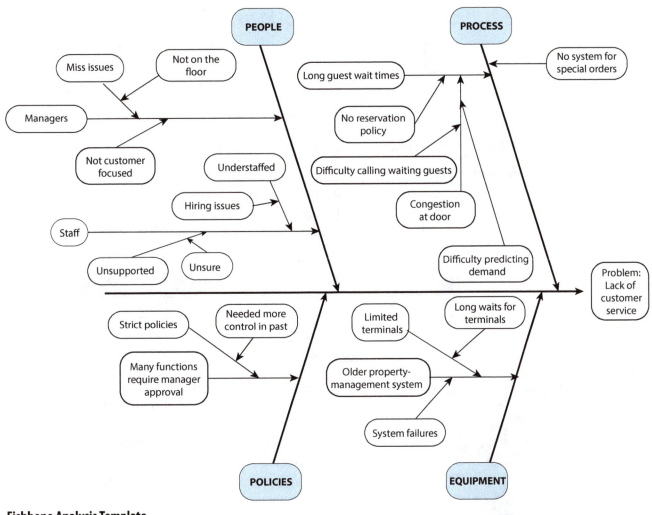

Fishbone Analysis Template
© Kendall Hunt Publishing Company

4 P's for Problem-Solving
- Environment
- People
- Products
- Process

4 P's for Manufacturing Industries
- People
- Machines
- Materials
- Methods
- (5th P = Measurement)

8 M's for Manufacturing Industries
- Machines/Technology
- Maintenance
- Management/Money Power
- Manpower/Human Resources
- Materials
- Measurement/Inspection
- Method/Process
- Mother Nature/Environment

FLOWCHARTS DIAGRAM

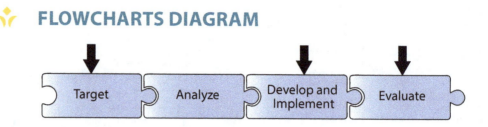

Definition: A graphic account of sequential steps in a process.

Helpful when:

▶ You need to break down each step to analyze a process
▶ Everyone needs to be together on a process
▶ Showing where a process speeds up, slows, and has other issues
▶ Training

Time	Cost	Labor	Difficulty
Medium	Low	Medium	Medium

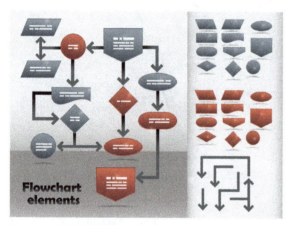

Flowchart Illustration
© Janos Levente/Shutterstock.com

Instructions:

1. Define process or inter-relating processes.
2. Determine beginning and ending points of the process.
3. Determine all steps and options within the process.
4. Diagram each step and option using the appropriate symbol.
5. Connect using appropriate symbols.

There is no universally-accepted legend of symbols but commonly-accepted meanings of symbols are as follows:

☐ Ovals or circles = beginning and endings
☐ Rectangles = typical processes
☐ Diamonds or triangles = decisions
☐ Arrows demonstrate flow of the process

SERVICE INSIGHT

Bottleneck

A bottleneck is a metaphor used to describe a type of issue in flowcharts. Just like the neck of the bottle constricts, forcing the liquid to gather and slow before exiting the bottle and completing the pour, so does a bottleneck slow the process in a flowchart. If you look around, you will notice many bottlenecks, like many people waiting to check out with only one register open.

FOCUS GROUP

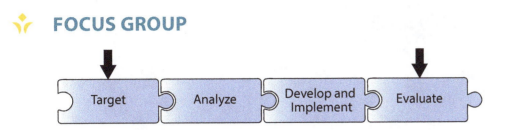

Target → Analyze → Develop and Implement → Evaluate

Definition: Qualitative (verbal) research in which a group (usually 4–11) are surveyed about their ideas and opinion toward a certain product, company, or field.

Helpful when: You need in-depth data from respondents.

Time	Cost	Labor	Difficulty
High	High	High	High

Description:

Focus groups are typically conducted by a Focus Group Facilitator, a trained professional who has superior communication and group skills.

It is qualitative research in which a group (usually 4–11) is verbally surveyed regarding their ideas and opinion toward a certain product or company. This method generates in-depth data from individuals that is difficult to obtain through alternative methods. A trained moderator leads the discussion. The group meets in a special room so that ideas can all be recorded and later interpreted. Each group lasts typically 30–120 minutes. Focus group participants are usually given a token gift in appreciation of their time. The moderator may conduct one or several different groups on the same topics.

Focus Group
© Roman Samborskyi/Shutterstock.com

FORCE FIELD ANALYSIS

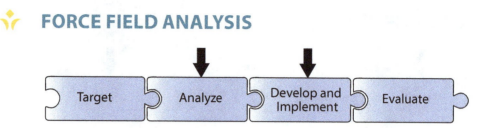

Target	Analyze	Develop and Implement	Evaluate

Definition: A technique for analyzing the forces that help and hurt a decision.

Helpful when: Determining and examining what is helping you and what is hurting you regarding a decision. Pros-Cons Sheets examine the product of a decision while this examines the other factors that may enable or disable your efforts in pursuing the decision.

Time	Cost	Labor	Difficulty
Medium	Low	Medium	Medium

Instructions:

1. List the decision in the middle of the page.
2. On the left, label: Forces for Change.
3. On the right, label: Forces Against Change.
4. Brainstorm and fill in both sides of the page with bullet statements (forces).
5. Rate each of the forces from 1 = (weak) to 5 = (strong).
6. Tabulate and interpret your findings, deciding whether or not your plan is sufficient given the forces for and against it.

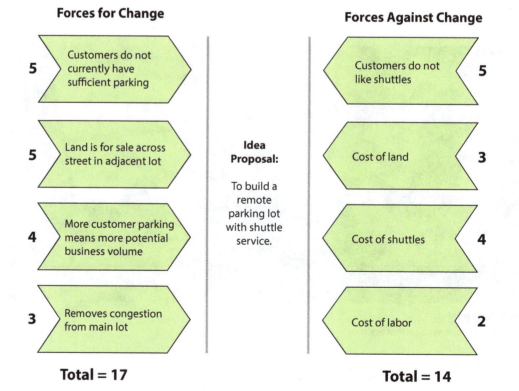

Forces for Change

5 — Customers do not currently have sufficient parking

5 — Land is for sale across street in adjacent lot

4 — More customer parking means more potential business volume

3 — Removes congestion from main lot

Total = 17

Idea Proposal:

To build a remote parking lot with shuttle service.

Forces Against Change

Customers do not like shuttles — 5

Cost of land — 3

Cost of shuttles — 4

Cost of labor — 2

Total = 14

GANTT CHART

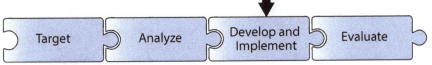

Definition: A project planning tool that clarifies who does what and by when.

Helpful when: You are setting up a project that requires coordination with others.

Time	Cost	Labor	Difficulty
High	Low	Medium	Medium

This tool helps to plan projects. It was developed by Gantt. A Performance Evaluation and Review Technique (PERT) is similar in that both are visualization charts intended to clarify and organize people, responsibilities, and due dates.

PERT was developed in the 1950s by the US Navy. It is very similar, but typically takes on more of a flowchart in appearance.

Instructions:

1. Determine tasks of project.
2. Determine order of these tasks and which tasks need to be completed before others can begin.
3. Determine due dates of tasks.
4. Determine who will be responsible for each task.
5. Apply steps 1–4 to the chart.

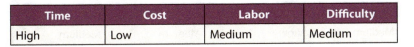

Week	0	1	2	3	4	5	6	7	8	9	10	11	12
Identify benchmarks to study	▬												
Present to Board of Directors		▬											
Devise team and set parameters		▬▬▬											
Present to Board sub-committee				●									
Develop details for pilot study				▬									
Conduct trial research				▬									
Process trial research findings					▬▬▬								
Set up major study details				▬									
Conduct research						▬─							
Process research findings						▬───							
Identify current business process									───				
Identify differences									──				
Outline new process									───				
Finalize new process											●		
Send to printing											──		
Present new process plan to Board of Directors											──		

▬▬▬ **Finished**   ─── **Unfinished**   ● **Presentation**

KANO MODEL

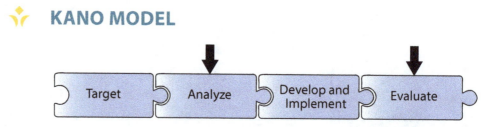

Definition: A tool that categorizes and evaluates levels of customer needs.

Helpful when: Trying to meet or exceed customer expectations.

Time	Cost	Labor	Difficulty
Medium	Low	Medium	Medium

Instructions:

1. Determine and categorize the needs of the customers. This might be achieved through use of a Focus Group or a Survey with a 5-Point Likert Scale.

2. Categorize data into three types of customer needs:
   - ☐ Expected needs (basic service requirements)
   - ☐ Expressed needs (typically conveyed from the customers before or during the transaction)
   - ☐ Excitement needs (extra, unexpected characteristics that are beyond expectations)

3. Determine one of three options to do with this data:
   - ☐ Improve (make existing better)
   - ☐ Innovate (develop new options)
   - ☐ Leave alone (it is presently sufficient)

Discussion:

These needs must be reassessed because they can shift over time. As a result, your business must be continuously monitoring the needs of the guest and creating new ways to please the guest in order to keep a competitive advantage.

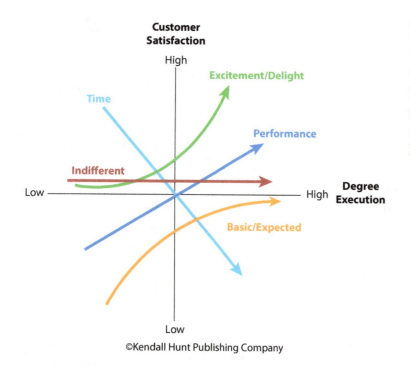

MULTI-VOTING

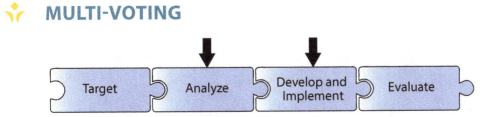

Definition: Prioritizes and narrows a large number of decisions to reflect the general favorite of the group. Other names: nominal prioritization.

Helpful when: A group must make a decision and equal input from all is a necessity.

Time	Cost	Labor	Difficulty
Medium	Low	Medium	Low

Instructions:

1. List all decisions or options, omitting duplication.
2. Determine a number of votes each participant will be given (ex: 5 votes each).
3. Each participant in the group will rank order their top choice (ex: 5 = top choice, 4 = second best choice, and so on).
4. Collect and tally all votes. The highest number is the group preferred choice.
5. This may be done once or with a few elimination rounds.

Votes in rank order:		
Kathy's votes: 4, 9, 12, 2, 8 Richard's votes: 11, 8, 15, 12, 11		
Carol's votes: 6, 11, 12, 9, 15 Patrick's votes: 8, 6, 11, 11, 4		
Kelly's votes: 2, 9, 14, 4, 6		
1. balloons	6. radio 5 + 1 + 4 = 11	11. celebrity 1 + 3 = 4
2. banners 2 + 5 = 7	7. television	12. food 3 + 3 + 2 = 8
3. neon	8. airplane banner 1 + 4 + 5 = 11	13. carnival
4. spotlight 5 + 2 + 1 = 8	9. LinkedIn 4 + 2 + 4 = 11	14. giveaway 3
5. spokesman	10. Facebook 4 + 5 + 2 = 11	15. open house 1 + 3 = 4

NET PROMOTER SCORE (NPS)

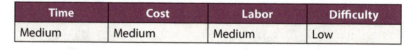

Definition: A measure of customer and employee loyalty, or how likely they are to recommend a product/service.

Helpful when: Monitoring customer satisfaction.

Time	Cost	Labor	Difficulty
Medium	Medium	Medium	Low

Instructions:

1. Customers are surveyed to determine how likely they are to recommend a product or service. The results of the survey are scored on a Likert scale of 0 to 11, with 11 being the most likely to recommend.
2. Results are then segmented into three categories as being a Promoter (9–11), Passive (7–8), or a Detractor (6 or lower).
3. Detractor percentages are then subtracted from Promoters percentages to obtain a Net Promoter Score.

Discussion:

This tool was invented by Fred Reicheld of Bain & Company. The idea of customer loyalty is highly correlated with the intent to return, and loyalty is typically tied to increased operating efficiency and profit, although never guaranteed.

PARETO CHART

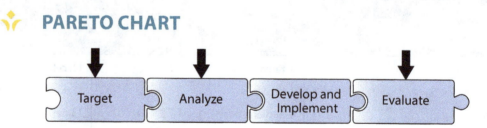

Definition: A bar graph that displays frequency of time, errors, or money.

Premise: Limitations prevent you from fixing every cause. The idea is that it displays the cumulative amount of errors the solutions would solve.

The Pareto Principle contains an 80/20 rule that states that 80% of the issues are caused by just 20% of the issues. This is an estimation, but the general idea holds true in many cases. In layman terms, "What gives you the best bang for your buck?"

Helpful when: Deciding on which problem/cause to focus on to resolve the most issues.

Time	Cost	Labor	Difficulty
Medium	Low	Medium	Medium

Instructions:

1. Construct a bar chart of categories of causes.
2. Arrange the categories (bars) in descending order.
3. Draw a line displaying the cumulative total.
4. Draw conclusions from the chart regarding percentage of problems.

Example: If you could only fix two of the five categories, how much of the errors would be resolved?

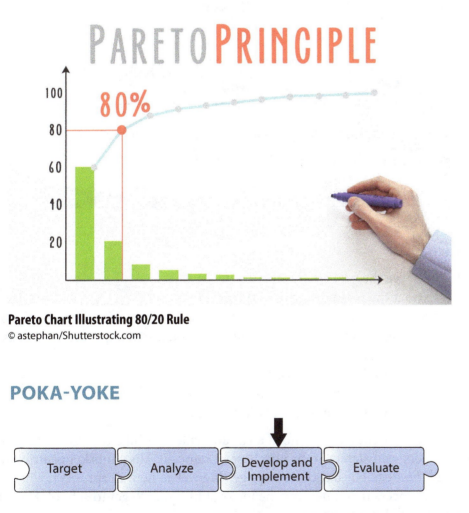

Pareto Chart Illustrating 80/20 Rule
© astephan/Shutterstock.com

POKA-YOKE

Target → Analyze → Develop and Implement → Evaluate

Definition: A system that helps to self-correct itself. Poka-Yokes are everywhere that you look. We take most of them for granted. They are engineered fail-safe systems.

Other names: Fail-proofing, mistake-proofing.

Helpful when: A process, function, or system is prone to a certain error.

Time	Cost	Labor	Difficulty
Medium	Medium	Medium	High

We see Poka-Yoke every day and do not realize it. Examples might be an overflow drain on a sink; a guard on a piece of safety equipment; or, a computer asking you if you want to save the file before exiting the program.

Instructions:

1. Observe the system for errors.
2. Select an error.
3. Revise the system to avoid or disallow the mistake to be made.

PROCESS REENGINEERING

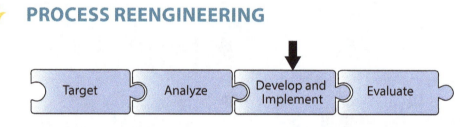

Definition: A dramatic redesign of a system, process, or business.

Helpful when: You require out-of-the-box thinking.

Time	Cost	Labor	Difficulty
High	High	High	High

Instructions:

1. Observe the process.
2. Extract the main purpose of the process.
3. Seek to engineer alternative methods to achieve main purpose of process.
4. Thoroughly review every step, asking fundamental questions such as:
    a. Why is it done?
    b. Does it have to be done?
    c. Is that the only way it could be done?
    d. Is that the best way it could be done?

Example: A student cannot afford a car and rides his bike to school every day. It has been very rainy lately, so he purchases a raincoat. His pants kept getting wet so he installs fenders. His backpack kept getting wet so he waterproofs it with a trash bag. With process reengineering, he looks at his goal: to get to school. He realizes that he can sell his bicycle and take the bus.

✦ PROS-CONS SHEET

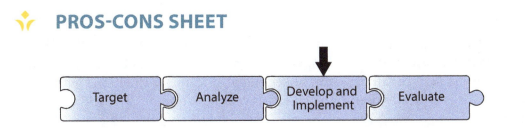

Definition: A comparison of the benefits and drawbacks of a given idea or solution.

Helpful when: A decision has many points to consider.

Time	Cost	Labor	Difficulty
Low	Low	Low	Low

Instructions:

1. Begin with two separate sheets of paper, one for Pros and one for Cons.
2. List all of the benefits of the idea on the Pros Sheet.
3. List all of the negative aspects on the Cons Sheet.
4. Devise a system to weight each of them. This can be stars or numbers (1–5) in order of importance.
5. Compare results. Keep in mind not only amount of lines on each list, but also priority or weight of the individual items.

✦ RISK MATRIX

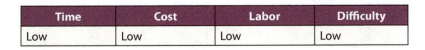

Definition: A matrix that evaluates *severity* (or impact) and *responsibility* (or fault).

Helpful when: Service staff encounter issues in need of quick interpretation and action.

Time	Cost	Labor	Difficulty
Low	Low	Low	Medium

Instructions:

1. Determine the severity of the situation.
2. Determine the responsibility of the situation.
3. Plot and solve accordingly.

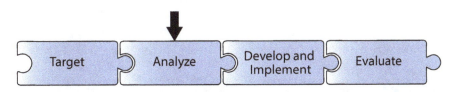

	Very Low	Low	Medium	High	Very High
Very Likely					
Likely					
Possible					
Unlikely					
Rare					

Risk Probability/Likelihood and Consequence/Severity
© Kendall Hunt Publishing Company

Discussion:

This matrix was originally created by Dennis Snow and Guy Smith of the Disney Institute. Walt Disney World Company has trained employees to use this model to help assess service failures. It has been adapted to many situations with similar labels. It is typically used to teach employees how to quickly assess customer problems.

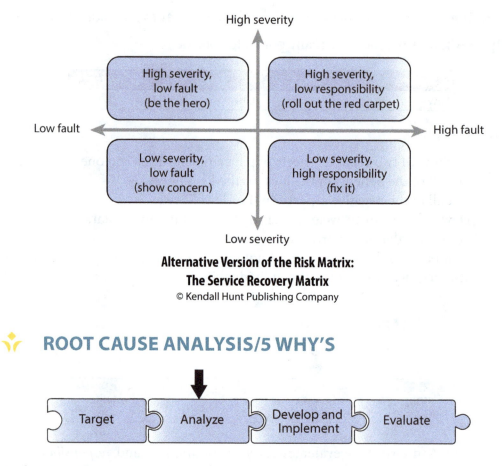

Alternative Version of the Risk Matrix:
The Service Recovery Matrix
© Kendall Hunt Publishing Company

ROOT CAUSE ANALYSIS/5 WHY'S

Definition: Determining the underlying reasons why something happens.

Helpful when: You want to explore why something happens so that you can solve it at the cause.

Time	Cost	Labor	Difficulty
Medium	Low	Medium	Medium

Discussion:

"Root Cause Analysis," or "The Five Whys," is a method for determining root cause. Instinct would tempt us to solve a symptom; however, solving a symptom does not typically solve the cause of the issue. This technique helps us to find a reason for symptoms that occur. It is commonly used in the Six Sigma DMAIC methodology and does not involve advanced statistical tools. By repeatedly asking the question "Why" to layers of symptoms, a root cause of a problem is revealed.

Instructions:

1. Determine the problem. Assemble a team who is familiar with the issues. Write it on a board or in a similar fashion. This will typically become the effect.
2. Ask "Why does this happen?" Note: There may be more than one reason. Record any and all responses.
3. State the response from #2 and ask, "Why does this happen?"
4. Record the response(s)
5. Repeat asking why until it cannot be answered. This may be any number of times, instead of precisely five. This is likely your root cause, which needs to be addressed.

Question	Answer
Why were we overcommitted on reservations?	Online reservations lost. People showed up that we didn't know about.
Why were the online reservations lost?	Our network went down and we couldn't retrieve the information.
Why did the network go down and information lost?	Our network administrator was on vacation and we couldn't reach him or his backup.
Root Cause Answer: So you were overcommitted because we don't have a reliable backup for our network administrator?	

Root Cause Analysis (Problem: Overcommitted on Reservations)

NOTE: It has been believed that when employing this tool that "Why?" is often asked five times, and that each "Why?" takes on specific characteristics; however, to assume that is often misleading. Each situation is unique. Therefore, despite being called the "5 Whys" process, one does not use precisely five "Why's" with each circumstance.

SCATTER DIAGRAM

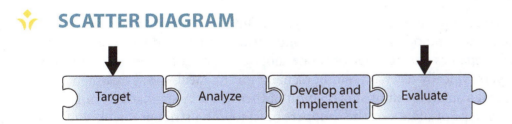

Definition: A graphing of pairs of numerical data. Other names: scatter plot; X-Y graph.

Helpful when: Examining for trends. Initial display and interpretation of coordinate data.

Time	Cost	Labor	Difficulty
Medium	Low	Medium	Medium

Instructions:

1. Collect or gather pairs of data believed to be related.
2. Plot on an X-Y graph.
3. Observe for patterns. Run regression analysis if warranted.

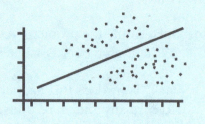

SCATTER DIAGRAM

Scatter Diagram
© garagestock/Shutterstock.com

SECRET SHOPPERS

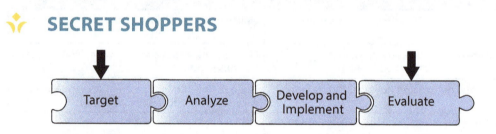

Definition: Evaluators who pose as customers and report findings to the management and owners.

Helpful when: Owners or manager want to test and ensure operational procedures are followed.

Time	Cost	Labor	Difficulty
High	High	High	Medium

Discussion:

A secret shopper is a customer in disguise. Outside contractors are sent to evaluate food, accommodations, services, and various other products in a covert fashion. Companies often change or rotate shoppers so as not to be discovered. Secret shoppers typically receive a reimbursement for the meal, show, treatment, or service, and a small token of appreciation of their time. A standard form is devised for each type of situation. The shoppers must follow a strict protocol, shopping at certain times, and ordering certain items. Shoppers hide forms and fill out immediately after the transaction. Owners use secret shoppers as a control device for operations. Managers usually have bonuses tied to shopper scores, and employees sometimes view it as spying. Nonetheless, it is relatively common, especially in chains.

Customer Service Evaluation Form

Last Name: _____   First Name: _____   Employee ID Number: _____

Date of Evaluation: _____   Arrival Time: _____ AM/PM   Time of Departure: _____ AM/PM

Property Number: _____   Property Location: _____

Order

	Poor	Below Average	Average	Above Average	Excellent
Greeting					
Accuracy					
Quality					
Timeliness					

Property

	Poor	Below Average	Average	Above Average	Excellent
Dining Room					
Kitchen					
Bathroom					
Counter					
External					

Staff

	Yes	No	Unsure
Was someone present at the door?			
Was the manager present?			
Did all staff have proper uniforms?			
Was it busy?			
Attendant's name:			
Description of order:			
Additional comments:			

Please complete, attach your receipt to the bottom portion of the page and scan and email to manager@XYZcompany.com

SERVQUAL

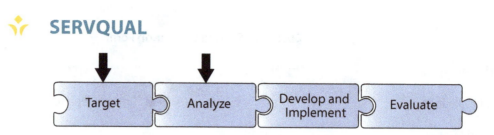

Definition: Measures five dimensions and assesses five different types of gaps in service organizations.

Helpful when: Owners or managers want to test or ensure quality service is present.

Time	Cost	Labor	Difficulty
High	Medium	Medium	High

Discussion:

Zeithaml, Parasuraman, and Berry developed SERVQUAL in 1985. They compiled the literature and blended it with practical use in industry. The SERVQUAL model has been widely used throughout the 1990s and after. The dimensions are widely accepted and the gaps have strong real-world application. It receives very little recent press, but the dimensions and gaps are widely understood to be a classic contribution to service research.

Servqual was originally developed with 11 dimensions: Tangibles, responsibility, responsiveness, communication (credibility, security, competence), courtesy, understanding/knowing customers, and access. It was later reduced to RATER which stands for:

- **Reliability:** Ability to perform promised service accurately and dependably. This includes customer service representatives responding in the promised time and providing error-free bills.
- **Assurance:** Employee knowledge, courtesy, ability to inspire trust and confidence. This includes the ability to answer questions and being capable to complete the services promised.
- **Tangibles:** Equipment, facilities, appearance of personnel. This may include appearing physically appealing and appropriately dressed employees.
- **Empathy:** Individualized attention and care to customers. This includes understanding their views.
- **Responsiveness:** Prompt service, willingness to help. This may include answering a telephone in two rings or less and meeting customers at the entrance.

Note: The last two dimensions combine the others previously mentioned.

After measuring these dimensions, it determines a measurement of five different potential gaps in the quality service process. The gaps are:

- ▶ Gap 1: Management expectation and customer exceptions
- ▶ Gap 2: Management perceptions and service specifications
- ▶ Gap 3: Service specifications and service delivery
- ▶ Gap 4: Service delivery and external communications
- ▶ Gap 5: Customer expectations and service delivery

Note: Lodging-specific measures were based on five SERVQUAL dimensions with 29 individual items of measurement.

✦ SIX SIGMA

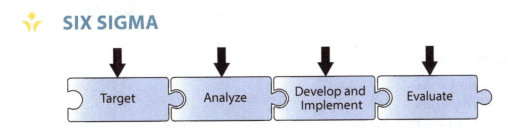

Definition: A complete program originally aimed at reducing defects to less than 3.4 in 1 million. Define, measure, analyze, improve, control (DMAIC).

Helpful when: A full embrace of quality control in a product is desired.

Time	Cost	Labor	Difficulty
High	High	High	High

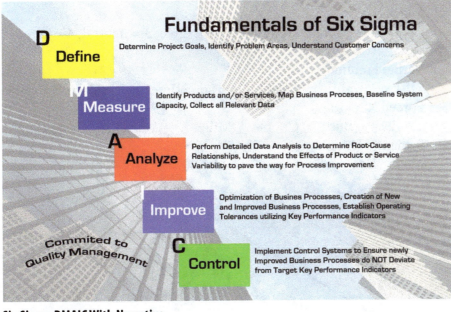

Six Sigma DMAIC With Narrative
© Fotoluminate LLC/Shutterstock.com

See Chapter 12 for a thorough description of this process.

SURVEYS

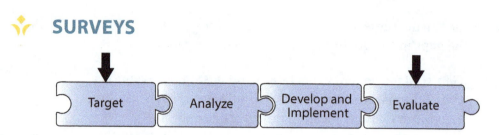

Definition: A polling of a group. Can be formal or informal. Works well with small to large groups.

Helpful when: You need to obtain a brief response from a broad audience.

Time	Cost	Labor	Difficulty
Medium	High	Medium	Medium

Could Be Administered To

▶ Employees

▶ Managers

▶ Customers (existing, potential, lost/dissatisfied)

Types of Questions (Note: Offer "no opinion" when appropriate)

▶ Close-ended Q's: Have specific options for an answer
  ☐ Ex: How old are you? ___<18 ___18–29 ___30–49 ___50–65 ___<66

▶ Open-ended Q's: Have no specific option for answering
  ☐ Ex: How old are you? _____

Types of Scales

▶ Likert Scale
  ☐ Ex: 1 = strongly disagree, 2 = disagree, 3 = neutral, 4 = agree, 5 = strongly agree

▶ Verbal Frequency
  ☐ Ex: 1 = always, 2 = often, 3 = sometimes, 4 = seldom, 5 = never

▶ Forced Ranking
  ☐ Ex: ___Bud ___Coors ___Miller ___ Amstel ___Guinness

▶ Semantic Differential
  ☐ Ex: Hot___ ___ ___ ___Cold

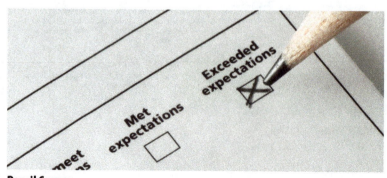

Pencil Survey
© 7505811966/Shutterstock.com

All Surveys Should Have

- ► Introduction briefly describing the situation: Who? What? Why?
- ► Body including the survey questions
- ► Closing
- ► Thank you

All Surveys Should Be

- ► Brief
- ► Focused directly on the subject
- ► Simple to follow
- ► Focused without extraneous information

Effective Survey Questions Should Involve the Following

- ► Clear/unambiguous to ensure consistent interpretation. (Poor Ex: What do you do?)
- ► Grammatically correct and free from spelling errors
- ► Free-flowing and easy to understand
- ► Leading questions that introduce bias or lead to a particular answer
  - ☐ (Ex: Would you favor random searches to keep people safe from bombers, assassins, and drug smugglers?)
- ► Inapplicable or overly sensitive questions (Ex: What are your children's names?)
- ► Overdemanding recall questions (Ex: When learning to ride your bicycle, how many times did you fall off your bike?)
- ► Double-barreled questions which include two questions in one. (Ex: Do you enjoy going to an event and getting a program?)
- ► Sensitive questions placed last.

Common Pitfalls

Too many resources needed to conduct study. Studies require time, knowledge, and money to conduct. As an alternative, research to see if anyone else has conducted similar research. Perhaps you could use their findings.

- ► Generalizing sample to all. It is tempting to want to apply your findings onto everyone. Keep in mind that who you sample might be representative of everyone else. Just because your survey showed that 35 women prefer your product does not mean that everyone else will feel the same way.
- ► Too much data. Surveys collect much data that might not be ultimately useful. Consider if you need to ask each question. Do you need to know their age and everything they ate or just if they were satisfied? Have a reasonable purpose for each piece of data that you collect.
- ► Results not implemented. With the best of intentions, many studies never make it through completion. Surveys are collected, and the data is interpreted, but implementing changes based on the data can require many other resources, and you may find resistance to change.

Try to Avoid

- ► Technical language or terminology
- ► Asking questions that you already have the answer to
- ► Too many questions assessing the same point
- ► Embarrassing/personal questions
- ► Too many questions
- ► Multiple changes in response patterns
- ► Questions that cannot be answered by the answers provided
- ► Difficult to answer questions in the beginning
- ► Influencing respondents to answer in a certain way
- ► Making cultural assumptions
- ► Assuming results will prove your point

SERVICE INSIGHT

Correlation Does Not Imply Causation

Your research may show that variables are seemingly related. Be careful of your interpretations and claims!

- ► Claim: Odd-numbered days have yielded fewer complaints.
- ► Claim: A recent rise in male travelers is followed by a lowering of guest complaints.
- ► Claim: A rise in gas prices relates to a decline in pool usage.
- ► Claim: An increase in service staff has led to a decline in room service delivery times.

When conducting research, be aware that just because two variables may be correlated, one does not necessarily cause another. They may not be related at all to each other.

- ► Incorrect: If the value of A rises as the value of B lowers, then A's rising causes B to lower.
- ► Reasoning: There could be many reasons why B lowers in value. There are many intervening variables that could cause B to drop in value. Just because the two values have correlation, does mean that one causes the other. Seemingly related or not, we cannot imply that.

Now let's review the previous claims:

- ► Incorrect: Odd-numbered days yield less complaints.
- ► Reasoning: Scheduling? Service staff? Property maintenance?
- ► Incorrect: A recent rise in male travelers is followed by a lowering of guest complaints.
- ► Reasoning: Did the manager/staff change? What other factors changed?
- ► Incorrect: A rise in gas prices relates to a decline in pool usage.
- ► Reasoning: What was the occupancy? Clientele? Weather?
- ► Incorrect: An increase in service staff has led to a decline in room service delivery times.
- ► Reasoning: That's illogical. The opposite might happen. There were likely other issues.

Technology Update

Simplicity in Technology

Consider this. Sometimes surveys don't have to be complicated. Picture yourself walking through an airport or out the exit of a business and you see a survey with a series of two, three, or four emoji faces ranging from happy to unhappy. You just touch the emoji or button that best describes your experience. Businesses can use this as quick feedback. Companies like "Happy or Not" and Smiley Answers offer quick customer assessments with very high completion rates. Typically placed at a front desk or exit, customers can use a button or a touch screen to quickly reply if they are happy or not with the current situation. These are anonymous stations that can be completed without even stopping. It may not tell their name or what happened, but the high response rate and time of the visit are recorded for further investigation. Places like Heathrow Airport and Levi's Stadium currently use these with great success.

CHAPTER REVIEW QUESTIONS

1. List the basic procedures of research methodology.
2. At what point in the research process might people be surveyed?
3. How is the research process begun?
4. After completing a brainstorming session, what next tool might be used?
5. According to the SERVQUAL tool, what does R.A.T.E.R. stand for?
6. What are the four different groups in which a tool could be divided?
7. List three tools that could be used for evaluating improvements.
8. List at least four common pitfalls to avoid in surveys.
9. Why might a Fishbone Analysis have different titles?

❖ EXERCISE

Analyzing a Survey

Directions:

1. Obtain a survey of a hospitality business in a field that interests you. This may be local or national.
2. Print out the survey and staple to the back of your assignment.
3. Reference the survey, fill in the example, and indicate whether or not it is correct in the chart below.

Component	Example	Was It Correct or Incorrect?
Introduction provided		
Clear instructions		
Type of scale used		
Free from introducing bias		
Avoids technical terminology		
Directions provided		
Thank you included		

Chapter 12

Systems, Ratings, and Awards

CHAPTER OBJECTIVES

After reading this chapter, you should be able to:

► Identify and explain the project management techniques.
► Apply the basic procedures Six Sigma to a project.
► Compare and contrast quality ratings.
► Identify quality awards.

TERMINOLOGY

Critical to Quality (CTQ)
Diamond Rating
International Standards Organization (ISO)
Kaizen
Lean Thinking
Project Management
Six Sigma
Star Rating
Team Project Charter
Voice of Customer (VOC)

Introduction

There are many approaches to quality systems. This chapter will outline some of the most popular and successful systems to date. The Japanese influence is still very apparent in the discussion of quality improvement. They share a partial origin. They still practice these techniques; and they work!

✦ KAIZEN

Kaizen
A Japanese quality term meaning improvement.

Kaizen is the Japanese word meaning improvement, or to get better. It is also referred to as a set of quality functions and techniques. This approach is typically continuous, practiced daily, and is instituted at all levels of the organization and to all processes.

There are different types of Kaizen:

► **Flow Kaizen** regards materials/information.
► **Process Kaizen** regarding workers/processes for small, quick changes or improvements.
► **Kaizen blitz** is used to describe shorter periods of improvement instead of a long-term, continuous approach. This version has been used more lately.

Kaizen has been applied to several industries. The Japanese began using Kaizen in the late 1940s. Toyota has benefited greatly from the use of it. An immediate goal is to eliminate waste and lessen work through scientific process.

Project Management

A project is a short-term, temporary set of actions and activities with the intention of achieving an objective or goal. The oversight of this should have a specific timeframe, scope, and allocation of resources. A business will likely have several projects at once and these projects could impact every part of the business.

Project Management
Short-term, temporary set of actions and activities with the intention of achieving an objective or goal.

Project management has been recognized as a formal discipline in the US since about the 1950s. Project managers typically oversee a project team. The team members could be from a specific department or from different departments or even different locations and organizations. Project managers must process the ability to apply knowledge, skills, tools, and techniques in an effort to meet the project goal within the established parameters.

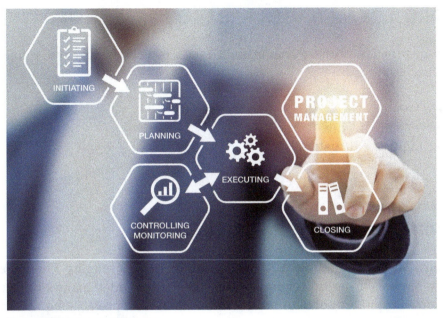

Project Management Diagram
© NicoElNino/Shutterstock.com

✦ STEPS OF PROJECT MANAGEMENT

According to PMI, project management falls into five distinct groups:

▶ Initiating
▶ Planning
▶ Executing
▶ Monitoring and Controlling
▶ Closing

https://www.pmi.org/about/learn-about-pmi/what-is-project-management

PROJECT MANAGEMENT GROUP DESCRIPTIONS

Initiating: providing the motivation to begin the project. The scope and boundaries or parameters of the project must be established. Often, a group charter will be established (see below for more on a charter).

Planning: assessing the situation and making accommodations and appropriations for work to be accomplished.

Executing: the actual performing of the plan.

Monitoring and **Controlling** oversee and devise changes to ensure goals are accomplished.

Closing: completing the project. Recommendations are made and success is celebrated.

PROJECT MANAGER AREAS OF RESPONSIBILITY

To manage projects, primary responsibilities of a project manager are refined to a few categories:

- ▶ Goals
- ▶ People
- ▶ Equipment/materials
- ▶ Time
- ▶ Budget

PROJECT MANAGER SKILL SETS

The ability to conduct Project Management in the Hospitality Guest Service Industry requires a multidisciplinary skill set that includes many of the topics covered in a hospitality curriculum and in this text. Most projects require abilities in the areas of:

- ▶ Knowledge of the Industry Sectors
- ▶ Quality Tools
- ▶ Analysis
- ▶ Teamwork
- ▶ Management
- ▶ Financial Accountability
- ▶ Performance Standards

As you can see, there is much that goes into being a project manager. No two projects are alike and these skill sets can vary depending on customers, location, timing, economic, and even political structure. Managing projects takes a well-rounded individual with flexibility and adaptability to coordinate efforts to reach the project goal.

A COMPARISON OF SYSTEMS

We see many similarities between project management and other quality management systems. Most projects are unique and specific to the business, goal, and environmental factors. Despite this, most of them follow a typical path of steps. Most of these steps are sequential, meaning that you typically follow them in order. There is a beginning point of sorting, assessing, and deciding on a plan of action. There is a middle point of performing and evaluating and altering the course of action. Also, there is usually an end point, which is closure.

Strategic Planning is

- ▶ Calculated plan with a common, chosen objective
- ▶ Formulation
- ▶ Implementation
- ▶ Evaluation

Six Sigma is

- ► Define
- ► Measure
- ► Analyze
- ► Improve
- ► Control

Lean is

- ► Start, enable, behavior, sustain, or—
- ► situation approach, process improvement.

TPS used by Toyota is

- ► (Adapted) stability, standardization, JIT, refinement

DDICA is

- ► Design
- ► Develop
- ► Initialize
- ► Control
- ► Allocate

While more **general project management models** are:

- ► Initiation
- ► Planning
- ► Execution
- ► Closeout

Management Functions are

- ► Plan
- ► Organize
- ► Motivate
- ► Control

The Five S's are

- ► Sort
- ► Set in Order
- ► Shine
- ► Standardize
- ► Sustain

Four E's are

- ► Educate (train, teach them about empathy, how to solve)
- ► Enable (qualify—give limits, guidelines)
- ► Encourage (reassure, inspire)
- ► Empower

Five Frames of Transformation are (McKinsey & Company)

- ► Aspire—Vision and method of engaging others
- ► Assess—Determining the mindset of the organization
- ► Architect—Plan path toward targets
- ► Act—Creating energy and momentum; quick wins
- ► Advance—Build skills and develop leaders

There are obviously many interpretations of the same idea. Though similar, each have specific approaches. They are structures to help you to:

- ► Accomplish your goals
- ► Have the procedures in place
- ► Make better decisions
- ► Add efficiency
- ► Add success and profitability

Team Project Charters

Team Project Charter

A document that defines the project, team member roles, objectives, and other pertinent information necessary to successfully begin a project.

The **team project charter** will act as a first step in team development, helping to bring people together and set the expectations.

After initial research is completed and the goal of the project is determined, a team is selected and a group charter is usually completed. There are parameters used to help solidify timeline, duties, responsibilities, and goals of the project. A group charter is a specific mandate in the Six Sigma process.

Project Charter Collage
© dizain/Shutterstock.com

Key aspects to the team charter might include

- ► Names and contact information
- ► Due dates and deadlines
- ► Team goals, what would make this a success?
- ► Team priorities
- ► Leadership
- ► Communication plan due dates
- ► Potential obstacles
- ► Backup plans
- ► Rules and responsibilities
- ► Strengths of individuals

Without a group charter, teams, processes, and goals have the potential to stray from their original intentions. Teams work better when expectations are made known and they are held to it. A charter can also help when problems occur, providing a plan to help realign the team.

Six Sigma

Six Sigma is a process approach that creates a business improvement. It focuses on measuring and improving product and service quality. GE and other manufacturers popularized the use of Six Sigma in the US in the 1980s and 90s. Its main goal is to find problems and solve them. A popular example of a Six Sigma was the space shuttle launches performed by NASA.

Six Sigma Collage
© Boris15/Shutterstock.com

There are different variations of Six Sigma depending on the situation.

- ▶ If *designing* a *new* process: DMADV Design, Measure, Analyze, Design, Verify.
- ▶ If *improving* an *existing* process: DMAIC: Design, Measure, Analyze, Improve, Control.

Below these terms are described in more detail.

Define

The first step of the project is mapping out the process. It sets up the project and brings everyone together. By the end of this phase, everyone should understand the process and begin to delve into the inherent issues.

- ▶ The problem is described and then clearly defined.
- ▶ The customer is identified.
- ▶ The team is established and the rules are established through use of the Team Charter.
- ▶ Project goals are determined.
- ▶ Voice of the customer (VOC) is identified.

Voice of Customer (VOC) is a term used for a process of attaining the wants and needs of the customer. Remember: VOC converts to CTQ's; meaning the customers' voices are converted into measurables.

The VOC typically has two or three and as many as five steps in the process. For purpose of illustration, this text will present a three-step process.

> **Voice of Customer (VOC)**
>
> A process of obtaining customer wants and converting them into measurable requirements.

1. The first are a collection of the customers' actual comments or surveys. This can be attained via any number of quantitative and qualitative ways. Focus groups, surveys, in-depth interviews, and observation are a few. The data is often called "Drivers."
2. The second step converts this raw data into key categories that are easier to process.
3. The last step takes these categories and converts them into applicable, measurable requirements that will serve as a target to delivering quality service. A number of terms are used for this, but the most popular is Critical to Quality (CTQ's). These may also be called "Critical to Customer" (CTC's) or "Critical Customer Requirements" (CCR's).

Critical to quality (CTQ): Items that are identified by the customer as being essential to quality service. These are measurable and specifically applicable to the operation and its staff.

Example

▶ VOC: "We waited too long to be seated."
▶ CTQ requirement: All reservations seated within 6 minutes of reservation time.

Example

▶ VOC: "The water in the pool is too cold."
▶ QTQ requirement: Pool heater set to engage at temperatures below 75°F.

Measure

In this phase the **baseline measurements** are established. This is important for declaring a starting point. These measurements will guide what will be improved and monitor the success of the project.

Analyze

After the baseline measurements of the project are established, the data must be analyzed in more depth. Many guest service tools might be used during this process including root cause, Histograms, Pareto charts, and scatter plots. The goal of analysis is to provide data for a solution strategy. The team charter might also need to be updated.

Improve

This is the implementation phase where improvements are made. The solution is first tested and confirmed to meet the objective. After that, the solution is instituted. This may involve allocation of resources, training, and interventions from organizational change agents.

Control

As you continue to implement solutions, adjustments will likely need to be made. In this final step, businesses monitor the improvements and determine if they are sustainable indefinitely. The team may decide to update or refine the plan. Other items such as resources or training will likely also need to be addressed. Finally, it is time to document, communicate, and celebrate the successes of the project.

Verify

Verification is present in designing a new process (DMADV). Since it was new, there was no pre-existing benchmark. The team only has data from tests and initial implementation. This step is important for assurance that goals were ultimately met.

Recognize

Occasionally there is an "R" in the beginning of DMAIC. This stands for the term recognize. It follows through with that wise adage, "The first step is recognizing that you have a problem." Consequently, DMAIC is changed to RDMAIC.

Standardize and Integrate

Depending on the application, standardization may be separated out. This is often combined into other steps. Integrate may also be a separate tool because of its importance. This can be useful when you have a solution that needs to be scaled to the rest of operations.

Team Member Roles

Six Sigma has levels of team members, much like that of karate or judo. The colors of belts are applied to the members of the team according to skill level and responsibilities.

> ► **Project Champions:** Comprised of senior-level management, they lead Six Sigma in their area of expertise. They help to support and initiate projects. They are also responsible for team motivation, outcomes, and a strong vision.
> ► **Master Black Belts:** Comprised of Six Sigma experts who lead the responsibility for operations. They are trained in all areas of Six Sigma.
> ► **Black Belts:** Comprised of Six Sigma experts who are advanced in their knowledge of methodologies and use of quality tools.
> ► **Green Belts:** Comprised of functional employees who have limited, introductory knowledge of Six Sigma.
> ► **Team Members:** Individuals who support projects in other ways but have no specific knowledge of Six Sigma.

Lean Approach

✦ LEAN THINKING

Lean thinking was originally part of Six Sigma. During the 2000s, Lean Six Sigma forked from Six Sigma. Lean thinking specialized primarily on waste reduction.

Lean thinking is a relatively simple methodology. The primary objective is increasing customer value through improving process flow, reducing/eliminating waste. Lean was first recognized in the US when Motorola employed its methodologies in 1986.

Lean thinking also aims to make something better than it was before. Typically, this is done through improving its efficiency.

Lean With Components
© Panchenko Vladimir/Shutterstock.com

Lean thinking tries to systematically remove things that are ancillary to the goal and have little to no value. If it is not useful, eliminate it because waste does not create value. Consequently, this reduces costs and saves money. A strength of lean thinking is its fast implementation. It quickly increases productivity, reduces errors, and leads to improved financial performance as well as customer satisfaction.

Variation is also closely related to waste when Lean Thinking is performed in manufacturing applications. They analyze defects, over-production, use of labor, inventory, motion, and many other elements.

Lean Thinking

A systematic approach to waste and cost reduction.

Lean Quality Tools

- ► Kaizen
- ► Process Mapping
- ► Error Proofing, Maintenance
- ► Time Reduction
- ► Standardized work

Quality Systems Conclusion

The above systems each have a different approach and are geared toward different applications. However, many similarities exist. They all use specialized terminology. All of them are geared toward quality and excellence. All of the processes are data-based and led by management with employees being a part of the solution. And, all have consultants that have specialties and various titles.

Deming: 14 Points

Below are Dr. Deming's 14 Points. He published these as practical advice for implementing quality systems. They were accurate when originally published many years ago and are still considered great advice today.

1. Create constancy of purpose for improving products and services.
2. Adopt the new philosophy.
3. Cease dependence on inspection to achieve quality.
4. End the practice of awarding business on price alone; instead, minimize total cost by working with a single supplier.
5. Improve constantly and forever every process for planning, production, and service.
6. Institute training on the job.
7. Adopt and institute leadership.
8. Drive out fear.
9. Break down barriers between staff areas.
10. Eliminate slogans, exhortations, and targets for the workforce.
11. Eliminate numerical quotas for the workforce and numerical goals for management.
12. Remove barriers that rob people of pride of workmanship, and eliminate the annual rating or merit system.
13. Institute a vigorous program of education and self-improvement for everyone.
14. Put everybody in the company to work accomplishing the transformation.

https://asq.org/quality-resources/total-quality-management/deming-points

External Awards, Certifications, and Recognitions

Awards, certifications, and recognitions are a way of letting the customer and others know what you stand for. They display a commitment and presence to your work. They are part of your brand image. They can show an affiliation or even a rite of passage in the field. However, they are also quite common. Customers have a difficult time keeping track of them and the granting organizations go to great lengths to make theirs appear as worthy as possible. A few stand out and many are lost in a sea of sameness. This section aims to explain many of the awards, certification, and recognitions common to the hospitality industry.

J.D. POWER AWARD

Features	Ratings of hotels, restaurants, rental car companies
Input	Randomly selected customer reviews
Award	Power Circles (out of five)
Difficulty	Medium
Customer Recognition	High
Field Recognition	Medium

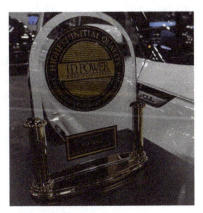

J.D. Power Award
© Ed Aldridge/Shutterstock.com

J.D. Power is a customer-rated service that reviews hotels, restaurants, and rental car companies, among many other non-hospitality industries. It is Canadian-based, but also has a strong presence in its US Division. It gained US popularity when car manufacturers began using it for marketing publicity. Since then, the restrictions for use in advertisements have tightened.

MALCOLM BALDRIGE QUALITY AWARD

Features	Award divisions for service and small business
Input	Strict and lengthy application process
Award	Granted or not granted
Difficulty	High
Customer Recognition	High
Field Recognition	High

Ritz Carlton Sign in Moscow, Russia
© Max_Ryazanov/Shutterstock.com

This is a national award given to companies who exhibit excellence. The Ritz Carlton Hotel Company won this award in 1992 and 1999. It awards up to two a year in the areas of manufacturing, service, education, health care, and small business. Other past recipients have been Federal Express, IBM, Cadillac, Verizon, Merrill Lynch, Xerox, Boeing, and Caterpillar.

INTERNATIONAL STANDARDS ORGANIZATION (ISO)

Features	Quality and standardization for many areas. ISO9000 series features quality
Input	Strict and lengthy application process
Award	Certification
Difficulty	High
Customer Recognition	Medium
Field Recognition	Medium

ISO 9000 Series Icon
© mushan/Shutterstock.com

ISO forms and maintains the largest set of commercial and industrial standards in the world. These are labeled by numbers. For example,

the ISO-9001 series provides standards on how to run a business that has a process for ensuring quality in their products. It can be found throughout most of the world, especially with European counterparts. Organizations pass a rigorous process to show they are conforming to commonly-accepted industry practices. Some businesses will only work with other ISO-certified companies. Others common organizations are ANSI (American National Standards Institute) and UL (Underwriters Laboratories).

FORBES–MOBIL GUIDE RATINGS

Features	Ratings of hotels, restaurants, spas
Input	Forbes unannounced inspectors
Award	Certification of star rating: one to five
Difficulty	High (for five stars)
Customer Recognition	High
Field Recognition	High

Forbes Star Evaluations

Forbes Travel Guide evaluates hotels, restaurants, and spas in the US, Canada, and Asia. Forbes has been evaluating since 1958. In 2009, Forbes merged with Mobil Travel Guide, another industry leader and assumed its **star rating** system. In it, hotels, restaurants, and spas are evaluated using a five-star rating system. Forbes primarily concentrates on four- and five-star properties. In 2019, Forbes Travel Guide awarded 209 hotels, 68 restaurants, and 64 spas the prestigious honor of five stars. The same year it also awarded 534 hotels, 151 restaurants, and 216 spas the four-star award.

Ratings are determined by the combined scores of a facility inspection (25%) and a service evaluation (75%). Facility inspection is a minimum of two nights and reviews aspects of the hotel including reservations, room service, laundry,

Hotel Five-Star Rating
© Andrey_Popov/Shutterstock.com

and concierge. Service evaluation is performed incognito and assesses up to 900 different items at each property.

- ▶ **Five-Star Hotels:** These are the most exceptional of all properties. They are nearly flawless, the staff is passionate and eager to deliver guest satisfaction beyond their expectations. The properties exhibit fine craftsmanship, comfort, and quality and are a destination unto their self. Examples: Montage Beverly Hills, Mandarin Oriental NYC.
- ▶ **Four-Star Hotels:** Distinctive setting, many interesting and inviting features, strong attention to detail in all aspects, staff is prideful and accommodating, personalized service. Examples: Wynn Las Vegas, St. Regis Deer Valley Resort.
- ▶ **Three-Star Hotels:** Are held to less inspection and evaluation standards than the four- and five-star candidates. They are still very nice properties with a strong sense of location, distinguishing style, ambiance, functionality, and ease of access to meetings or tourist attractions.

In 2005, Forbes began offering an additional consulting practice which shares the extensive inspection criteria with the hotels. This allows them to more appropriately gauge what they need to change in order to achieve the four- and five-star criteria.

AAA RATINGS

Features	Ratings of hotels, restaurants, campgrounds
Input	AAA unannounced inspectors
Award	Diamond rating of 1–5
Difficulty	High
Customer Recognition	High
Field Recognition	High

The American Automobile Association (AAA) approves and rates hotels and restaurants. They cover more establishments than any other rating association. AAA began approving hotels in 1937 and began the rating system in 1963. The lodging ratings evolved into the presently-known **diamond rating** system in 1976. Diamond ratings were rolled out to restaurants between 1986 and 1991. They rate hotels and restaurants on a scale of one to five Diamonds. One is the lowest and five is the highest. The ratings assess extensiveness of services, amenities, and décor. AAA inspectors visit every property and rate them every year. The five-star rating is highly coveted. Candidate properties for five-star awards undergo multiple evaluations and an expert panel. Only 121 (in US, Canada, Mexico, Caribbean) were awarded in 2019. This represents .4% of the 27,000+ hotels that it evaluates. In 2019, 1,722 hotels were awarded the four-star rating, representing just 6.3% of the total hotels evaluated.

ISO 9000 Series Icon
© Shahin Aliyev/Shutterstock.com

Hotel Diamond Rating

Diamond Rating

AAA rating system of 1 to 5 diamonds scoring hotels, restaurants, and campgrounds. The largest guide of its kind.

▶ **1 Diamond:** Is the lowest level. This is a no-frills property, but satisfactorily meets the basic requirements. It is suitable for the budget-minded traveler.

▶ **2 Diamonds:** Is a modest designation of a property. It has more to offer than a one-star property, and offers modest accommodations.

▶ **3 Diamonds:** Is a property for a traveler with more needs.

▶ **4 Diamonds:** Are properties that are located in upscale areas. They are refined, stylish, and feature a high level of quality throughout.

▶ **5 Diamonds:** Offer the highest level in all manners. These properties offer the best of everything. They are the pinnacle of luxury, with impeccable service and amenities. Names like Ritz Carlton and St. Regis are common in this category.

AAA also visits and evaluates over 32,000 restaurants a year. Restaurants must first meet a criteria of having set minimum requirements to even be evaluated. Diamonds represent level of food, décor, and service. Only about .2% make the 5-Diamond Rating and about 2.1% make the 4-Diamond list.

Restaurant Diamond Ratings

▶ **1 Diamond:** "Good food" meets basic, essential requirements of food, management, and overall quality. Limited food selection, limited service, (self-service) basic décor, and surroundings. Lower-priced.

▶ **2 Diamonds:** "Family fare" reasonably-priced. Better dishware, garnishes, familiar surroundings with a theme, elevated level of food and service. Upgraded.

▶ **3 Diamonds:** "Entry-level fine dining" has a chef and highly-trained cooks, skilled menu, complementing beverages, dining room manager, skilled service staff, fine dining, comfortable, typically adult-oriented.

▶ **4 Diamonds:** "Fine dining" has an executive chef, highly-trained kitchen and dining room staff, fresh-market ingredients, first-class impressions in all respects.

▶ **5 Diamonds:** "World-class dining," the best in every aspect. Renowned, world-class cuisine, "haute cuisine." The best of everything from the staff, to the menu, to the beverages, to the décor, to the food. Typically very expensive.

https://newsroom.aaa.com/diamond-ratings/

Quality Around the World

Quality is not just known to Japan and the US. Each country or region has their own quality award. Most are sponsored by the government to promote and reward quality excellence. Following is a list of a few:

- ▶ Australian Business Excellence Awards
- ▶ Canadian Awards for Excellence
- ▶ China Quality Award
- ▶ Dubai Government Excellence Award
- ▶ Dutch Quality Assessment
- ▶ Egypt Excellence Quality Award
- ▶ Indonesian Quality Award
- ▶ Korean National Quality Award
- ▶ Phillipine Quality Award
- ▶ Premio Qualità Italia—Italy
- ▶ Prime Minister's Quality Award—Malaysia
- ▶ Russian Government Quality Award
- ▶ Singapore Business Excellence Award
- ▶ Thailand Quality Award

❖ CHAPTER REVIEW QUESTIONS

1. Describe Project Manager skill sets.
2. Describe the basic objective of Lean Thinking.
3. What are the common steps used in implementing Six Sigma?
4. What is the importance of establishing a Group Charter?
5. Why do you think that The Ritz Carlton was the only hotel to receive the prestigious Malcolm Baldrige Quality award?
6. What is the difference between a star rating and a diamond rating?
7. What substantiates a 5-Diamond rating in a hotel?
8. What substantiates a Five-Star rating in a restaurant?

CASE STUDIES

6-Star Restaurant

6-Star Restaurant had an ideal location. It is located in downtown Chicago in an area surrounded by other restaurants, hotels, and major businesses. Several of the restaurants in this area were considered world-class. The owners and design staff had an idea to make 6-Star Restaurant stand out from those. They envisioned a restaurant that was better than the rest. They decided upon a name that would help it to stand out, "6-Star Restaurant." They based this name upon the star rating system of one to five stars, placing their establishment off the scales. Although it was never formally rated, the owners believed they deserved an extra star above the rest because of their ability. They believed they would have a restaurant like no other.

Much work went into substantiating their claim. They trained their staff to deliver outstanding service. They chose some of the nicest place settings available. They recruited the best chef and kitchen staff available. They were off to a great start. They were delivering outstanding food and service.

Despite this, customers were left feeling slighted. Many of the competitors were also delivering outstanding food and service in that area. It was good, but not that overly impressive. 6-Star Restaurant was not an entire step above the competitors to warrant their claims. Due to these claims, the customers' expectations were not met.

1. Describe the concept of 6-Star Restaurant.
2. Describe the expectations of the customers.
3. In your opinion, is it possible to deliver 6-Star service?

Jose's Travel

Jose's Travel is a small, private company that prides itself on serving the people of the greater L.A. area. It is a full-service travel company with a strong clientele speaking mostly Spanish. To assess his customer service, Jose e-mails all of his customers an electronic survey 1 week after their trip. It includes questions in the main areas of accuracy of service, friendliness of service, and price/value of service. Four questions are listed in each area, each approaching the topic from a slightly different point of view.

Of the surveys sent out, Jose realizes that only about 25% of his customers reply. When analyzing the responses, he sees two trends emerge. One group loves everything and is quite pleased with all aspects of the service. Another, yet smaller group is displeased with nearly every aspect of the service. He believes that customers generally appear happy and quite pleased in the store and on the telephone, so he is unsure how they could have received such poor ratings across the survey from a few of the customers.

In an effort to rectify the bad experiences of his customers, he has historically e-mailed them back, offering a coupon, although he seldom received a return to his e-mail offer. To probe into this further, Jose has recently begun calling each of the customers that responded with an average of less than 60% satisfaction. He has been unable to reach most of these people on the telephone. He leaves messages, but continues to receive little or no information as a result.

1. List the research steps that Jose has taken until this point.
2. In what step might Jose have failed?
3. Outline tips or advice that you would give to Jose to help him better gauge his customers.

The Suggestion Box

The Operations Department at the Van Arena consists of 15 full-time help, with several others brought in on an as-needed basis. Jeff has recently been promoted to Director of Operation of the department. He has been at the arena for 7 years. He began as a part-timer in high school, eventually working his way to full-time after graduating from a local college. He has always gotten along with the other members of the department, and considers many of them close friends.

In the storage room, Jeff noticed a comment box gaining dust in the back corner. He decided to place it on the wall outside his office with blank cards in a rack above it. He didn't know what would happen, and he didn't really think about it until he decided to open it one day.

To his surprise, it was quite full. Jeff spent the next two hours in his office pouring over the comments. He was very upset, but decided to wait until the next weekly staff meeting.

Jeff could barely stand waiting, but the meeting finally came. He walked into the room last and stared at everyone. He took out a folder containing the comment cards from the suggestion box. He then proceeded to read all of them off, one by one. The room was silent and the air was heavy. Jeff was obviously mad. Everyone froze as he began:

- ► "You stink"
- ► "You give preferential treatment to your friends"
- ► "We could use new uniforms"
- ► "Sometimes people sneak in through over the fence after dark"
- ► "We could save money by getting automatic devices in the restrooms."

Overall, there were many good suggestions, but there were also two very negative ones. Jeff could not get over how someone could write those two. He looked around the room to survey their faces. He had a few ideas who it was. It even looked like the two negative comments were of the same handwriting. Jeff was mad at everyone.

1. Was the Comment Card Box a good idea? Explain.
2. Rate the responses that were read. Overall, what did they say?
3. If you were Jeff's boss, what advice would you give him regarding the interpretation of these comments?

❖ EXERCISE

Diamond Rating

Directions:

1. Choose a local hotel or restaurant that can be observed for this assignment.
2. Review it according to the Diamond Standard Rating according to AAA.
3. Provide examples to support your decision.

Name of Property: _____

Location of Property: _____

Number of diamonds awarded according to your review: _____

Justification:

List at least seven aspects of the property that substantiate your star rating.

	Aspect
1.	
2.	
3.	
4.	
5.	
6.	
7.	

Chapter 13

Developing a Staff

CHAPTER OBJECTIVES

After reading this chapter, you should be able to:

- ► Identify the proper hiring attributes.
- ► Describe the importance of verbal and nonverbal communication in delivering quality service.
- ► Explain and apply the concepts of successful nonverbal communication.
- ► Understand the importance of corporate culture and in developing a brand.
- ► Identify the attributes of successful service industry candidates.
- ► Recognize the stages of team development.
- ► Contrast the importance and different views of training, managing, and developing.

TERMINOLOGY

Body Language
Cross-Functional Teams
Employee Turnover
Empowerment
Internal Customer
Job Description
Job Specification
Organizational Culture
Standard Operating Procedures (SOP)
Synergy

The magic formula that successful businesses have discovered is to treat customers like guests and employees like people.

—Tom J. Peters

Introduction

The employees are at the frontline of the company. They are what the customer sees. They are the ones interacting with the customer. They can seize or lose opportunities. How well you hire, train, and develop your employees determines your future as a manager. If you could hire, train, and promote precisely the right people:

▶ You would have little or no employee turnover,
▶ You would have excellent customer service, and
▶ You would work a lot less, and smile a lot more.

Hiring

Today's society is filled by design with positions at hourly rates where employees clock in and out, performing duties with little sense of responsibility for true guest satisfaction. Managerial positions are overly controlled by financial goals. Numerous policies and procedures inundate staff, and management is overwhelmed with forms and reports. Everyone has talents. Most employees can be really great with customers if trained, supported, empowered, and given the opportunity.

Developing a staff is something that is crucial to any hospitality business. We can't train employees for every unique situation, but instead we could give them a "bag of tricks" or a "bag of tools" that would be helpful to apply to most situations.

We aim to hire for attitude, traits, and abilities, and then train for precise skills. Policies and procedures, stories, examples, demonstrations, and corporate culture are all ways to indoctrinate them. Employees could then use their discretion in the application. Through practice, we monitor them and they hone their craft.

It is often said in the hospitality industry, "We hire for attitude and train for specific position-related skills." That is true to a certain extent, but candidates must also present the satisfactory level of mental abilities such as judgment and comprehension skills. They must be familiar with basic procedures and methods or at least have transferable skills. They also need to possess organizational skills to work on projects alone and with others. But in the end, the Hospitality Industry has little use for candidates with poor attitudes and poor people skills.

Job Description Collage
© Sampien/Shutterstock.com

WHAT DO HOSPITALITY SERVICE COMPANIES LOOK FOR IN A NEW HIRE?

A well-performing Human Resource department is an essential first step to fostering quality guest service staff members. They plan, recruit, train, and develop employees who will serve the guest. Each of these responsibilities require proper forms and documentation of which you should be familiar.

Standard forms for the hiring process include the job description and the job specification. The job description explains what they do in the position, the duties and responsibilities. It is often used in interviewing, training, and evaluation. The job specification explains what they need to successfully complete the job. It is primarily used in hiring. It includes knowledge, skills, abilities, education, and certifications. It gives much insight into the qualifications of the ideal candidate. Occasionally, these two documents are blended into one and referred to as one name or the other. The important thing is that a business has this information and uses it appropriately.

Most hospitality companies seek similar traits and ask themselves similar questions when hiring someone:

- ▶ How do they appear?
- ▶ Do they get along with others?
- ▶ Can they communicate?
- ▶ Are they sensitive to others?
- ▶ Can they foster customer relationships?
- ▶ Do they know and understand your business and your customers even if they're not from the same background?

Job Description

Details what the position does: duties and responsibilities.

Job Specification

Details what the position requires: knowledge, skills, and abilities.

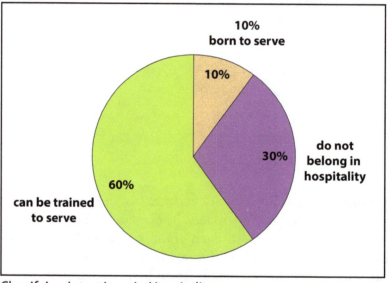

Classifying Interviews in Hospitality
Copyright © Kendall Hunt Publishing Company

Only about 10% of the general population is born to serve others and have an attitude to please. About 60% can be trained to serve, and about 30% don't belong in hospitality. Seek out and hire the 10%, sort through the 60%, train them to act like the 10%, *and then run from the other 30%!*

Successful hospitality professionals share certain common qualities. Some are innate, while many can be developed. As you read these, you will begin to see a model of an ideal candidate to hire. Below is a list:

- ▶ A genuine desire to please others. They find reward that comes in a job well done
- ▶ Motivation from within—an energetic personality
- ▶ Bring a positive attitude to work—leaving personal issues behind
- ▶ Adaptability to situations, but consistency in performance
- ▶ Ability to anticipate needs and demands before they occur
- ▶ Duty of loyalty to the company
- ▶ Sensitivity and consideration to the needs of others
- ▶ Sincerity
- ▶ Knowledge of rules, procedures, and products (which is different from rules that can be broken/not broken?)

- A thirst for continuous learning
- Knowledge of themselves (+/−)
- Pride in themselves
- Knowledge of standards of excellence—what to strive for
- Positive habits
- Great listening skills
- Great communication skills

Hiring correctly is crucial for guest service. Your staff will be more content, they will perform better, and a momentum will pick up that will make the manager's job much easier. Another benefit of this is lowered **employee turnover**, which is a measure of the gains and losses of employees. It is typically expressed as a percentage during a given period, such as a year. A higher turnover percentage means that employees work at the business for a shorter amount of time before leaving or being terminated. Lowered turnover means less time spent training, a lower training expense, and the aggravation that comes along with it, hence causing even more turnover. Reducing turnover means more content employees and is a general indication that your operation is well-run. All of this contributes to successfully implementing customer service.

To calculate employee turnover:

1. First, determine the period of time to be used (month, quarter, or year).
2. Determine number of the separations (number of employees that have left and been replaced). Each full-time employee counts as 1. Adjust accordingly for part-time employees who will equal a fraction relative to their hours (ex: 2 half-time employees equal 1).
3. Divide the number of separations by the total number of employees during that same period (again, adjust for part-time employees).
4. Multiply this number by 100 to receive a percentage. (Note: Sometimes the calculation is simplified by only including full-time workers. It can also be calculated for management, employees, or new hires separately. You may also need to adjust for adding employees or downsizing.)

Employee Turnover

A measure of the rate of employee losses and gains during a given period.

SERVICE INSIGHT

Duty of Loyalty

It is probably in the manual. Employees should have a duty of loyalty to their company. That means that they should always be acting in the best interest of the company.

This means at work and sometimes extends to outside of work. Most companies agree and are doing something about it. Companies are cracking down on employee social media presence. Companies can and do terminate employees for lessening the reputation of the company.

Loyalty, Integrity, Trust, Support, Agreement
© EtiAmmos/Shutterstock.com

Communication

When you communicate, you are revealing much more than you might initially realize. As a customer approaches you, an identity of them begins to form. Without them saying a single word, you have formed a detailed picture of who they are. Consciously or subconsciously, this often directs how they will react in a situation. It will direct their questions and their responses. Be conscious of this. Your guesses are often correct, although you continue to hone this skill throughout life. You can expound and put together such descriptors as:

- ► Confidence
- ► Education
- ► Knowledge of surroundings
- ► Mood or demeanor
- ► Accent—country or region
- ► Gender
- ► Sexual orientation
- ► Social status
- ► Respect for others
- ► Energy level
- ► Age
- ► Personal lifestyle
- ► Ambitions
- ► Health

It goes both ways. As they look at you, they are also doing the same thing. This changes the service experience. It alters their expectations. A certain profile will cause customers to assume and thus change how they are going to react or "play it!" A profile may remind them of someone or they may associate a communication/presence with a certain outcome. Not everyone is so open and unjudgmental.

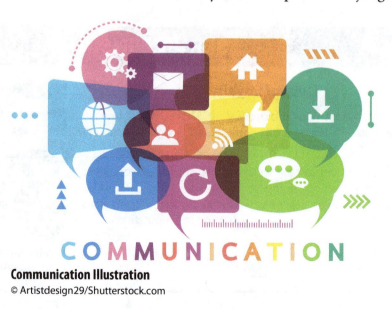

Communication Illustration
© Artistdesign29/Shutterstock.com

Owners Warmly Acknowledging Presence of Guest
© Dmytro Zinkevych/Shutterstock.com

10 and 5 Rule

Knowing when to greet a guest can be made simple with a few tips on distance and the "10 and 5 Rule" can help. As a staff member comes in contact with a customer, they should respond accordingly. They should stop what they are doing and acknowledge their presence with a smile and eye contact at a distance of 10 feet. This should continue. When they come within 5 feet of the guest they should present them with a greeting. It is as simple as that! The 10 and 5 rule is easy to train others in and easy to remember.

VISUAL

You only have one chance to make a first impression. These visuals will tell much without ever speaking a word.

Dress and appearance: what works well for one situation may be very inappropriate for another. People judge each other. People are all taught that they should not do this, but most often do make these snap judgments of others. A business must control what it is able to, and the employees' initial appearance is something that can be controlled. Customers are approaching front-line service staff with needs that often have to do with their trust in them for their health, safety, money, entertainment, status, and comfort. The first impression can make a big difference!

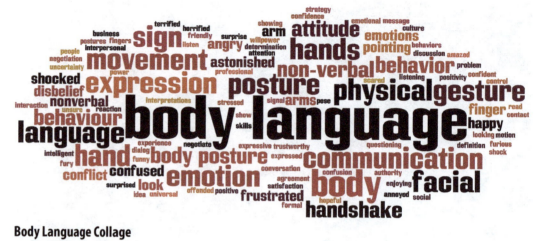

Body Language Collage
© Boris15/Shutterstock.com

BODY LANGUAGE

Many ideas are communicated without ever speaking a word. Because many people mistrust the spoken word alone, they look for other clues in body language. All must be synchronized in order to do this. People pick up on these clues very quickly, often without realizing it.

Hidden feelings and thoughts may be revealed through body language. This could help to interpret a customer, or help them to gain a trust or professional image for you.

Humans use many senses. Body language can give subtle clues as to the underlying premise of a person's motivation. Communication occurs in many ways, and verbal is only a part of the equation of communication. In other words, you can tell what someone is thinking by watching how their body reacts. The same is true for the customer. You could be saying all of the correct things, but if your body tells a different story, you are sending a mixed message. They must be synchronized.

Body Language

Nonverbal communication that gives clues to one's underlying premise.

OTHER DEFINITIONS

Eyes: People often desire eye contact during a conversation. They are comforted by another giving them this. Looking away when someone is speaking conveys an attitude of disrespect or insincerity. You want to give them your undivided attention or they may feel unimportant.

Head: Nodding of the head also conveys active listening skills. Shaking, bobbing, and facing any other direction than directly at the guest should be avoided.

Face: Avoid blank looks. Smile whenever possible. Be aware if you naturally scowl or frown.

Hands: Avoid excessive hand gestures. Point with open hands conveys trust. Avoid waving continuously, using a tightened fist, hands in pockets, or fumbling with keys or jewelry.

Arms: Never folded arm and keep at your sides. Behind your back is fine. Never lean.

Torso: Turned toward the guest, as straight as possible. Note your posture. Be professional.

Legs: Stance should be about shoulder-width apart. Avoid leaning on one side or shifting back and forth. Crossed or together for women; together for men, they should always be bent at the knees while sitting and never apart.

Feet: Should be flat to the floor and pointed at the customer. Avoid shifting and tapping.

Distance: How close is too close? This depends on the occasion: closer for personal (24–48 inches). Further for social, formal, or public. Watch if the guest gets closer or backs away or appears uncomfortable.

Remember that your body communicates. All must be instinctive or it will look rehearsed or contrived. You must practice these principles to appear genuine. When dealing with customers, it is important for you to be able to discern their body language. It is also important for you to convey the appropriate body language. You typically know when you get it right.

✦ VOCAL

Vocal expression is even more difficult to control. Few people focus on it, but it is essential. Have you listened to yourself on a recording? It is probably very difficult to do this. If you are serious about your presence, you should. When doing so, observe:

- ► Inflection: variation in voice
- ► Pitch: high, low, or monotone
- ► Timing: fast or slow
- ► Volume: loud or quiet

Ask these questions:

- ► Is it strong enough to resonate confidence?
- ► Is it firm enough to command a presence?
- ► Is it distinctive?
- ► Does it enunciate?

As an exercise, try listening to others for these qualities. It quickly makes you aware of your vocal abilities. Also try to learn phrases that parallel the organizational culture. Examples of training responses are:

- ► Please and thank you.
- ► May I?
- ► It is my pleasure.
- ► That would be great.
- ► With your permission.

- Would you consider?
- I regret to inform you that.
- Great question.
- That makes sense.
- Have you considered?

Also consider integrating other key words that identify with the organizational culture such as:

- Opportunity
- Challenging
- Options
- Fine
- Well

There are also words that should be discouraged and removed from your vocabulary. It is difficult to remove them "just at work." Instead, remove them from your personal life as well. Otherwise they will creep in when you are relaxed or in times of stress. Avoid words such as:

- Vulgarities
- Profanities
- Religious, political, and sexual references
- Honey, babe, or sugar
- Kid
- Axe (a question)
- You's
- Fittin'
- Fixin'
- OMG

Also remember to be optimistic and avoid negative phrases such as:

- Hang on.
- You have to.
- Not my job.
- I don't know.
- I don't have time.
- I haven't had the time.
- I can't.
- I won't.

SERVICE INSIGHT

Making a Connection: Using Guests' Names

Consider how effective these questions can be when using names:

▶ Mr. ___ or Ms. ___, where are you coming from?

▶ Mr. ___ or Ms. ___, how was your travel in today?

▶ Mr. ___ or Ms. ___, have you been to any of our properties before?

▶ Mr. ___ or Ms. ___, can I provide suggestions for any part of your stay?

Other tips for making a connection:

▶ First, observe the guest. Make eye contact. Read the guest, but don't presume.

▶ Realize that these questions cannot be forced. Skip the questions if they are rushed or bothered.

▶ Stay in the moment. And focus solely on their presence.

▶ Listen to what and how they are saying it. This allows better and more unique experience specifically tailored to them.

ANSWERING THE TELEPHONE

Everyone speaks on the telephone. It is very natural, but the rules change at the workplace. A business must train the employees to use a protocol. These tips can truly make a difference when answering the telephone:

▶ Use the standard greeting.
▶ Identify yourself by name and company, thank them for calling.
▶ Minimize background noises.
▶ Listen and do not interrupt.
▶ Be patient and don't rush them.
▶ Pretend that you are looking at them.
▶ Envision them as being in front of you.
▶ Smile, it will come through in your voice.
▶ Avoid multi-tasking, most people can tell that you are doing something else.
▶ Take note of their name and use it if possible.
▶ Restate and reply to each comment or question individually.
▶ Apologize for any inconveniences.
▶ Tell them what you are doing to satisfy their need.
▶ Apologize, give estimated time, and ask permission before placing them on hold.
▶ Ask if you have answered their question.
▶ Ask if there is anything else you can help them with.
▶ Keep notes, follow up as needed, and do what you said you would do.

Employee Answering Telephone With a Smile
© LarsZ/Shutterstock.com

Initiating the Call

- ▶ Have a plan, script, or flowchart to follow.
- ▶ Greet and identify your name and company and department.
- ▶ State your reason for the call.
- ▶ Ask if they are the correct person.
- ▶ Refer to them by name.
- ▶ Write down notes—have a phone record sheet.
- ▶ Remember that you are repeating this many times, but it is the first time they have heard it.
- ▶ Have the computer system, calendar, and telephone directory available.

Leaving a Message

- ▶ Speak slowly and clearly.
- ▶ Leave date and time of call.
- ▶ Identify yourself and company.
- ▶ Leave basic information.
- ▶ Suggest options or tell them there is nothing else for them to do at this time.
- ▶ Leave a number and contact information.
- ▶ Leave a pleasant closing.

Training, Managing, and Developing

People get on the bus. People get off the bus. Your job as a leader is to keep driving the bus and make sure that people don't get run over by it.

—Abstracted from Jim Collins' *Good to Great*,
HarperCollins Publishers 2001

Employees may come and go. A few need to move on, but many can and should be developed. It is your job as a manager to keep the momentum. Your job as a manager will be much easier if you have a great staff. Hiring the right person is only half of the battle. You must properly train, manage, and develop them. In doing so, you will surely be rewarded.

This section details a four-step process for training, managing, and developing:

1. Demonstrate personal and procedural expectations.
2. Integrate and initiate into culture.
3. Demonstrate service standards.
4. Monitor, assess, support, and reward.

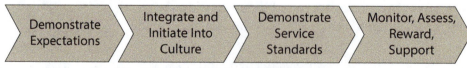

Four-Step Process for Training, Managing, and Developing

DEMONSTRATE PERSONAL AND PROCEDURAL EXPECTATIONS

| Demonstrate Expectations | Integrate and Initiate Into Culture | Demonstrate Service Standards | Monitor, Assess, Reward, Support |

Goal Setting

Everyone should be challenged. Setting goals helps establish expectations. It also helps to ensure that objectives are completed and goals are met. It keeps employees on track and allows management to fulfill its expectations from the ranks above.

Let the employees know what is expected of them. This should be detailed in the job description. It is continued through orientation and initial training. It also comes up in reviews. As simple as it is, using ABC Prioritizing is quite successful.

ABC Prioritizing

► Record all of your tasks on a list as bullet statements.
► Rank each of them as A, B, or C.
 ☐ A = the tasks that must be completed today.
 ☐ B = the tasks that are important, but could wait a day if necessary.
 ☐ C = the tasks that can wait.
► If something is of utmost importance, label it an AA, or even an AAA. Work on those first.
► A task labeled B may soon become an AAA, but it doesn't have to be done on the prior day.
► Now, begin the day working on the A's first. Then completing the B's. And, as time permits, work on the C's.
► Place a line through items as you complete them.
► Write up and revise a new list at the end of each day while it is still fresh in your head.

As a manager, you should also set goals. Keep a close notice of what consumes the majority of your time. Delegate whenever appropriate and don't be embarrassed to ask for help. You will be setting the employee expectations. Keep them informed and promote cross-training. Consider your role as an enabler of customer service.

Use of Terms

Nearly every business has terminology. A great example of this is Walt Disney World who uses the terms to help demonstrate expectations:

Onstage and Offstage

- ► Similar to front of house and back of house.
- ► Everyone is to perform a role when in front of the customer.

Cast Members

- ► All employees are in a play or performance.
- ► Employees are all dedicated to the same cause.

Guests

- ► All customers are really guests of ours.
- ► They are invited to join us in the performance.
- ► They aren't a nuisance, they are welcomed.

Standards

Standard Operating Procedure

A formalized method. Crucial in training to achieve consistency.

Every business needs standards for control and consistency. For example, "Try to refer to a guest by name whenever possible." Standards are used in training and evaluation. Without them, employees would have no idea what to do, or if they are doing it well. It may seem contradictory and controlling, but the employee discretion and **standard operating procedures (SOP)** can co-exist.

INTEGRATE AND INITIATE INTO CULTURE

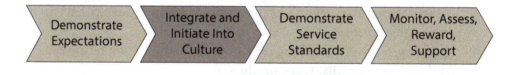

Demonstrate Expectations → Integrate and Initiate Into Culture → Demonstrate Service Standards → Monitor, Assess, Reward, Support

Internal Customers

If you're not serving the customer, your job is to be serving someone who is.

—Jan Carlzon

Internal Customers

Staff that are served by other employees. This mindset helps employees to recognize they are serving those who serve the customer and the importance of assisting them in their roles.

Internal customers are an idea that staff who serve other employees should think of them as customers that are internal to the organization. Those employees go on to serve the customer. By contrast, typical customers outside of the organization are referred to as *external customers*. This mindset helps employees to recognize that their service to other employees can have a direct impact on the customer. The idea is that an employee will deliver better service to another if they think of them as a customer. Employees also need to get along with each other when in front of customers. The public can easily notice when employees are fighting and it makes them feel awkward.

Developing a Culture/Managing an Image

An **organizational culture** is a personality of a business. It answers many of the questions that are difficult to place in procedure manuals. It can be designed and managed and it also has a life of its own. Your business can have a culture of helping customer service or hurting customer service.

Does your staff feel as though they are part of the family?

A culture directs many of the small details that cannot easily be expressed or managed. It should be facilitated at all employee contact points including orientation, training, in the policies and guidelines, and in the verbiage or terminology. It should dictate:

> **Organizational Culture**
>
> The personality of a business: The style, pace, and attitude. It can be managed while also having a life of its own.

- ▶ Work pace
- ▶ Work style
- ▶ Attitude toward each other
- ▶ Attitude toward customers
- ▶ Presentation—appearance
- ▶ Skill sets
- ▶ Accountability
- ▶ Activities
- ▶ Priorities

INDUSTRY EXAMPLE

Corporate Culture at the Marriot International

Marriott International is an example of a company with a strong corporate culture. If you've ever spoken to an employee, you will know this is true. In the words of J. W. Marriott, Jr., "Culture is the life-thread and glue that links our past, present, and future."

Marriott is committed to fair treatment of associates and to providing training and advancement opportunities to all. Marriott's reputation for superior customer service rises out of a long tradition that started with J. Willard Marriott's simple goal for Hot Shoppes to provide:

- ▶ Good food and good service at a fair price.
- ▶ Do whatever it takes to take care of the customer.
- ▶ Pay extraordinary attention to detail.
- ▶ Take pride in their physical surroundings.
- ▶ Use their creativity to find new ways to meet the needs of customers.
- ▶ Actively support the community.
- ▶ Encourage associate volunteerism through a variety of organizations.

Marriott employees have such a strong, caring nature that many donate their personal vacation time to be transferred to other employees in need of leave.

http://www.marriott.com/corporateinfo/culture/coreCulture.mi

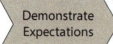

DEMONSTRATE SERVICE STANDARDS

| Demonstrate Expectations | Integrate and Initiate Into Culture | Demonstrate Service Standards | Monitor, Assess, Reward, Support |

Empowerment

A family is walking through an amusement park, enjoying the day. The children each have an ice cream cone in hand when suddenly the smaller child's ice cream cone falls on the ground. The child immediately begins to cry. The parents are consoling the child, and considering options. They look over and see a long line for ice cream.

A nearby employee sees this and walks behind the counter, serves up a replacement cone and brings it over to the crying child. The child is pleased and the parents are relieved.

Certainly controls are in place, and items must be accounted for, but customer satisfaction comes first. Actions like this are common at Walt Disney World. In fact, they share this story with employees at orientation, describing the idea of **empowerment**. This is enabling the employees with the authority, or power, to make decisions in the best interest of the guests. This is done with training and trust. It permits guest service issues to be handled more quickly. It gives the employees a feeling of accomplishment and trust. It frees time from management. To implement this:

▶ Establish a culture.
▶ Detail the guest service expectations.
▶ Give examples.
▶ Set limits.
▶ Have a reporting procedure.
▶ Management must back up employee decisions.

Empowerment
Enabling employees with the authority to make decisions in the best interest of the guests.

Empower Collage
© ibreakstock/Shutterstock.com

- ► Recognize great decisions.
- ► Be constructive with lesser decisions.

Empowerment permits employees to make a difference. It reduces frustration by removing the need to involve managers and speeds up the resolution process.

An amazing example of empowerment: When the two-time Baldrige Award-winning Ritz Carlton first applied for the Malcolm Baldrige Quality Award, they empowered employees to resolve customer situations as they saw fit up to $2,000. See if they still were awarded the Malcolm Baldrige award.

INDUSTRY EXAMPLE

Ritz-Carlton Hotel Company Standards

Ritz-Carleton's motto, credo: *three steps of service, service values,* and the employee promise can all be found at this link:

http://corporate.ritzcarlton.com/en/About/GoldStandards.htm

MONITOR, ASSESS, SUPPORT, REWARD

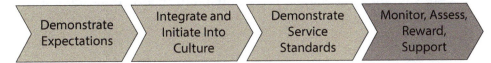

Demonstrate Expectations → Integrate and Initiate Into Culture → Demonstrate Service Standards → Monitor, Assess, Reward, Support

Monitor

There is a belief that a manager should let little things go. They should not constantly police and monitor their employees. Instead, they should train their staff, trust them, empower them, and be more like a coach. Another belief is that a manager must begin strictly because once they let things slip, it is very difficult to resume control and employees will respect the strictness of the manager. While yet a third idea is that lenient (and coaching) is fine and strict is fine, but inconsistency causes frustration and dissention. Most agree with the third idea.

SERVICE INSIGHT

Explaining the Purpose

There was once a chef who demanded that all of the warming boxes were to be wiped out every night. This seemed unreasonable to the employees because the warming boxes were never dirty. The food was wrapped and there was no need to clean the boxes. This task was left undone when the chef was away on vacation. After a few days, employees realized that food was being left in the warming boxes. What the chef was really getting at was that he didn't want food left in the boxes. If they were wiped out, they were emptied out, and extra food would not be wasted. Sometimes there is much wisdom behind rules that employees don't understand. <u>People need to understand why things are done.</u> It was a joke that "Generation Y" would be renamed "Generation Why" because they needed to be told the purpose behind it. Surely other generations also wondered, but it is prevalent in new entrants of today's workforce. Explaining the *why* is yet another practical tip to gaining buy-in with employees.

Assess

Evaluations can be difficult to give and receive. Evaluations should be a formality with no surprises. Employees should receive continuous feedback and know how they are doing all along. Feedback should be treated as an opportunity to improve.

Meetings are another chance to meet with employees and let them know how they are doing. Managers should also have day-to-day conversations with employees, and meetings should be for things that cannot be done through other methods. Below are tips for conducting successful meetings:

▶ Have an agenda and try your best to stay on it.
▶ Make meetings short, less than than 30 minutes.
▶ Attention spans are short, so should be the topics of meetings.
▶ Stick to the important things making meetings meaningful or don't hold them.
▶ Show the same respect for others at meetings and the people and others will reciprocate.
▶ If it is dissemination of information, ask if it could it be done in another way.
▶ Ensure that all participants can see and hear each other.
▶ Pre-shift meetings should be essential information only and last 5 minutes or less.

Support

Front-line workers have various priorities. Some want to excel in management and others only want it for a short time until they finish school or complete something else. They are using this as a stepping-stone or buying time with it. Some have limited options for their future. Others are out of work and this is a job until they get a better job. It's important to know where employees come from and where they want to go and what they want out of a job.

However, the business also has priorities and everyone needs to realize this. When discussing this with employees, address the idea of their future in the industry and with your company. There is a relationship between the needs of the business and the needs of an employee. Those priorities must be balanced. Just like a traveler stops by a hotel for a short visit and then is on his or her way, so do employees. However, an employee must pay with hard work and dedication just like the traveler must pay with money for the accommodations. It is a trade-off, and both parties need to know where each other stands.

Another point to mention is that of conflict. When conflict occurs, realize that some conflict is acceptable. People are different and without it we would grow stagnant. Try to realize what is behind the emotions, and always be professional. As a manager, you should anticipate problems before they occur.

Reward

Incentives and reward are key motivators. Why does a dog bark at the mailman? Because every time the dog sees the mailman, he barks and then the mailman goes away. So, why wouldn't the dog bark?

SERVICE INSIGHT

Checking in With Employees

One manager would walk around every day and say good night before he left for the day and have a brief conversation with each and every employee. What was he really doing? Was he a really friendly guy? Perhaps. Did he really want to say good-bye? Probably not. He was monitoring the employees. He was checking on their status, the accomplishments, trouble-shooting, and keeping a general view on what was happening within the ranks. He developed a relationship with each employee. Everyone knew him and felt comfortable speaking to him. This was his way of monitoring operations.

How are your employees motivated? Employee reward systems should have clear goals and address the appropriate behavior and actions. When done properly, it has a great impact. The rewards should be consistent. They don't have to be monetary. Rewards can be intangible. Rewarding specific actions and service works better than an overall reward. Remember, providing good service should be more of a habit than a reward.

The opposite of rewards is punishments. If a company punishes based on complaints, the employees and managers will hide the actual number of complaints.

SERVICE INSIGHT

Saying Yes

Being optimistic can work. As a manager you should learn how you can say yes to an employee's request. Instead of saying that they are crazy for their request or that the employee is ridiculous, you could take a different more optimistic approach. Show them how their request could be accommodated, but in what situations and circumstances that it could work. The circumstances might be steep, but it sets goals and allows them to make the steps to advance and fulfill their goals.

Team Management

Implementing service rarely occurs with just one person. It is usually part of a team effort. Team management has been very popular in the literature and practice over the last 20–30 years, providing much insight on team practice. The original idea of teams was to use a cohesive group instead of passing problems and customers from department to department. A group effort was seen as a solution to the disjointed, "silo effect" that plagued organizations. The goals of the teams were to improve productivity, quality, and efficiency in an effort to best serve the customers. Teams have offered many benefits such as:

- ▶ Work load distribution
- ▶ Idea generation
- ▶ New perspectives
- ▶ Oversight for responsibility and objectivity

TEAM Effectiveness, Precise, Creative, Communicative
© ivosar/Shutterstock.com

Despite these advantages, many teams have not been entirely successful. Teams must be run well so the benefits exceed the costs. If not, the demands of resources on a team could easily exceed the costs. At an early age, most people have already been exposed to a team environment that was unfavorable. As a result, some employees dread the idea of teamwork and prefer to work alone. Why then, do teams fail? Teams fail for a number of reasons. Communication, personality, planning, and roles are a few. Below is a list of the most common reasons why groups fail to become highly successful:

- ► Communication and Awareness
  - ☐ Lack of communication leading to a lack of understanding
  - ☐ Unaware of expectations
  - ☐ Unreal expectations
  - ☐ Unaware of the pitfalls
  - ☐ Misjudgment of conditions
  - ☐ Lack of contribution to group communications
- ► Personalities and Traits
  - ☐ Not realizing personalities
  - ☐ Bad blending of personalities
  - ☐ Insecurity within self
  - ☐ Lack of flexibility
  - ☐ Lack of concern
  - ☐ No trust between members, in process
  - ☐ Self-importance
  - ☐ Not managing known weaknesses
  - ☐ Lack of diversity
  - ☐ Fear of conflict
  - ☐ Lack of commitment
  - ☐ Lack of ability

- ► Planning and Scheduling
  - ☐ Lack of motivation resulting in a lack of timeliness
  - ☐ Poor time management of members
  - ☐ Inappropriate allocation of assignments
  - ☐ Failure to have a backup plan
  - ☐ Lack of recognition of work
  - ☐ Not given proper resources
  - ☐ Lack of accountability
  - ☐ Inappropriate management of strengths and weaknesses
  - ☐ Loss of focus on objectives
- ► Past team issues

✦ TYPES OF TEAMS

Teams can be classified in many ways. The most common classifications use characteristics of functionality, purpose, duration, supervision, and dependency.

Functionality of Team

Functional teams

- ► Description: Within the same area, but with different levels of supervision. Typically focused on specific issues.
- ► Frequency: Several times/week or constant
- ► Size and duration: 4–20 in size and relatively permanent
- ► Example goals: Quality customer service

Cross-functional teams

- ► Description: From different areas of organization, but at about the same supervisory level. Teams are problem-solvers, created for specific assignments.
- ► Frequency: 1–3 times/week
- ► Size and duration: 4–12 in size; a few weeks to 1 year or until problem is solved
- ► Example goals: Improved efficiency or communication

Purpose of the Team

Operational

- ► Goal: Production oriented
- ► Example: A staff team at a box office

Problem-Solution

- ► Goal: Solving specific issues; implement solutions
- ► Example: Waste-reduction team

Product Development

- ▶ Goal: Developing new or improved products or systems
- ▶ Example: Adding a new boutique line

Employee Development

- ▶ Goal: Staff development
- ▶ Example: Group bonding at ropes course

Duration of Team

- ▶ Terminal: Team disbands when project objectives are completed
- ▶ Non-terminal or ongoing: Team is permanent until re-assigned

Supervision

Self-directed teams

- ▶ Description: All responsible for objective/goals. No formal supervisor. They vote, evaluate each other, and form a group consensus.
- ▶ Frequency: 1–3 times/week
- ▶ Size and duration: 4–15; until problem is solved, a few weeks to 1 year
- ▶ Example goals: Efficiency, customer service

Directed teams

- ▶ Supervisor directs efforts and monitors

Dependency

Interdependent

- ▶ Description: Interdependent teams rely on each other to reach objectives
- ▶ Example: Security team at a concert

Independent teams

- ▶ Description: Independent teams work mostly independently; one is not supporting the role of the other
- ▶ Example: Waitstaff team at an ala carte restaurant

Virtual Teams

- ▶ Description: Meet, communicate and work through problems from a distance through the use of electronic methods: telephone, video, and so forth. Virtual teams have both advantages and disadvantages. Despite this, they have become very popular, particularly with larger organizations that have multiple properties. They work especially well when the group members do not need to work together or continuously depend upon each other as in the case of independent teams. Below are some of the advantages and disadvantages of virtual teams.

Advantages

▶ Not geographically-specific, location does not matter
▶ Easily allows members to join from outside the organization
▶ Permits those who might never had been able to join due to logistical reasons

Disadvantages

▶ Lack of nonverbal communication cues
▶ Exchange of information can be difficult
▶ Technology-dependent

A common type of team in the 1980s was known as a Quality Circle. This was a team of about 8–10 employees and supervisors. They met regularly to discuss quality issues, research the causes, and recommend solutions or corrective actions. They didn't actually implement the changes. They were very successful. According to the above characteristics, it would have been described as nonterminal, directed, and interdependent.

⁂ TEAM STAGES OF DEVELOPMENT

The most commonly used framework for team development stages was devised by Bruce W. Tuckman in the 1960s: forming, storming, norming, and performing. Tuckman's model has been given alternative names, but the general idea has withstood the test of time and is still used to describe the progression of groups.

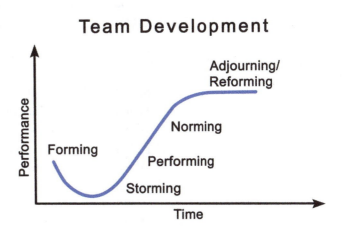

1. Forming: Familiarization, getting acquainted with leadership issues
2. Storming: Fighting, goal/objective issues
3. Norming: Beginning to trust and form a structure
4. Performing: Productive teamwork
5. Adjourning: Closing, reflecting, celebrating

Team Stages: Forming, Storming, Norming, Performing, Adjourning
© arka38/Shutterstock.com

Groups are yet another key to customer service. Recognition of these stages helps the team leader and members to realize what is occurring and what is to come. Expecting these stages, realizing these stages, and working with the stages helps the group to progress through them more efficiently and effectively. As a result, they can progress to the fourth and final stage of performing in a productive manner.

TYPES OF TEAM MEMBERS

Everyone brings something to the team. Hopefully, it is a positive attribute. Recognizing and channeling the characteristics of others is the key to successfully working together. Diversity of characteristics often leads to conflict, but also produces some of the best results when overcome. There are many classifications of team members. Many combine a few variables and give descriptive names, such as, "Dominator," "Invisible Man," or "Diplomat." Most are categorized by the following headings:

Approach to Problems

▶ Acceptance: Do they accept problems or question them?
▶ Solution style: Do they seek an immediate answer or wish to collect more information and suspend judgment?

Interaction/Expression

▶ Communication: How do they prefer to communicate? How frequently? How involved are they? What is their preferred tone?
▶ Ability to negotiate: Do they seek a win-win, dominate, or give up?
▶ Conflict: Is it welcomed or avoided? Do they argue loudly or softly?
▶ Transitions: Can they move on from a topic or an argument?
▶ Empathy: How concerned are they for others?
▶ Introversion: Do they generally prefer interacting with others or alone?

Work Style

▶ Stage: Do they prefer to begin, work on, or complete a task?
▶ Work pace: Are they fast or slow?
▶ Work quality: Is their work sloppy, average, or perfect?
▶ Balance: Are they most concerned with completion or perfection?
▶ Work focus: Are they detail-oriented or are they focused on the big picture?

Personal/Emotional

▶ Motivation level: Are they naturally motivated?
▶ Honesty: Are they straightforward, or do they downplay or embellish?
▶ Ability to control: Can they control their emotions?
▶ Priority: What level of priority are the group objectives?
▶ Comfort: Are they comfortable with the group?
▶ Confidence: How confident are they in their abilities?

Expertise/Intellectual

▶ Specialization: What is their specialization?
▶ Capacity: Are they below, at par, or above the average intelligence of the group?

✦ HOW TO MAKE TEAMS WORK

To make teams work is an ongoing refinement of many qualities. To begin, have knowledge of the team members and the issues. Then, assess and regulate the members, activities, and environment. Have the ability to stay focused and meet the objective, yet be flexible enough for changes. While seemingly contradictory, all of these things must be kept in mind. In order for teams to be successful, you must:

- ► Know the types of teams and assign appropriately
- ► Know the typical roles of the members
- ► Keep the pitfalls in mind
- ► Stay focused on the objective and monitor

Knowledge of members, objectives, and progress is key. Know the resources available. Analyze the risks. Understand the goals. Interact with the other members as much as possible. Understand the realities of the environment and situation. Monitor progress; have them e-mail progress regularly.

Objective is the purpose of the team. It is easy to get off-topic and lose sight of the reason why the team is in place. Begin each shift with a goal. Monitor timeframes, keeping responsibilities in mind. Ensure that employees are aware of the meaningful purpose of what you ask them to do. Often they will think that their job is not important. Let them know what would happen if their duties were not performed.

Balance the members and work. Manage the change. Be willing to be flexible, lend help, and be ready to re-group, re-design. Provide prompt and honest feedback. Give employees a chance to improve, set goals, and strive for something more. Always have a backup plan, and then have a backup plan for your backup plan.

Culture of the team will supersede the other directives. Have a team culture that fits the tasks, members, and organization. The culture is the personality that develops the unwritten rules and expectations. Foster communication with each other, realizing the different styles of the group members.

Planning will guide the process, utilizing the members, keeping the available resources in mind, and allocating workload appropriately.

SERVICE INSIGHT

Work to Live or Live to Work

A speaker was sharing his experience of recently opening up a restaurant. He told the class that he was in three other industries prior to opening up the restaurant. He said that as he was learning about the restaurant industry, many people told him that it wasn't a lifestyle for him. They said that it took too many hours and that it wasn't as glamorous as he thought. Now that he is in business, he states that it doesn't seem to have many more hours than the other industries that he was involved in; however, people in restaurants tend to brag more about how many hours they work. Some people live to work and others work to live. The ones that he encountered loved to talk, or complain, about how they lived to work. He went on to say that restaurateurs just seem to have a larger soapbox on which to stand. In a distorted way, they enjoy bragging about how much they hated to work.

Conclusion

You need to manage your own career and assist employees in managing theirs. The hospitality industry is an awesome industry, with challenges just like every other industry. It can be a win-win. Encouraging employees to plan requests off for the days they want far in advance and to have a life outside of work promotes balance of work and life. Allow them to enjoy other hobbies, and live their lives as we all want to and should. When this happens, employees will enjoy coming to work and it will surely be evident in the service they provide.

CHAPTER REVIEW QUESTIONS

1. List the most important attributes that hospitality companies look for in hiring candidates.
2. Why is nonverbal communication so important to delivering quality service?
3. List and briefly describe five aspects of body language that you would seek in a concierge position.
4. Explain the concept of employee empowerment.
5. Why is developing an organizational culture crucial to developing a brand?
6. Should a manager be strict, or lenient, or consistent? Explain.
7. When should you devise a list when ABC Prioritizing?
8. Outline the stages of team development.
9. Ideally, how long should a meeting be in length?

CASE STUDIES

Special Privileges

Agents Field is a mid-sized, outdoor venue. It has a small-town feel. It seats crowds of up to 9,000 people for concerts and events. It is seasonal and weather-permitting. Keeping a core staff is very difficult, and many are temporary workers for the summer. It is difficult to hire and train the staff because of the small prime season. It is, essentially, all or nothing. Roger is staffing manager. He is in charge of all staffing.

Rhonda is one of his core employees. She is a very talented worker. Other employees look up to her and Roger has always valued her. She is able to fill in on nearly every station, although she prefers bartending because of the tips.

Roger notices that Rhonda is changing. She is beginning to become very persistent. She begins to complain and demand certain shifts on certain stations. She invents and argues seniority which didn't exist prior. She tells Roger that it isn't worth it if she cannot make $200 a shift. He also hears that she told other employees how they don't need to cater to the guests' needs.

As he learns this, Roger asks Rhonda to come into his office for a discussion. He explains that she has always been a valued employee but that he is very concerned with the recent change in her behavior. He explains that it is against the standard practice to give seniority all of the preferred shifts. Instead, Agents Field has always divided the prime shifts and stations equally. Rhonda is clearly upset at not getting her way.

1. Outline the issues of Roger, the staffing manager.
2. In your opinion and according to the advice in the chapter, did Roger handle the situation with Rhonda appropriately? Explain your reasoning.
3. What kind of communication would best be used with Rhonda?

Train the Trainer

Karen is a dock captain at the Sunshine Marine Club, a 58-slip yacht club located in southern Florida. She has worked there part-time for 6 years through high school and college. Karen performs to minimum standards. She has become complacent and tired of the job. She does the basics just to get by. Stacia is the club manager. She is always very busy solving problems and runs from one thing to another the entire time she is there. The Sunshine Marine Club does not have a formal training system. Instead, they utilize an unofficial train-the-trainer system. Basically, the person who is available and has worked there the longest trains the newest workers. This is typically done by the new worker following, or shadowing, the tenured person. Eventually, the new person is left alone. A few standards exist, but they are not often reviewed, and Stacia is very busy tending to the rest of the club. She only responds if there is a problem, so the employees on the dock try to keep the problems down and enjoy being left alone.

One day, a new hire named Amy begins. She appears young and eager and very conscientious. It is obvious that she wants to do well. Her paperwork is complete and Stacia walks her to the dock and introduces her to Karen, a dock captain, working that day. Karen is very polite in front of Stacia and welcomes Amy. She assures Stacia that everything will be fine and that she will be glad to allow Amy to shadow her and train under her. As soon as Stacia leaves, Karen goes in the dock house, sits down, and lights a cigarette. She turns toward Amy and says, "I hate it here. Just stay out of trouble and everything will be fine." Karen then picks up a book and begins to read.

Amy is unsure what to do. She doesn't want to tell on her coworker and wreck the job. She wants to learn what to do and would like to do a good job. She feels like she is stuck.

1. Outline the training system at the Sunshine Marine Club.
2. Describe Stacia's train-the-trainer style.
3. In your opinion, what should Amy do to correct the situation?
4. What standards should be in place to ensure this doesn't happen again?

Body Language

Mike is a new manager at the Loco el Loco, an airport bar. He has worked at other bars, but just landed this position because the prior manager had to suddenly quit due to health issues. Since Mike has begun, he noticed something different about a bartender named Sabrina. Mike has noticed that customer counts have remained consistent, but sales per customer have steadily declined at the bar during her shifts. New to the location and employees, he decides to secretly observe her one day without her being aware. He notices that she does everything required. She greets the guests, she pours timely, she distributes menus, and everything else required.

Upon running additional reports, he notices that her tip percentage is substantially lower than any other bartender on any other shift. He decides to confront her with these reports. She immediately gives him an evil eye. He feels very uncomfortable, but continues to show her the reports. She says very little. She is unsure of the reports. What she says is technically fine, but the way that she says it strikes Mike as being odd. She technically says and does the right things, but just doesn't have a service personality or click with the customers.

As he observes her more, he notices that no one warms up to her at the bar. People sit down for one drink and leave, looking as if they just want to leave. People linger for hours with the other bartenders, almost causing a problem with seat turnover. Mike is perplexed.

1. Assess the personality and communication traits of Sabrina.
2. Was Mike handling the situation appropriately?
3. What are Mike's options with rectifying the issues with Sabrina at this point?

The Whinery

The Whinery is a local winery with a catchy name. The Whinery was established by a local college professor a few years ago as a side project. He loved wine and turned his hobby into a reality. He has since retired and expanded the business to include a tasting room and gift shop. The problem is that he was a better professor than he was a winemaker. He makes wines according to his own methods, and will only produce wines that please him personally. To add, his arrogant attitude as a wine snob ceased any possibilities of him hearing constructive criticism. This occasionally worked, as some customers would admire his bold, new ideas. More often, the customers would be snubbed if they didn't agree with him and his ideas. The same held true to his staff. In the beginning, the staff was very polite to the customers. The winemaker was generally a likable and kind man in all other respects. Consequently, the staff would cover for the winemaker's eccentric nature. They would minimize it in front of customers, smoothing over most conflicts. The staff members were loyal and consequently instrumental in helping to best serve the customer. Recently, the staff had begun to tire of the antics and change their ways.

They didn't always agree with the winemaker and would secretly tell the customers that some of the wine was horrible. They would often imitate the winemaker's actions behind his back and do very little to help his cause.

The winemaker's wife was a kind woman. All of this time, she had remained on the sidelines, only observing and never interfering with his art and craft. One day she decided to enlist the help of the winemaker's lead staff, Susan. She told Susan that she was well aware of the situation, to which Susan hesitantly agreed. They decided that they would change things.

1. Outline the issues relating to customer service and staffing problems at The Whinery.
2. What are the options for Susan and the winemaker's wife?
3. Outline steps for positive change according to instituting change theory in the chapter.

❖ EXERCISES

Exercise 1: Expectations and Culture

Directions: Describing expectations is a very important part of management. Expectations should always be clear. Outline the expectations of your class.

1. Expectation_____
2. Expectation_____
3. Expectation_____
4. Expectation_____

Directions: The organizational culture is the personality of a business. It is the behavior, the conduct, the pace, and the style. Your class also has a culture. Describe the culture of your class:

1. Behavior: _____
2. Conduct: _____
3. Pace: _____
4. Style: _____

Exercise 2: Hiring Attributes

Directions: You are commissioned to hire for the position of Concierge at a 4-Star Resort. Consider the top five attributes that you would desire in a candidate. Fill in the chart below to describe the attributes that you would look for in a successful candidate. Then, devise an interview question to assess that quality.

Position: Concierge at a 4-Star Resort

Priority Rank	Desirable Trait	Interview Question to Assess Trait
1.		
2.		
3.		
4.		
5.		

Exercise 3: Moral Codes

Directions: You work at a restaurant. Everyone is required to ring in and purchase all food and drink at an employee discount. You and your colleagues regularly drink soda without ringing it in or paying. Use the chart below to detail your responses.

Ethical Checklist	Response
Is it legal?	
Is it fair?	
How do I feel about it in my conscience?	
Would the court of public opinion find my behavior incorrect?	
Am I fearful of what those I trust and respect would say of my actions?	

Directions: Your friend's ride is leaving a couple of minutes before the end of the shift. He is required to stay until the end of the shift. He asks you to punch out for him. No one will notice.

Ethical Checklist	Response
Is it legal?	
Is it fair?	
How do I feel about it in my conscience?	
Would the court of public opinion find my behavior incorrect?	
Am I fearful of what those I trust and respect would say of my actions?	

Chapter 14

Marketing and Establishing an Image for Service

CHAPTER OBJECTIVES

After reading this chapter, you should be able to:

▶ Explain and apply the concept of marketing as it applies to a service organization.
▶ Define and apply the concept of brand image to a service organization.
▶ Define and apply the 5 Ps of Marketing.
▶ Define and apply the four steps of the marketing process.
▶ Contrast the expectations of quality customer service as a marketing tool.

TERMINOLOGY

Brand Image
Corporate Responsibility
Customer Intelligence
Expected Turnover
Fam Trips
Generations
Market Segmentation

Marketing
Relationship Marketing
Reputation Management
Unexpected Turnover
Word-of-Mouth
5 Ps of Marketing

Introduction to Service Marketing

MARKETING AND CUSTOMER SERVICE

Marketing and customer service work in tandem. Below are excerpts from marketing literature:

- ▶ "Place the customers first."
- ▶ "Without our customers we have nothing."
- ▶ "The purpose of a company is to serve the customer."
- ▶ "The purpose of a company is to create and maintain satisfied customers."
- ▶ "Reward the employees. They will take care of the customers."
- ▶ "Establish an organizational culture that cares for the customers."
- ▶ "Develop a service culture."
- ▶ "Customer service is in the hands of the front-line workers."

Most of these marketing quotes involve quality customer service. Marketing embraces customer service because neither can exist alone. Marketing and customer service go hand in hand. They are part of a larger system of business processes.

EVERYONE HAS CUSTOMER SERVICE

These days, everyone is dedicated to customer service. They boast of personalized guest service, whether or not they actually deliver it. It is in their mission statements, their training manuals, written on business cards, and on the walls behind the counter. Why then, isn't everyone actually delivering quality customer service? Why does service suffer miserably? Do customers or staff even belief the statements? The answer is no. Customers don't typically believe quotes that boast quality service because they are over-used and without delivery.

MARKETING DEFINED

Marketing

The coordination of the exchange of goods and services in an effort to fulfill the wants and needs of the customers. This involves a deliberate control of research, advertising, and brand management is put in place.

Before we go further, let's examine what marketing is. **Marketing** is the coordination of the exchange of goods and services in an effort to fulfill the wants and needs of the customers. This involves a deliberate control of advertising and brand management.

Now, let's take this definition apart to better understand it. Marketing is:

the coordination

Coordination means that it does not just happen spontaneously. It is a deliberate process. It is analyzed and planned and executed with intention.

of the exchange of goods and services

The exchange is open to include the many distribution channels such as in-person, through a website, or through a distributor such as a travel agent. Goods and services embraces hospitality in that there is typically both a tangible and intangible component to what is provided.

in an effort to fulfill the wants and needs of the customers.

This is a hallmark of customer service. Marketing aims to fill the wants and needs of its customers.

This involves a deliberate control of research, advertising, and brand management is put in place.

The term deliberate means that it is by design and on purpose. It is something intentionally orchestrated, or controlled, by the business.

It is important to first understand the unique characteristics of your potential customers, in doing this market research. Ideally, it is done before sales are begun. If not, market research will be handed to you in the form of sales and customer feedback. At this point, it is often too late if the results are unfavorable.

Advertising is the actual act of getting the message out to the customer. It may be passive (remember us) or active (buy now). It can involve many forms such as print, e-mail, direct mail, phone, website, or through a third party.

Brand management is maintaining the brand image. It is the end product of marketing. Brand image is what your business stands for and what it means to others. It is what the customers think when the name of your business is mentioned. It is an ongoing process that involves every aspect of the business. It is represented in the uniforms, the greetings, the signage, the greetings used, and so on. Brand management is key! It is important that your customers believe that you deliver quality service!

Brand Image
The end product of marketing. It is what your business stands for. It is evident in every aspect of your business.

✦ THEMES IN MARKETING

As outlined above, marketing is an integrated system that encompasses the customer and the brand, but it was not always this advanced. Marketing was once quite primitive. Within the last century, it has been heavily influenced by the society, education, technology, and industry. These themes have greatly changed how marketing is performed in businesses. Below is a general timeline to give light to the many changes that marketing has seen in the last 100 years.

(1930s and prior) Focus on Manufacturing

This is considered to be the early years of marketing. Advertisements were not well constructed and had a manufacturing emphasis because of the heavy manufacturing focus of the US.

(1940s) Focus on Sales

Technological advances meant increased competition and marketers began to understand the importance of sales. The primary focus was on making the sales quotas. The needs and wants of the customer were considered but not as important.

Today we refer to these actions as primarily advertising and sales, which are only considered a portion of the marketing as we know it today.

(1950s) Management Discipline

Business schools realized and embraced the ideas of marketing as a discipline in the field of education and important for success of business. The idea of the 4 Ps became popularized. Customers had more choices and there was a shift to focus on ensuring that products matched specific needs. Quality of service and customer satisfaction became part of organizational strategy. Businesses began to have internal marketing departments.

(1960s) Marketing as a Business

Businesses continued to realize the importance of marketing as it became a major division of businesses. The full-service advertising agencies became popular (recall the television show *Madmen*).

(1970s) Societal Concerns

Organizations grew more aware of the communities and the society in which they operate. They began to show an increased concern for saving the Earth. As they made this known and began to use it in their marketing, **Societal Marketing** evolved.

(1980s) Service Economy

The US continued to change from a manufacturing to a service economy. The need for marketing of services became essential. **Service Marketing**, or the idea of marketing services as opposed to products, became more recognized as a field of its own with unique needs.

(1990s) E-commerce

Electronic commerce produced new marketing channels, the increased management of reservations, and customer feedback. They were now able to analyze market data and sell goods and services with the use of technology. This had a dramatic change on the way that goods and services were marketed.

(2000s–present) Social Media Marketing

Social media became popular. User-generated content became easy to obtain and very credible. This, again, changed the way that many market to customers.

The Four Steps of Marketing for Quality Guest Service

This section discusses the process of marketing as it relates to customer service. It is divided into four steps that flow from one to another as the concepts of marketing are applied to a business. Each section is further divided, delving into details within each of the four steps. We begin with a presentation of the four steps because it is important to keep in mind the big picture. This will help to better place the details into their proper context.

1. Analysis and Identification of Needs.
2. Establishment of a Marketing Plan.
3. Implementation of Controls to Position.
4. Follow-Up After the Sale.

STEP 1: ANALYSIS AND IDENTIFICATION OF WANTS AND NEEDS

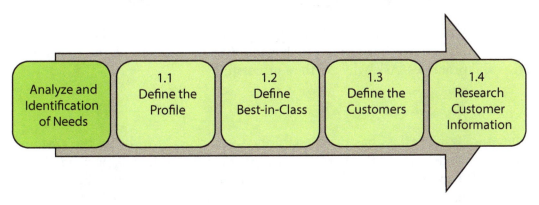

What defines a buyer's choice of brand, type, amount, timing, and expectations? By answering the questions below, you will begin to piece together a picture that will answer this question.

The term *Big Data* is used quite frequently to describe the vast collection of guest preferences. It is used to customize a guest's experience. It can be an interactive display that can change as an identified customer approaches it. A server can provide customized suggestions based on a guest profile. The mass customization of preferences and services can be endless if this data is discerned and implemented appropriately.

1.1 Define the Profile

Establishing a profile requires answering a barrage of questions to help define the market and competition. Below is a list of questions to begin the classification and establishment of a profile.

- ▶ What business are you in? This may seem obvious, but it established a foundation.
- ▶ What are you known for?
- ▶ Who is your competition?
- ▶ What is the competition known for?

1.2 Define Best-In-Class

Answering these questions will produce a profile and an initial list of competitors. The next section begins to rank the competition by providing a list of Best-In-Class. This list can be used as a ranking to strive for, and a benchmark for adapting best practice methods. Below is a list of questions to begin the ranking of competitors for your industry.

- ▶ Who first comes to mind when your industry is mentioned?
- ▶ Who is the best at quality service?
- ▶ Who has the overall best product?
- ▶ Who has the nicest property?
- ▶ Who has the nicest options or amenities?
- ▶ Who leads in innovation?
- ▶ Who leads in market share?

Learn what the competition is doing. Go visit them. Talk to others. Read the journals and reviews. Take note of what the Best-In-Class are doing to excel in areas and processes. Ask, why are they successful?

1.3 Define the Customers

After the Best In-Class has been established you must also define the customers. So, what defines a customer? The customer can be explained, or divided into groups. The information is referred to as customer intelligence and the divisions are called market segmentation. They could be internal or external. Most people think of customers as being internal, but quality service utilizes the concept of internal customers. First, they are served by other employees. Also, they are a great testimonial to your business if they love the product. For example, a server who shares knowledge of their personal favorite dish is likely to enhance the experience. Product knowledge is so important. Henry Ford wanted to give his employees time off to enjoy driving their Fords.

The other customers could be potential, actual, or former. Below is a chart to illustrate this point. Once this is determined, it is easier to learn their motivations and respond accordingly.

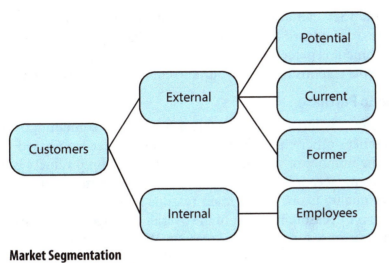

Market Segmentation
© Kendall Hunt Publishing Company

Customer Intelligence

The process of gathering information regarding your customers. Includes history of use, demographics, and psychographics in an effort to understand former, future, and current customers. Used in marketing, strategic planning, and training.

Market Segmentation

The process of dividing the market into groups, typically demographically. However, numerous ways exist.

- ► What do the customers want?
- ► What do the customers expect?
- ► How do customers define value?
- ► Is there such a thing as an average customer? Perhaps not in that they are all unique and deserve respect and attention, but there can be certain averages.
- ► What is the average lifespan of a customer?
- ► Is it one-time or continued?
- ► Where do new customers come from?
- ► Why did former customers leave? Customers leave for a variety of reasons. Some relocate and others change lifestyles. These reasons are known as **expected turnover** which is part of the nature of sales. That is when they leave for natural reasons beyond the control of the business. What a business can control is the **unexpected turnover**, or loss of business due to a fault of the business. This could be from poor service, inferior products, or a number of other controllable aspects.

Why did potential customers choose to never patronize your business? Many customers could choose to never patronize your business. Customers could be turned off by a telephone conversation without even patronizing your

Expected Turnover
When customers leave for reasons beyond the control of the business.

Unexpected Turnover
When customers leave for reasons within the control of the business.

establishment. They can also be turned off by something that they heard from someone else or an advertisement that they saw. Perhaps it was an image or what your establishment is perceived to be like.

Who accepts responsibility for your current and potential customers?

Decision to Purchase

Have you ever wondered what makes a person buy something? We ask what are the customer's other choices? Are they making a decision based on price? Is it based on the number of stars it received? Is it based on product? Is it based on location, convenience, or lack of alternative choices? Or, maybe it is based on service? Service quality is one of the main reasons why consumers purchase items, but it isn't the only reason. It is part of the overall message they receive. People are motivated to purchase for a variety of reasons. We must gauge the customer interest in a product or service. We assess this with individuals and as a demographic segment. Every customer is slightly different, and some reasons overlap.

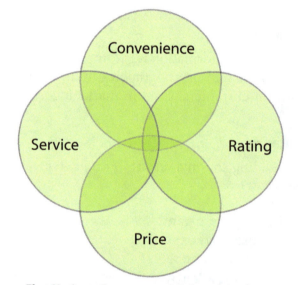

Reasons That Motivate Customers to Purchase a Product or Service

Generations

Generations are a common way to segment the US market. People are divided according to the year they were born. Three of the most common generations are the Baby Boomers, Generation Xers, Generation Ys, and Generation Zs.

Baby Boomers (born 1946–1964): 77 million

The Baby Boomer generation was the biggest generation the US had ever seen. Consequently, the shift in demand of goods and services had increased as their age demanded it. They are now nearing or entering retirement age. They have grown up and raised children and had careers and are now experiencing empty nest syndrome. They are now earning more money than they have ever made in their life. They are cautious but also beginning to branch out to spend and experience technology in their empty nest age. Consequently, they present a new challenge. They are beginning to spend their money for new and different reasons. Providing service to them is a unique blend of appreciation, quality, and price. They know a quality product, great service, and reasonable price and they are fully aware of how to find an alternative if they don't receive it.

Generation X (born 1965–1974): 45 million

Generation X was originally given the name X because it was deemed worthless. It turned out they, like every other generation, was just misunderstood. They have given us the X-Games and the 1980s. They are now in their family-formation years and steadily climbing in their careers. Consequently, they are now patronizing hospitality with a different set of eyes. Finally set free from the Baby Boomers, they are the core of the market. Providing quality service to them is a challenge. They have always been held to a standard and they hold others to that same standard.

Generation Y (born 1977–1994): 72 million (Millenials, Echo Boomers)

Generation Y is the first generation to grow up with good economic times and dual-income households. Consequently, they have eaten different than any generation before them. They grew up consuming food from a box, from a can, from the freezer, or from a restaurant. There was little time for a home-cooked meal as other generations have experienced. We now have the first generation that does not know how to cook.

Their lifestyle and eating habits will forever be changed as a result. Add in the proliferation of television shows dedicated to food, wine, travel, gambling, and events and you have a very different customer. Their lifestyle is conducive to eating, traveling, and enjoying hospitality as a leisure, a necessity, and a way of life. This has produced a very different, unique blend of customer. This new type of customer has a little bit of knowledge about many things that interest them. Their patronage is not as often a celebration but a pastime and a way of life.

Generation Z (born 1995–2012)

Generation Zs are quickly becoming the primary segment. They currently represent over half of the workforce in the US. They fully embrace technology and have a heavy influence on their parents. They have less discretionary income due to their age, but spend a higher percentage of it. They care, but about different causes, and don't make assumptions. Marketing and providing services to them is much different than any other generation before. They were always accustomed to technology and have much higher expectations of speed of service and communication responses. Like other generations, they really don't care about "how it used to be" because they only know how it is today. This, again, changes the landscape of expectations and service.

1.4   Research Customer Information

Now that you have the best-in-class and the profile of the customer, it is important to look at it from the customer's point of view. What do they see, hear, and experience? A secret shopper is a great way to monitor procedures, but there is much else to be researched. Begin by asking:

- ► What are the sources of customer information?
- ► How are you represented?
- ► Who is the face of your business?

It is often the front-line employees. In addition, there may be suppliers, marketing intermediaries, websites, blogs, reviews, or advertisements. All of these need to be monitored and managed to be in line with your brand image.

- ► What does the customer see and experience?
- ► Analyze the service process. Try to see the organization through the customers' eyes.
- ► Are they taken care of within each step? In the bed and breakfast segment, the innkeeper spends nights sleeping in each of the different rooms. They jokingly refer to this as "sleeping around."

Management Information System (MIS)

An MIS is more than a computer. It is everything in a system of people, equipment, and procedures to collect and interpret information in an effort to make the best management decisions. This includes comment cards, surveys, focus groups, company records, POS, and information.

Property Operation Systems (POS)

All POS's are part of the MIS. They may also be referred to as Property Management Systems (PMS). Nearly every business has a system. Several great brands are on the market to help manage information. PosiTouch, Micros, Fidelio, Squirrel, and Aloha are just a few of the most popular systems available. All serve as registers, schedule reservations, and inventory. Newer features permit staff scheduling and projections. All of this information can be used in the research collection process.

STEP 2: ESTABLISHMENT OF A MARKETING PLAN

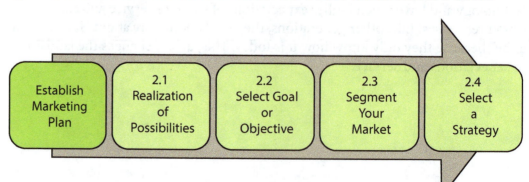

2.1 Realization of Possibilities

The first step is to open your mind and brain-storm. Be creative. Open it up to unlimited possibilities. Enlist the help of others. Benchmark others to see what is out there.

2.2 Select Goal or Objective

Then, begin to narrow it down. Tools could assist in narrowing the options. Think about the answers for the prior sections:

- ► What business are you in?
- ► What does your brand stand for?
- ► What is your selling point?

2.3 Segment Your Market

In the prior section, you began to profile markets. Now it is time to put these profiles into action, deciding which will be most appropriate. Consider these questions in determining which you want to go after:

- ► Which market do you currently serve?
- ► Which market does the competitor serve?
- ► Which market is most profitable?
- ► Which market is emerging?

"You want fries with that Chardonnay?"

Customers Confused With Different Levels of Product Offerings
© Cartoon Resource/Shutterstock.com

2.4 Select a Strategy

Next we select a strategy which would best fit our needs. It will be the vehicle to transport us to meet our objectives.

Options

- ► Are you changing the:
  - ☐ Product
  - ☐ Service
  - ☐ Reputation
  - ☐ Overall package
- ► Are you going to sell the heck out of it?
- ► Are you to earn profits through:
  - ☐ Volume
  - ☐ Price
  - ☐ Increased sales per customer

SERVICE INSIGHT

Corporate Responsibility

Corporate responsibility means that a company has values and ethical standards aligned with good stewardship to its community and environment. It ensures proper conduct of actions, therefore benefitting its stakeholders. Marriott International is a hotel company that is very committed to corporate responsibility. Their business values ensure that they are good stewards to their customers, employees, investors, communities, and environment. They are not just in it for the profits. They are in it for the benefit of all and their words are backed up with actions.

This idea of social responsibility shines through in their brand image and makes a difference in how they serve the customers. Customers notice and investors appreciate the lengths to which Marriott and others go to respect the communities and resources that have made them so successful. The employees feel good about being on a team that cares about the community in which they work and live.

Corporate Responsibility

The idea that a company upholds values and ethical standards to be a good steward to its community and environment.

After the direction of the strategy is determined we must

- ▶ Establish a timeline.
- ▶ Dictate resources.
- ▶ Support our brand.

All of these decisions impact customer service.

☀ STEP 3: IMPLEMENTATION OF CONTROLS TO POSITION—THE 4, 5, OR 8 PS

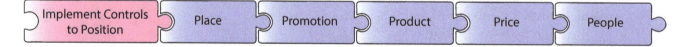

Implement Controls to Position | Place | Promotion | Product | Price | People

5 Ps of Marketing

Common to any marketing plan: place, promotion, product, price, and people.

Now that you have selected a goal and a strategy, it is time to implement the controls. These were established in the previous section, but here is where the actual changes are made. Strategies come to life and begin to take hold as they are transferred from paper to practice. A great way to begin is by considering The **5 Ps of Marketing**. These are common to any marketing plan. They are: place, promotion, product, people, and price. Occasionally there are one or two more Ps included, and on rare occasion, a P is omitted, but the five are the core as they relate to marketing and serving the customer. Each of these should be considered and controlled in the overall plan.

There is also an alternative 3 Ps of Service Marketing:

- ▶ People: Employees (staffing, hiring, training, development, internal marketing)
- ▶ Physical (design, location, signage, appearance used to make claims tangible)
- ▶ Process (the way it is packaged or delivered, level of ease and participation)

Other versions will lengthen the service marketing mix with characteristics such as:

- ► Performance
- ► Programming
- ► Partnerships
- ► Competition comparison
- ► Consistency
- ► Serviceability

Place

The place includes the atmosphere, the environment, and all of the surroundings. It involves the capacity, the décor, the amenities, and the physical appearance. Place is like a headache or hiccups. Most people don't think about it until there is an issue. The physical attributes that make up the entire guest experience. Even smell has recently become a big consideration.

Servicescape

Servicescape was a concept developed by Bitner in 1992, building on the work of Baker in 1987. Servicescape describes the physical surroundings that facilitate service. These include both tangible and intangible elements to help communicate or deliver the service experience. It incorporates all of the senses. Examples may include colors, decorations, scenery, temperature, lights, sounds, and smells.

Below is a table that helps to illustrate some of the colors, their degree of perceived warmth, and common human responses to them. These should be taken into consideration when designing servicescapes.

Color	Degree of Warmth	Common Human Responses
Red	Warm	Stimulating, high energy
Yellow	Warmer	Intellectual, clarity
Orange	Warmest	Emotional, warmth
Green	Cool	Nurturing, serenity
Violet	Cool	Spirituality, calming
Indigo	Cool	Meditative
Blue	Coolest	Relaxation

Adapted from Lovelock and Wirz, 2007

Promotion

The promotional mix is a combination of advertising, public relations, and promotions. They include word-of-mouth, television, newspaper, familiarization (fam) trips, online, and presence including social media and publications. All need to be controlled. Monitoring and improving this is called reputation management.

Word-of-Mouth

Opinions expressed by the general public regarding your business. This may have a very powerful influence on customers and is often difficult to control or quantify.

Fam Trips

Short for familiarization trips. Typically used by hotels. An invited, all-expense paid trip to people who will purchase or influence the purchase of future sales.

Reputation Management

The science of monitoring and consistently improving or maintaining your assessment among the public and outside constituencies. This often involves surveys and entire brand management. With social media, people advertise for you by promoting your brand on social media and in other reviews. These are now essential for any hospitality business. Many guests only write reviews when their experience was either very good or extremely poor. The 2015 J.D. Power study of guest satisfaction in hotels reported that 80% of highly satisfied customers also confirmed that they would tell others. This translates into more revenue and is essential for maintaining a competitive advantage.

Product

Earlier we analyzed our product, now it is time to control it. Everything the customer experiences and consumes constitutes a product. This includes service. Draw upon those findings and consider everything that goes into the product, both tangible and intangible.

SERVICE INSIGHT

Community Involvement

Does it matter if a company is involved in the community? The community believes so. Most respondents surveyed think it is a good idea, but would they patronize an establishment because it is involved in the community? Would they boycott a company because it doesn't help the community? Do companies do it for the employees, the core belief, the image, or the marketing? Sure, it is a good idea and the most successful companies engage in community activities, but the opinions of the motive are mixed. Estimates also vary greatly between demographics, type of businesses, and communities.

Price

Price is often an indicator of quality. Prices change and customers notice. Price must be in line with all of the other Ps. Numerous pricing strategies exist:

- ▶ Comparative pricing
- ▶ Mark-up pricing
- ▶ Desired profit pricing
- ▶ What the market will tolerate pricing
- ▶ Market skimming pricing

The customer will always consider price as a factor. It must be determined *how* much they will consider it. Based on this assessment, pricing adjustments can be made.

The 4 Ps help to set the expected level of service. Below is a chart illustrating three hospitality companies as they adjust each of the Ps.

The Four Ps and Expectations Related to Hospitality Organizations			
Four Ps	**Universal Studies**	**Carnival Cruise Lines**	**Holiday Inn Express**
Product	Hotels, amusements, dining, shopping	Leisure cruise ship, accommodations, destination, activities	Hotel, business center, amenities, meetings
Price	~$120	~$1000	~$125
Place	Orlando, FL Hollywood, CA	Ports, ocean, destinations	Country-wide
Promotion	TV, radio, print, Internet, social media	TV, print, Internet, social media	Print, Internet
Expectations	Fun	Fun cruise	Business stay, reasonable accommodations at reasonable price

People

People are sometimes referred to as the fifth P, although purists maintain that people would fit in under another P. Despite where it falls, the Human Resource function is key! All should be considered in hiring, promoting teamwork, satisfaction, training, and development. Your employees make the difference. Everything else can be controlled with the exception of the human element. Humans must be cultivated and managed, and what they are capable of is often beyond belief. Your strategy should prepare and adjust for new customer situations and also take into account the physical and emotional labor involved.

Additional thoughts

- ▶ Do employees treat customers as if this is the last time they will ever see them?
- ▶ Are dissatisfied customers treated as problems or opportunities?
- ▶ Do your employees believe that you are a great company?

▶ Every organization has some type of customer. Just saying terms without backing it up is insincere and will be noticed.
▶ Treat your front line workers as well as you want them to treat customers.
▶ Give customers a reason for returning in future.

Internal Marketing

Internal marketing is the idea of marketing to the employees. It is the idea of conveying information regarding the company to the employees. It is publicizing the accomplishments of the employees. It provides them with news regarding the company. It may be directed to their department and the company as a whole. It allows them to feel part of a team and realize their important role as a member.

Remember that employees are either directly involved with the customer, or serving someone else who is directly involved with the customer. They are the window to the company. Many intrinsic points are conveyed through your employees:

▶ Company image
▶ Corporate culture
▶ Hiring criteria
▶ Training
▶ Efficiency
▶ Concern for guests
▶ Concern for employees
▶ Empowerment

Conveying these points might utilize an employee newsletter, pre-shift meetings, in-services, or meetings with management. To orchestrate internal marketing to the employees, steps to follow involve motivating, involving, reminding, and maintaining the communication to the employees.

To do this, consider the following points extracted from Deming's Service Profit Chain:

—Recruit, hire, set standards, train, establish a culture of service.

—Use service quality tools to evaluate and improve.

—This should result in increased customer satisfaction.

—Which turns into increased customer loyalty.

—And creates more profits.

The idea of Internal Marketing is really something that Deming preached many years before this concept was derived.

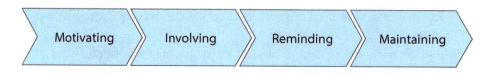

The Four Steps to Orchestrating Internal Marketing to Employees

Motivating

- ► Getting them interested
- ► Getting buy-in
- ► Providing regular product samples
- ► Showing value
- ► Providing incentives
- ► Presenting incentives

Involving

- ► Letting them know their role
- ► Showing them how to perform their roles

Reminding

- ► This cannot be a one-time event
- ► Be aware that over-reminding is just as bad as underdoing it
- ► Remember employees are intelligent individuals

Maintaining

- ► Follow-up is key
- ► Check to ensure they are getting the true message
- ► Maintain consistency

SERVICE INSIGHT

Service Expectations

How else are expectations and services changing? With Social Media, also known as Web 2.0. Below is a list of the most popular sites that are changing the landscape:

- ► Facebook check-in and Four Square: Geolocation via mobile device
- ► Blogs (sharing experiences)
- ► Forums (seeking, sharing, and answering questions)
- ► Social Networks (referrals, connecting)
- ► Twitter (discount and dialogue)
- ► Second Life (which partially designed the new Aloft Hotel concept by its virtual residents)
- ► YouTube (make your own ad, comment, or viral videos)
- ► Trip Advisor (online reviews)
- ► Urbanspoon, Orbitz, Expedia (online reservation)
- ► Yelp (restaurant reviews)
- ► AAA (travel ratings)
- ► Twitter (with hashtag the concierge with questions)

Consumer Decision-Making Process

As a customer goes through the sales and marketing process, it can be important to analyze it through a different lens, referred to as the Decision-Making Process. This begins with realizing there is a need and then evolving through searching, evaluating, purchasing, and even afterthoughts. The Process is outlined and described below in four combined steps:

▶ Recognition of Need: The customer might know they have a need or desire, or they might be enticed by your offerings. This could be an ad, a post on social media, a free sample, a sign, or number of other means that prompt a stimuli.

▶ Education and Comparison: A comparison of the possibilities, reviews, costs, competitions, and any other information they can attain.

▶ Purchase: A transaction is made.

▶ Post-Purchase Judgments: After the purchase and at least some use, judgments and assessments are made against prior expectations. Essentially, are they pleased with the purchase? Larger purchases are typically related to increased deliberations. Businesses go to great lengths to monitor and stop "buyer's remorse" before items are returned by instituting HELP-lines, and customer FAQ's along with other online resources.

Adapted from Bruner & Pomazal (1993)

STEP 4: FOLLOW-UP—SERVICE AFTER THE SALE

Follow-Up After the Sale

What Is the Post-Purchase Behavior of the Customers?

Transactional Customers

Transactional customers are one-time patrons. This isn't always bad. They could be traveling through, changing life segments, or be looking for other great experiences. Customers who are pleased may talk well of your establishment. The main thing is to make sure they aren't displeased. Surveys and tools can assist with this.

Tourist Traps are a term for businesses that take advantage of transactional customers. The business knows that it will be a one-time purchase, and looks good on the outside. Service and quality is often greatly lacking.

Relationship Customers

Returning customers are the key to businesses. It estimated that it costs three times more to attract a new customer as it does to retain a return customer. Relationship management is crucial. Loyal customers speak well of the business, require less

Technology Update

Beacon Technology

This is a newer technology that pushes messages and information based on the location of a guest. Beacon technology consists of devices that are placed in strategic locations throughout the property which send marketing information such as coupons, specials, or event information.

customer-training, and are more forgiving. Technology has facilitated the customer connection a great deal. Websites, e-mails, tweets, and fan pages all help to build and maintain a relationship.

Often, the relationship is begun well before the sale, but the after-sale period is crucial.

Service does not stop with the sale or transaction. A few will move on, but for many it should be the beginning of the relationship. You should make sure the customers feel good about their decisions and work on building a long-term relationship with them. This is commonly called **relationship marketing**.

Customer Relationship Management (CRM)

CRM is the strategy behind relationship marketing. It is used by businesses to identify and maintain the quality lifetime customer relationships. As we know from above, some customers are more likely to return than others. This strategy helps to retain and increase the profitability of customers. Following through with this mindset, an objective could be to make your brand "Top of Mind," meaning that it is the first brand people think of when asked about your services. A similar objective would be to make your brand "Top of Heart," meaning that it would be the optimally desired brand people think of when asked about your services.

At the core of CRM are programs that identify and build databases of frequent customers. These utilize apps, social media, loyalty programs, and other push programs to promote to specific customers, catering to their independent needs. This drives customer loyalty and, hence, sales.

Relationship Marketing
The process of fostering and cultivating a long-lasting relationship with your current customer base. Can be in person or through the use of electronic media.

✦ TECHNOLOGY AND ITS INFLUENCES

Much of the hospitality industry occurs off-line. You cannot dine online. What **IS** changing is the way that we interact with our guests. They can:

- ▶ Sell the product encouraging new and return guests.
- ▶ Receive services like concierge, reservations, and advance purchase.
- ▶ Refer others.
- ▶ Offer promotions with last-minute deals, or just a soft sell.
- ▶ Place complaints into the public sector.
- ▶ Determine guest expectations.

Customer Completing a Mobile Review
© Andrey_Popov/Shutterstock.com

In the past, customer care and personal service went hand in hand. Consumers had little choices due to a lack of communication, transportation, and technology. Customers were treated as regulars, and they appreciated the comfort of being known. The world was, in a sense, small. Now information can be shared anywhere with anyone who wishes. Technology continues to personalize the experience, but it has changed it dramatically.

Social media is a general term referring to Web-based applications that promote the exchange of user-generated content. The idea of user-generated content appears to have a higher credibility than marketers or expert reviews at a much lower cost. A problem with users generating the content is the control of their posts. This leads to a need for enhanced reputation management.

INFLUENCES PURCHASE DECISIONS

Ratings can play a substantial role in the decisions of perspective customers. A survey by Phocuswright (2017) found a direct correlation between user-generated reviews and purchase decisions. The better the rating, the more likely they were to choose the business. Three out of four travelers cited reviews and photos as influential in choosing activities.

Leads to Increased Sales

This can lead to a direct increase in revenue. An increase in ratings can be very advantageous. A study by Harvard Business School (2016) determined that independent restaurants with a one-star increase in Yelp ratings led to a 5 to 9% increase in revenue.

Customers Photographing Food Before Eating
© Twinsterphoto/Shutterstock.com

Leads to Increasing Prices

You can increase rates. A study at Cornell (2012) determined that, with all other things being equal, a single point in a Travelocity hotel average rating permits an 11.2% increase of average daily rate without affecting demand.

Over half of all websites are now accessed on mobile phones. In addition, applications or "apps" have become common for enhancing the customer relationship. Properties are finding that numerous meaningful possibilities are possible to assist the guest and increase revenue. Many of the successful apps permit guests to do nearly everything, seamlessly at their fingertips. Features include:

- ▶ Local events and points of interest
- ▶ Ability to browse through services
- ▶ User-generated and expert reviews
- ▶ Property pictures
- ▶ Checking of availability
- ▶ Real-time contact for questions
- ▶ Making reservations
- ▶ Checking in
- ▶ Ordering food
- ▶ Room temperature
- ▶ Media controls
- ▶ Paying the bill
- ▶ Checking out
- ▶ Loyalty programs
- ▶ Easter eggs (small, hidden features)

More recently, there have been many changes in the way businesses market to the public. The world has become quite larger and more knowledgeable. Smartphones are ubiquitous. Consumers can access information from numerous methods, purchase from anywhere, and drive or travel much further than ever before. As a result, customers now have much more knowledge and freedom of choices than ever before. Newer technologies like voice-activated (e.g., Apple's Siri) and map-activated are also changing how hospitality markets and provides guest service.

Online travel agencies (OTAs) have also dramatically increased. They are used in browsing, reservations, concierge, shopping, and travel planning. In the past 10 years, the percentage of hotel rooms booked on these third-party OTA sites has increased from 1% to about 9%. Trip Advisor and Booking.com receive millions of hits each month.

According to Smith Travel Research and Market Matrix, 89% of respondents claimed to be influenced by the online reviews, making these very important to hoteliers. Never before has the expectations of guests been so heavily influenced by other guests. In fact, they rated guest experience factors (past experience, recommendations, and online reviews) at 51%, making it the biggest predictor of purchase. Second was location, and third was price.

✦ INTEGRATED MARKETING COMMUNICATIONS

Integrated Marketing Communication (IMC) is a concept of alignment. All marketing communications must work together. It must appear seamlessly to produce a directed, specific message to the intended customers. Everything that a service business says, does, and is should be aligned with a consistent message of establishing the expectations of the guest.

Everyone knows that a business cannot say one thing and do another, but it happens quite frequently. Consider all of the decisions that a service business makes with how it portrays itself through its communications. Immediately, things come to mind such as:

▶ Website
▶ Pricing and discounts
▶ Signage
▶ Social media
▶ Advertising
▶ Apps

These are certainly important ways of communicating and they should be aligned to produce a consistent message with consistent resources being devoted to them. Additionally, there are many other things that should also be aligned:

▶ Location
▶ Décor
▶ Food
▶ Beverage

- ▶ Accommodations
- ▶ Guides
- ▶ Entertainment
- ▶ Seating
- ▶ Elevators
- ▶ Corporate culture
- ▶ Billing

It happens with brands, it happens with independent properties and entertainment venues, and it happens with destinations. There must be a vision and a plan that coordinates the mix of elements so that it ensures each activity is aligned with a common goal. When it is coordinated properly, expectations are met. Guests know what to expect and there are far less unsatisfactory issues.

SERVICE INSIGHT

High-Tech–High-Touch Dilemma

There is an issue in practice and literature referred to as the high-tech–high-touch dilemma. As technology progresses, the need for service workers has been reduced by automated services such as online reservations and self-check-in. Customers and technology drive service automation to advance. Speed of service is increased and costs are reduced. As this is done, personalized service is being replaced by machines and technology. At what point is it too much? At what point are we losing the customer contact that is so desired in hospitality? There are many different points of view and the dilemma continues.

⚹ AUGMENTED REALITY (AR)

Virtual Reality (VR) uses technology to create a different, new environment. This is not as user-friendly to the average guest and poses some challenges in implementation. The use of AR in guest service is expected to grow substantially because it utilizes a similar technology but enhances the guest's current environment and does not require as difficult of an implementation. It can add to what they have to provide features or information. It can provide personalized experiences with regular mobile devices, including smartphones and tablets without needing bulky wearables. It uses 3-D programs that layer images over the existing environment. We have gotten accustomed to it without realizing it. An example of AR is the yellow line identifying a first down on televised NFL games. Other common applications include seeing images or video when a smartphone is held over a restaurant menu. It is also used for interactive maps of cities. It can provide location markers sites or other transportation options.

❖ CHAPTER REVIEW QUESTIONS

1. What is servicescape and why is it important in marketing?
2. Explain the importance of IMC.
3. List and briefly describe the four steps of the marketing process.
4. List and briefly describe the 5 Ps of marketing, relating them to customer service.
5. How has marketing recently changed?
6. Why is a return customer preferred to a transactional customer?
7. What is the relationship between marketing and customer service?
8. What is internal marketing and how can it help a business?
9. Which generation are you from? Outline five tips that you could give a business owner to best accommodate to your generation.

CASE STUDIES

Up-selling at the Cost of Service

Increasing average sales per guest has been a common theme in hospitality as well as all retail. Consequently, up-selling, or selling more to the customer, has become a popular push in most settings. There are several approaches to this:

▶ Suggestions Method: "We have a nice king suite with a view of the pool."
▶ Ask Method: "We have you in a bed in our standard room, is that suitable for your needs?"
▶ Listen and Watch Method—watch for guest needs: "We have a great restaurant and award-winning spa."
▶ Top-Down Method—starting with the highest-price rooms and moving down: "We have our diplomat room available for $195." If no, "We have a suite for $150."
▶ Lowest-Plus Method: "Did you want to upgrade to water view for $25?"
▶ Random-Choice Method—present all available options at once: "We have a diplomat room for $195, a standard room for $75, and a suite for $150."

Businesses mandate their staff up-sell using these techniques. Staff are evaluated based on use of these techniques and their jobs are compromised if they do not "make the ask." Consequently, their heart is not in it. Other properties are motivated to up-selling through contests, encouraging them to sell at any cost. Sometimes this works and sometimes it does not. Average dollars per guest are increased, but at what cost? Guests are accustomed to sales pitches. Most are immediately turned off to high-pressure sales gimmicks. They are on guard and vigilant, cautiously scrutinizing the staff for hidden tactics of all their transactions. As a result, trust has diminished. Staff are placed in awkward positions and the guests feel taken advantage of if they are sold beyond their personal level of comfort. At this point, guest service has eroded and there is no opportunity for customer service. Some guests will change brands when presented with sales tactics.

On the other hand, the guests may enjoy the upgrade. They might have never experienced it if not suggested. Perhaps they could receive it complimentary once and like it so much that they pay for it in the future. In these cases, everyone wins.

1. What are the benefits to up-selling?
2. What are the disadvantages to up-selling?
3. What are ways that hotels can up-sell but still deliver great customer service?

Profiling Burgers

Bobby's Burger Palace is yet another creation by the famous Bobby Flay. It features artisan-crafted burgers that are difficult to beat. Its no-frills layout and open design promote a bare-bones approach to consuming the ultimate burger. It features the best grade of beef and other ingredients in combinations that surely please. It also offers a full bar with plenty of cheer and competent service.

Red Robin is another chain that has also seen recent growth. A bit larger in volume, Red Robin has undergone a marketing blitz to promote its slogan "Red Robin—Yummmmm." Also offering full-service, it looks more like a typical casual restaurant, although it specializes almost exclusively in burgers. It also has a bar and encourages drink specials.

Wendy's is a well-known burger restaurant. It features counter-service and drive-thru. It makes fresh burgers to order, and boasts that it never freezes its meat. Wendy's offers a sit-down area and is priced much lower than the competition. Wendy's menu also features salads, wraps, and other diversions from the typical burger.

1. Describe the profile and class of each of these restaurants.
2. Identify the brand image of each of these restaurants.
3. In your opinion, who is most successful at conveying their image?
4. Which concept is the most appealing to you? Explain.

An Old Lodge

The Log Lodge is a huge, old log lodge located in the Catskill Mountains. It features a view of a private lake, mountains, and vast arrays of wildlife. It is absolutely peaceful and is located less than 2 hours from New York City. The Log Lodge is also known for being a past host of such celebrities as Rodney Dangerfield and Frank Sinatra. It has enjoyed a loyal clientele from New Jersey, New York, and Connecticut for many years, but this is beginning to change. More recently, the clientele has also begun to progress into an age where it is becoming difficult for them to travel and be comforted by the lodge due to their deteriorating health conditions. Nowadays, it features lesser-known acts and is lesser-attended in its Grand Ballroom and has become a sleepy, tired old lodge. The owners are considering attracting a newer, younger demographic to the Log Lodge, but do not have the capital to make major renovations or take out major newspaper advertisements. They aren't even sure what they could offer the younger demographic. They also compete with entertainment options provided by casinos, and crowds no longer want to travel to the Catskills. They aren't sure which direction to take.

1. Are the owners correct in wanting to attract a younger replacement crowd?
2. What constraints are preventing the owners from targeting a new demographic?
3. List the positive aspects of The Log Lodge.
4. What are the options that owners could take with a limited budget and all of the other constrictions?

Benny's Restaurant

Benny graduated from a culinary program in high school and worked for several small restaurants for years. He had always dreamed of opening his very own restaurant. Now was his chance. He didn't have much of a plan, but had much desire and passion and knew that he could make it work. He just loved the cuisine. He recalled reading a quote in a food magazine that stated, "If you build a simple restaurant, and prepare a truly great dish, they will come in great numbers." Essentially, if you prepare it, they will come. Benny was rather idealistic and his personality and passion was quite appealing. He believed in the power of cuisine as a motivator for business. He watched several shows on television and was sure that he was as good, if not better, of a chef.

Benny finally got his break when an old bakery went out of business. It was the first place that Benny found that he could afford rent. He immediately placed a security deposit on it and began to make his dream a reality. He couldn't sleep for over a week. He spent every spare moment at the restaurant. He loved it. He decided that he would open as soon as he possibly could. This meant that he would have to go without a few things, but he was sure that he could manage.

He couldn't think of a great name, so he called it Benny's. He wasn't sure of a precise cuisine so he decided that he would use a chalkboard as he had seen at other establishments. He had two servers to start, his girlfriend and her brother. He would find the rest as needed. Then, he decided to open.

1. How successful do you think Benny will be with his initial opening?
2. Assess Benny's marketing from the standpoint of the 5 Ps.
3. From a marketing standpoint, what advice would you offer Benny?

❡ EXERCISES

Exercise 1: Advertisement Review

Directions:

▶ Research hospitality-related journals and choose an advertisement.
▶ Attach the advertisement to the back of your assignment. Answer the below questions with your related responses.

Audience: What generation were they targeting?

Tactic: Was it an impulse (purchase now) or passive (remember us) advertisement?

Brand: What image did the advertisement portray?

Success: Do you believe it is a successful advertisement? Explain.

Exercise 2: The 5 Ps

Directions: Invent a hospitality business of your choice and relate it to the 5 Ps in the chart below.

Name of Establishment: _____

Type of Establishment: _____

Ps	Description
Place	
Product	
Promotion	
People	
Price	

Exercise 3: Analysis and Identification of Customers

Directions: Choose a hospitality company within the segment of your choice and answer the following questions relating to the analysis and identification of customer wants and needs.

Define the Profile

► What business is it in?
► What are they known for?
► Who is their competition?
► What is the competition known for?

Define Best-In-Class

► Who first comes to mind when your industry is mentioned?
► Who is the best at quality service?
► Who has the overall best product?
► Who has the nicest property?
► Who has the nicest options or amenities?
► Who leads in innovation?
► Who leads in market share?

Define the Customers

► What do the customers want?
► What do the customers expect?
► How do customers define value?
► Are customers one-time or continued?
► Where do new customers come from?
► Why do potential customers choose to never patronize the business?

REFERENCES

Bruner, G. C., & Pomazal, R. J. (1993). Problem recognition: The crucial first stage of the consumer decision process. *Journal of Consumer Marketing, 5*(1), 53–63.

King, D. (2012, November 29). Cornell study links hotel reviews and room revenue. *Travel Weekly*. Retrieved from https://www.travelweekly.com/Travel-News/Hotel-News/Cornell-study-links-hotel-reviews-and-room-revenue

Lovelock, C. H., & Wirz, J. (2007). *Service marketing: People, technology, strategy.* Upper Saddle River, NJ: Prentice Hall.

Luca, M. (2016, March 15). Reviews, reputation, and revenue: The case of Yelp.Com. Harvard Business School NOM Unit Working Paper No. 12-016. Retrieved from https://ssrn.com/abstract=1928601 or http://dx.doi.org/10.2139/ssrn.1928601.

Merlino, D. (2017, September). User-generated content has moved into the marketing mainstream. Phocuswright. Retrieved from https://www.phocuswright.com/Free-Travel-Research/User-Generated-Content-Has-Moved-Into-the-Marketing-Mainstream.

Smith Travel Research and Market Matrix. Competitive marketing. Retrieved from https://str.com and https://www.marketmetrix.com/hospitality.html

Index

CPSIA information can be obtained
at www.ICGtesting.com
Printed in the USA
JSHW061045030223
37218JS00007B/115

9 781792 4